THE **NATIONAL TRUST** GUIDE TO

# Savannah

116 West Hull Street. Drawing by Christopher Murphy, Jr., given by him to Susan and Walter Hartridge on the occasion of their marriage. *Photograph courtesy of Walter Hartridge, Jr., and Susan Hartridge.*

# THE **NATIONAL TRUST** GUIDE TO
# Savannah

---

## R O U L H A C
## T O L E D A N O

PRESERVATION
PRESS

**JOHN WILEY & SONS, INC.**

New York • Chichester • Weinheim • Brisbane • Singapore • Toronto

A cooperataive publication with the National Trust for Historic Preservation, Washington, D.C., chartered by Congress in 1949 to encourage the preservation of sites, buildings, and communities significant in American history and culture.

This text is printed on acid-free paper.

This publication is designed to provide accurate and authoritative information in regard to the subject matter covered. It is sold with the understanding that the publisher is not engaged in rendering legal, accounting, or other professional services. If legal advice or other expert assistance is required, the services of a competent professional person should be sought.

*Library of Congress Cataloging in Publication Data:*
Toledano, Roulhac.
    The National Trust Guide to Savannah / Roulhac Toledano.
        p.   cm.
    Includes index.
    ISBN 0-471-15568-3 (pbk. : acid-free paper)
    1. Savannah (Ga.)—Guidebooks    I. National Trust for Historic
Preservation in the United States.    II.Title.
F294.S2T65    1997
917.58'7240443—dc20                                        96-43875

Printed in the United States of America

10 9 8 7 6 5 4 3 2 1

# Contents

# Preface

"I recollect a principle laid down by you. . .live as if each day were the last, but in building, build as if I was [sic] to live. . .forever. I feel my pride a little roused and I want these buildings to excel all others," said William Gibbons in an 1820 letter to his father, Thomas, mayor, entrepreneur, and Savannah's wealthiest man. He was speaking in reference to Gibbons Range at 102–116 West Congress Street, about to be rebuilt after a fire. Thomas Gibbons had gone to New York, and had retained Daniel Webster as his lawyer to break Aaron Ogden's monopoly of steamboats operating on the Hudson River. Chief Justice John Marshall's Supreme Court in 1824 decided in Gibbons' favor in Gibbons v. Ogden, defeating attorney Edward Livingston's client and establishing the supremacy of the commerce clause of the Constitution, which is the lynchpin of the federal government's power

"The building of cities," wrote Edmund N. Bacon in his study *The Design of Cities,* (New York: Penguin Books, 1987) "is one of man's greatest achievements. The form of his city always has been and always will be a pitiless indicator of the state of his civilization."

General James Edward Oglethorpe, founder of Savannah in 1733; copper engraving, "Ravenet sculptit" engraved on plate; from Tobias George Smollet's Compleat History of England (London: 1757). *Courtesy V. & J. Duncan Antique Maps and Prints.*

GENERAL OGLETHORPE.

James Edward Oglethorpe's 1733 plan of Savannah is North America's outstanding contribution to urban planning and to civilization. Savannah is a city as it should be, planned with the capacity to grow in an orderly fashion with a cohesive scale and a balance between landscape and buildings.

Savannah's founder made a design so organized and comprehensive that although not one building remains of his period, the whole today, largely a mid-nineteenth-century city, reflects the spirit as well as the design of the 1733 plan.

The city, planned before the arrival of its early inhabitants, continues today to express the civilization of its citizens, some of them descendants of those who arrived in Oglethorpe's time. Savannah, designed with such thoughtfulness, and practicality, expresses the ideal of an enlightened, responsible, and educated English society of its founding period.

Savannahians today find themselves thrust into the position of living up to their city and its history. Conversely, the city, through its leaders, struggles to indicate the state of civilization of the inhabitants and to strive toward the goals that Oglethorpe intended. Terrible failures alternate with notable successes.

This book is dedicated to two Savannah citizen-scholars who have represented the spirit and hopes of the founder and who reflect the civilization imprinted with Oglethorpe's plan. Walter Charlton Hartridge (1914–1974) and Joseph Frederick Waring (1902–1972) personify Savannah's complex and interlaced history. The Walter Charlton Hartridge Collection and the J. Frederick Waring Collection at the Georgia Historical Society provided the foundation for this book.

Walter Charlton Hartridge's careful research notes, articles, books, and photograph collection helped me to understand his city and that of nine generations of his antecedents. He was a pioneer in Savannah historical scholarship and in the preservation movement, the city owes much to this quiet citizen-scholar. The Hartridges have produced other writers, like Anne (Hartridge) Green and her brother Julien Green of Paris, a member of l'Academie Française. Their works made mine possible.

While writing this book I resided at the 1816 Federal-style rowhouse at 116 West Hull Street that scholar Walter Charlton Hartridge had inherited and where he and his wife, Susan, and their son, Walter, lived.

J. Frederick Waring carefully dissected the appearance of the city as depicted in Joseph Louis Firmin Cerveau's celebrated 1837 view, and he wrote an illuminating book in 1973 about Savannah's architecture and its inhabitants, documenting each structure in the Cerveau painting and providing its provenance. The book is available at the Georgia Historical Society. Bay Street's presevation is just one of his successful volunteer efforts for his city. Like the Warings before him, J. Frederick practiced an enlightened liberalism, which the family held dispite criticism during both the nineteenth and twentieth centuries. The tradition of community responsibility continues from century to century.

Hartridge house, 116 West Hull Street. Entrances to a pair of Federal houses built by and for John H. Ash in 1817. *Photograph by Keith Cardwell, courtesy Savannah College of Art and Design.*

These two Anglo-American men and their extended families, the houses they have lived in, the books they have written, and their libraries, churches, organizations and educational institutions represent what is good about Savannah as well as what is controversial. This is appropriate; Oglethorpe established a philanthropic project of constructive benevolence for Englishmen and for persecuted Protestant Europeans in the new thirteenth colony. Ideological and physical struggle preceded and followed each accomplishment. Whatever the population statistics for Savannah through 350 years (it has had a black majority in the past and has one today, with the Irish next and Germans strong in numbers and contributions to the city from 1733 on), it remains an English-style city in looks, in attitudes, and in culture.

I have seen within both families, Hartridge and Waring, leaders in historic preservation, in cultural, religious, and political activities, in gardening, in preservation of antiquities, in teaching, and in community service. Most of all I have seen family life as it has been through the centuries in the South, extended and adapted but never straying much from tradition.

Propitious marriages to neighbors, distant cousins, and co-religionists have made Savannah cohesive and have focused the community and social life of its inhabitants. The Hartridges have brought into their family descendants of Noble Jones, the original citizen-soldier of Savannah, and have emulated his traditions. Jones, with his wife and 10-year-old son Wimberly, arrived with Oglethorpe on the Anne in 1733. When Georgia became a Crown colony in 1754, the Jones family members were the only original colonists in Savannah from the first ship with forty families in 1733. The various Hartridges and their relatives — the Charltons, Barrows, Bells, Jones, McIntires, Jacksons, Lamars, Greens, and Foleys — whom I have known or whose houses I have known, are people who have adjusted to their old houses and their old city. They are loyal in their family dealings. Among them are strong and well-educated women who have moved beyond the expected family and civic responsibilities to contribute to their city in memorable ways. You will see examples of their service to the community throughout this book.

Like most Savannah families, the Hartridges and Warings have interacted with serious repercussions. For example, one Dr. Waring, following the enlightened and liberal tendencies of that family, provided a surety and bond for a young black man who was running for public office during Reconstruction. The Medical Society of Georgia met over Waring's action and decreed that such an act was not fitting behavior for a doctor of medicine. Waring's license to practice medicine was rescinded. Julian Hartridge, who had fought for the Confederacy, served two terms in its Congress and returned to Savannah to practice law, defended his neighbor Waring before the Georgia Supreme Court. The lawsuit resulted in reinstatement of Waring's license.

Families like the Hartridges and Warings instill in their children the same habits, sense of responsibility, and attitude toward civic and family service that pervaded earlier life here.

My times in Savannah have included afternoons with the late Walter Hartridge and his wife, Susan, in his library at 116 West Hull Street; walks through the city with his namesake, Walter Hartridge II; and stories of the Hartridge and Waring boys from Julian Hartridge, not the first of that name. In fact, it's hard to know which generation one is talking about because generations merge in their attitudes and work — lawyers and judges among Charltons and Hartridges, physicians among Warings, scholars among both.

The houses and buildings of the Hartridges and Warings and their allied families span the historic district and represent all types and styles of Savannah architecture. In Savannah it's not that you can't go home again. The question is which home to settle in; family residences or related buildings abound among Morels, Lanes, Hartridges, Warings, Stoddards, and many others.

On visits to the Georgia Historical Society bordering Forsyth Park I saw one of the most impressive of the colonial revival houses in Savannah, built for Mills B. Lane in 1909 after designs by Mowbray and Uffinger; Mrs. Mills B. Lane, Jr., born a Waring, lived there. I also passed Walter Hartridge II's mother's grandfather's house — Captain John David Hopkins' house at 304 East Gaston Street — where Walter grew up. Savannahians often grow up in houses descended from their mother's family (an antiquated extension of the early dowry system).

I saw these Gaston Street buildings while walking to the Georgia Historical Society. I also passed the Armstrong house, which houses the law firm of Bouhan, Williams, Levy, where Walter Hartridge II is a partner.

Georgia Historical
Society, 501 Whitaker
Street, designed in 1876
by architect Detlef
Lienau;
photograph by Adams
Studio, about 1905.
*Courtesy V. & J. Duncan
Antique Maps and Prints.*

View along West
Jones Street.
*Photograph by Keith
Cardwell, courtesy
Savannah College of
Art and Design.*

I wandered past Mrs. Wilkes' boardinghouse on Jones Street and saw that it is a Hartridge house. I passed another Waring House and two Hartridge houses walking to 119 East Charlton on Lafayette Square. There, Walter and Cornelia McIntire Hartridge live in yet another family home, built in 1852 for William Battersby, an Englishman and Savannah cotton merchant.

I spent many afternoons in their library and at dinner. Meals are much like they have been in this house over the past hundred years. The inhabitants of such historic houses, with their inherited furniture and decorative arts, adjust to their house plan and its accoutrements. They don't rebuild or manipulate the house to suit their present needs. They like the way their forebears lived, just as they appreciate their religion, education, and customs; historic Savannah churches are full of families on Sundays.

Thomas Usher Pulaski Charlton by John Wesley Jarris. Like many Savannah families through the generations, the Charltons named their children after the Revolutionary War Heroes. *Photograph Courtesy of Walter Hartridge, Jr., and Susan Hartridge.*

Breakfast rooms are nonexistent in such houses. Meals are meant to be served in the dining room. The old banquet table that serves twenty when the leaves are extended has been reduced to a small round for family intimacy. This makes the dining room large and empty, waiting for a wedding or a dinner party. I noticed the same arrangement at Wormsloe when I dined with Elfrida DeRenne Barrow.

Collective knowledge can provide strength: Let us hope that future generations of these families benefit from this communal and interrelated aspect of Savannah life. Perhaps the traditions and customs brought with the early settlers, promoted by the founder, and developed through the generations in the houses and squares of the city can continue to reflect the civilization envisioned by the Trustees of Georgia.

# Acknowledgments

First of all, gratitude to Scot Hinson, who provided a place to stay in his historic residence, the Federal paired house off Orleans Square built by and for John H. Ash in 1817. Previously it was the home of Walter Charlton Hartridge, Savannah scholar and author. Scot also gave me his time and talent, and he refamiliarized me with a historic city that I had known only casually for thirty years.

We walked together through every ward, street, avenue, and lane in the historic district. He made hundreds of study photographs for me, as well as some of the photographs published in this book. He assisted me in my research at the Georgia Historical Society, providing valuable information about the city where he came to study at the Savannah College of Art and Design.

I am grateful to Walter Hartridge II and to Cornelia McIntire Hartridge, who shared their daily lives with me, and to their son Tom, who endured the extended lectures provided by his parents.

Forsyth Ward house, built in 1897. *Photograph by Keith Cardwell, courtesy Savannah College of Art and Design.*

xiii

I am also grateful to old friends and acquaintances such as Susan Riley Myers, who lives in the Dasher house of 1844 on Chippewa Square that Reid Williamson inhabited when he was active in local preservation. Susan's expertise in the legal means to acquire deserted housing for renovation is helping to revitalize the Beach Institute area through the Live in a Landmark program.

My thanks to Ginger and John Duncan. John, a twelfth-generation Charlestonian, did what Charleston men and women started doing in 1733 and in greater numbers after 1750 — he came to Savannah. He has taught for thirty years at Armstrong College. He and Ginger have a rare book, print, and map shop in the basement of their astounding Second Empire baroque revival townhouse on Monterey Square.

My gratitude is extended to Beth Lattimore Reiter, whose ancestor Henry Hays Lattimore provided Savannah with its first automobile suburb, Ardsley Park, about 1910. She has devoted her energies as a volunteer, professional consultant, and author to the preservation of historic Savannah. She is now the historic preservation officer for the city of Savannah. Her book *Coastal Georgia* (Savannah: Golden Coast Publishing Company, 1985), with Van Jones Martin, is available at the Fort Pulaski Historic Monument. Her published works, surveys, and studies, particularly of the Victorian districts, reveal the depth of her knowledge and understanding of her city.

The Savannah College of Art and Design (SCAD) not only provided me with a better, more lively and organized Savannah than was here before its advent, but it offered almost forty renovated historic buildings to enjoy and walk past each day. Friends and assistants came to me from among students, faculty, and staff, including Marlborough Packard, Maureen Burke, Elizabeth Hudson-Goff, Jeff Eley and Susan Clinard.

Photographer Goeff DeLorm, of the Savannah College of Art and Design, is talented, and thank goodness, fast and efficient. We whipped across Savannah's squares as he photographed buildings for this book.

Photographer Keith Cardwell of London, now teaching at SCAD, tromped through the waterfront and Victorian district with me to capture the sunlight and the flatness of Savannah with its surrounding salt marshes and myriad waterways. The humid sun provokes a special light on Savannah's pine millwork in the Victorian districts and Keith was determined to capture it. Nancy White, whose antique wedding dress I provided, in turn provided photographs for the book's cover.

Leonard Zimmerman, graphic designer at SCAD's Design Press made Savannah easier to understand and enjoy with the fine maps he designed that illustrate the neighborhoods. SCAD's Jason McKay, Christine Moore, and Goeff DeLorm spent long hours at the computer scanning the photographs onto disks.

The Savannah College of Art and Design participated in the production of this book and made these services available to me and to the National Trust for Historic Preservation in a gracious and enthusiastic gesture of appreciation for my focus on the historic value of their city. I've written and had published some ten books in tandem with volunteer organizations to promote historic preservation and I do not remember unsolicited participation for a volunteer project like that from SCAD.

Sam and Pat Zemurray offered their hospitality and enthusiasm; they brought me together with many of their friends interested in the culture of Savannah, and they provided me and my volunteer assistants and friends a home in Guyton, an antebellum village with its own historic ambiance on a sand ridge northwest of Savannah. Their library provided rare books that had not previously been available to me.

Among many helpful Savannahians were Esther Shaver of Shaver's Bookstore, Anita Raskin at the Book Lady, and Odette Terrel des Chenes, her brother Gordon Gale, and his wife, Angela. Dot Lambert, a former Savannahian who as a newborn baby was found on a stoop on Liberty Street seventy eight-years ago and grew up in such a colorful way that a book demands to be written about her, also gave me background material. Alvin Neely, a descendant of patriot and Governor John Berrien, and John Macpherson Berrien, U.S. attorney general and senator provided a resting place in his marvelous Romanesque revival landmark, as well as information, humor, and lunches. Sam Ross and Michael Sullivan, students at SCAD, did all-around work assisting me.

As always, Emmaline and Robert Cooper were both host and hostess supreme, as well as acute contributors on the subject of Savannah historical and cultural environment. Emmaline's guide to Savannah, written with Polly Cooper, provides up-to-date information and the acumen that only natives have.

It takes a lot of nerve to write about a city that is not your own. The directors, curators and volunteers at museums, research institutions, and libraries gave their time and resources. These include the Historic Savannah Foundation; the Telfair Museum of Art, especially Tania Sammons and Charles M. Johnson, for use of his manuscript on the Telfair family; the Davenport house museum, Richard Betterly, curator; the Juliette Gordon Low house and birthplace, Stephen Bohlin-Davis, curator, the Andrew Low House of the National Society of the Colonial Dames of America in the state of Georgia, Betty Arnold, administrator, and Alice Daily, furnishings chairman; the Owens-Thomas house, Olivia Alison, curator; the Green–Meldrim house, Joanne Hardwick, volunteer curator; Ships of the Sea Museum; the Beehive Press; the Georgia Historical Society, especially Kim Ball; the staffs at the Chamber of Commerce and the city of Savannah, especially Robin Gunn; and the Special Projects Department of the Savannah School of Art and Design, with its helpful staff.

Jo Ann Gunn, Reid Williamson, Audry Dunn Platt, Beth Sheehan, Preston Russell, co-author with Barbara Hines of *Savannah, A History of Her People*

*Since 1733,* (Savannah: Frederick C. Beil, 1992), National Trust trustee Camille Jones Strachan, Emma Morel Adler, and trustee emeritus of the National Trust, Lee Adler, were part and parcel of the effort to research and write this book. Volunteer photographers, computer consultants, and editors without whose help there could be no book include Dr. Will Waring, Rosemarie Fowler, Sharon Hinson, Jenny Williams, Susan Hartridge, Walter Hartridge, Jr., Melinda Cardell, Clement Speiden, Jemison Gale, and Lewis Rector.

# Foreword

## By John Berendt

For five years in the late 1980s I had the good fortune to live in Savannah, and to tell you the truth, I reveled in it. At least once a day I would stop work and wander through the city's 3-square-mile historic district, strolling from one garden square to another, as if walking through the rooms of a magnificent open-air mansion. You do not have to be a specialist in urban design (and I am not) to recognize that Savannah's twenty-two squares are its treasures. The city was laid out by James Oglethorpe, founder of the Georgia colony. He placed the squares at regular intervals to serve as meeting places and sites for such public amenities as water pumps and baking ovens. Today, 260 years later, the squares are no longer needed for their original uses, and they have evolved into peaceful, tree-shaded urban ornaments. The marvel is that they accommodate automobile traffic and, at the same time, exert a moderating influence on it: cars must slow down as they negotiate the turns around the periphery of the squares; they cannot race through the middle.

During my walks, I would always pass a fair sampling of Savannah's other main attraction: its architectural gems. The sheer number of distinguished buildings is astonishing for a city of Savannah's size, but this is easily explained. Early on, Savannah became a city of rich cotton traders who wanted, for themselves and their city, the best townhouses and public buildings money could buy. Knowing they would have to go far afield to accomplish this goal, they imported the leading architects of the day to design buildings that incorporated the latest popular tastes. Master builder Isaiah Davenport came down from Rhode Island at the beginning of the nineteenth century and built Federal-style dwellings in brick. The young Englishman William Jay designed several buildings in the Regency style (very rare in the United States), and the great Boston architect William Gibbons Preston left Savannah a legacy of Romanesque revival brick buildings.

If it was money that built the city, it was money that nearly destroyed it, too. In the early years of the twentieth century, merchants began knocking down old buildings to make way for gas stations, parking lots, and commercial structures. They also drew a bead on the squares, proposing to pave them over as parking lots or at least slice roadways through the middle of them so that traffic could rush through unimpeded.

In reaction, concerned citizens formed a preservation movement; it began in the 1930s and gathered momentum with each stunning new loss. It was the deep dismay over demolition of the beloved city market in 1954 that finally tipped the balance in favor of the preservationists and resulted in the formation of the Historic Savannah Foundation. The following years saw the spectacular restoration of 1500 dilapidated downtown buildings and the landscaping of the squares, which by then had become bare and neglected.

The heroes of Savannah's restoration and preservation movement are well known and justly celebrated. There are, in addition, a number of unsung heroes whose efforts have been equally important, and I used to see one of them in action as I took my daily walk through the squares. She was a tall, gentle woman who always wore a broad-brimmed hat and carried a long, thin walking stick that looked very much like a classroom pointer, which in fact it was. She was always trailed by a double line of 20 or 30 well-behaved children. Her name was Sarah Parsons, and she was a teacher at the Massie School on Calhoun Square. Massie is the oldest functioning schoolhouse in Georgia, and some years ago it was turned into the Massie Heritage Interpretation Center. Its purpose is to introduce grade-school children from all over Georgia to the state's history, particularly its architectural history.

Mrs. Parsons was the heritage classroom teacher, and she had an amazing rapport with children. It was said she could walk into an auditorium full of 750 boisterous students and have them listening to her in rapt silence within two minutes. Each morning in her heritage classroom at Massie, she would take a new group of students under her wing by first asking each child to stand and say his or her name. "I will remember all your names," she would promise, "because every one of you is important. If I do forget your name, you can eat my lunch!" Mrs. Parsons would compose little rhymes in her head for each child ("Benny has a penny," "Mike rides a bike") in order to remember the names, and in all her years as the heritage classroom teacher, she never forfeited her lunch.

"Today I am going to teach you 50 things you didn't know when you came in here," she would tell them, "and you won't have to read one word! But you will have to listen. And you are going to learn by looking. Today I am going to introduce you to Palladian windows, to mansard roofs, to leaded glass, to terra-cotta, to cupolas, and to fish-scale shingles. I am going to increase your visual knowledge." She would show the children slides of the world's greatest buildings and then tell them, with a hint in her voice that they were about to embark on a great adventure, "Today, you are going to see the triangular pediments of the Parthenon, the Roman arches of the Coliseum, and the Gothic arches of the Cathedral of Notre Dame—all right here in Savannah!"

Then off they would go on a tour of the squares, the brim of Mrs. Parsons' big hat aflutter, her pointer held high in the air like a mizzenmast. "One-two-three: Follow me!" she would call out so loud and with such gusto that a passing adult or two would usually fall in step at the end of the line for the sheer joy of it.

Before long, Mrs. Parsons would come to a stop, tap her stick on the sidewalk, and say, "Who can show me Greek revival?" The children would look eagerly at the buildings, while she sang out, "Greek re-viiiiii-val! Greek re-vii-iiii-val! Let me know with your hands—and not your voices—when you have found one!" The children were well prepared for this game, and, one by one, they would raise both hands, forming a triangle with their thumbs and forefingers to show that they had spotted a Greek revival building with its distinctive triangular pediment. They would jump up and down, hoping to attract Mrs. Parsons' notice.

"Angela's found a Greek revival building!" Mrs. Parsons would declare. "Point it out to us, Angela! Point it out! Very good! Mark, where's yours? That's good, too!" Then she would start walking again, exhorting the children not to fall behind—"Quickie-wickie, 'cause I got a stickie!" Soon she would ask if anybody could find a Romanesque building. "When you find it, hold your hands up and make the best horseshoe arch you can, and say 'Round Romanesque! Rowwwwwwwwnd Romanesque!'" Later, she would ask the children if they could find a Gothic revival building, and the hands would shoot up again, this time with palms almost touching as if in prayer, approximating a Gothic arch.

Mrs. Parsons told me she felt privileged to be the one to introduce so many young people—at least two thousand a year—to the wonders of architecture. "When their parents and grandparents were children," she said, "nobody bothered to tell them about Savannah's architectural treasures, so they never learned to appreciate them and they came very close to letting the bulldozers knock them down. The generations to come will never let that happen. Nowadays, I'll be walking downtown, and I'll hear someone call my name, and I'll look up and see a young adult waving at me from across the street—and they'll put both hands in the air in the form of a triangle. They remember. They'll never forget."

Mrs. Parsons is retired now, but I often think of her when I visit Savannah and walk through the squares. I also think of the people who, each in his own way, helped rescue it from destruction, and then I think back to the colonists who built the city in the first place. Inevitably, these thoughts remind me that Savannah's greatest saving grace has always been its people. They are headstrong, insular, and often marvelously quirky. They are also very proud, and the way I see it they have every reason to be.

THE **NATIONAL TRUST** GUIDE TO

# Savannah

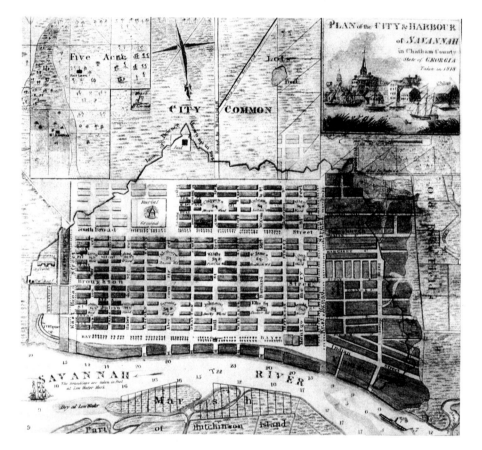

**Figure 1** Plan of the city and harbor of Savannah, 1818, by I. Stouf. The map indicates the line of defense thrown up in the War of 1812. Some of the city common is shown with the 4½-acre garden plots, assigned according to Oglethorpe's original plan, to the holders of associated tithing lots within the city. Fairlawn is indicated, as are rice fields. An inset shows the city exchange (now demolished) and the steeple of Christ Church when it was a little Federal building, before its remodeling as a Greek temple. *Courtesy V. & J. Duncan Antique Maps and Prints.*

# 1

# IMPRESSIONS RESPECTING SAVANNAH: MANY TIMES A GIFT

In 1864, General W. T. Sherman telegraphed President Lincoln, "I beg to present you as a Christmas Gift, the city of Savannah with 150 heavy guns and plenty of ammunition and also about 25,000 bales of cotton" (Figure 1).

This was the third time that Savannah was given away. General James Edward Oglethorpe, the founder, made the first gift. In 1733 he bequeathed the laid-out city to the new settlers, a charitable benefaction for the worthy, working poor of Britain and persecuted European Protestants (Figure 2).

Twenty years later, when the tiny port city failed to flourish, the Georgia Trustees gave Savannah and the entire colony to the Crown of England; one more time the city was given away. In 1754 the first royal governor landed at the dock to take over the newly acquired city of Savannah. Between the three gifts and intervening wars, the fortunes of Savannah ebbed and flowed, much like the tide it depends on for sustenance.

**Figure I** Gordon block, 110–129 West Gordon Street, 1853. High stoops projecting into the sidewalk from the rowhouses and townhouses characterize Savannah's street scenes. *Photograph by Clement Speiden.*

**Figure 2**  "Peace Between Governor Oglethorpe and the Indians in 1733," relief frieze at the U. S. Capitol; from *Art in the United States Capitol* (Washington, D.C.: U. S. Government Printing Office, 1976). *Courtesy V. & J. Duncan Antique Maps and Prints.*

After World War I it became evident that Oglethorpe's creation was worth holding onto. At that time Savannah simply wasn't being given away for the fourth time: It was being thrown away, not by a military enemy this time, but by the city and its citizens. Stellar residences designed by such architects as Jay, Norris, Cluskey, and Preston had become tenements and were sliding one by one, then in blocks, toward demolition. Weed-infested squares became candidates for parking lots and thoroughfares.

Town meetings started again, to preserve Savannah. The inhabitants did again what the Trustees had done in the 1730s and 1740s. They met, petitioned the government, and raised statewide consciousness and money. In 1921 the Society for the Preservation of the Parks was formed to thwart attempts to eliminate certain of the ancient squares. They failed in 1935 when the Montgomery Street squares were destroyed. In response to the Historic American Building Survey project, Savannah Mayor Thomas Gamble began the Savannah Commission for the Preservation of Landmarks. They met to block efforts to make Habersham Street a throughway. This threat spurred the forming of the Society for the Preservation of the Squares of Savannah. All was hit and miss until the 1950s, when the city market was demolished and a parking lot was built on Ellis Square.

The feud continued from 1933 to 1956. By that time, thirteen of Savannah's fifty-six major historic landmarks that the Historic American Buildings Survey (HABS) had selected for recordation were demolished. Mary

Hillyer managed to begin the turning of the tide. She took up the area where Mrs. Marmaduke Floyd and her Pirates House had kept a spark of interest alive, on the east side of town in the Old Fort area. Mary Hillyer was a pioneer in the 1940s when she saved the Trustees Garden area to make it a successful real estate investment for the Savannah Gas Company, which had planned the demolition of all the extant buildings on its property.

Finally, the seven women who saved the Davenport house and spurred the establishment of the Historic Savannah Foundation kept Savannah from being given away, indeed thrown away: its plan, its buildings, its heritage. These women knew that preservation of the built environment of Savannah was the ultimate gift to future generations.

Savannah, with its strong tradition of civic leadership, was up to the challenge laid down by the women. Its size was manageable, with the 1733 plan still intact. Eighty percent of the building inventory between the Savannah River and Victory Drive, and East and West Broad Streets, was historic. Much of it looked like a mess, though—too deteriorated to appear picturesque.

The preservation movement prospered over the next thirty years, after 1956. Thousands participated, and hundreds must be remembered as leaders (see pp. 9–26). The Historic Savannah Foundation led the fight, first under Reid Williamson, with associated organizations such as the Junior League and participating churches. Exhilarating successes have been intermixed with heartrending failures. As preservation methods have become more sophisticated and preservation a respectable career as well as a philosophy, Savannah's preservation-interested base has spread, but certain players' names stand out.

Besides the women themselves (see pp. 9–26), the Historic Savannah Foundation has led the fight and coordinated many of the efforts of other individuals and organizations. Among the people who have worked with the foundation are Lee Adler, who has received the National Trust for Historic Preservation's highest award for the work he continues; the Lane family, both individually and collectively, through the Lane Foundation; the late Jim Williams, who used the money he made to make his adopted city beautiful; and more recently, civil rights leader W. W. Law, who has brought the black community into active participation in the city's preservation. Following in the footsteps of the Historic Savannah Foundation, the Savannah College of Art and Design has had an impact on all areas of the historic city through its role in the rehabilitation of so many monumental brick anchor buildings that had been abandoned, such as jails, schools, and other institutional buildings. In addition, the Coastal Heritage Society has initiated a vast project to preserve the Central of Georgia railroad complex and the site of the 1779 seige of Savannah (see p. 42).

The foundation went to work just as a century of owner-occupancy of vast numbers of Savannah's building stock was ending. Using the foundation's $200,000 revolving fund, buildings were purchased and resold at or below cost. In addition to the rescue of individual houses, such as the Davenport house, Oliver Sturges house, and Scarbrough house, the foundation assumed the task of salvaging a commercial block of Italianate buildings on West Congress Street near the city market in Decker Ward. Later it was the Troup Trust and Mary Marshall Row. After saving Pulaski Square and Jones Street (Figure 3), the Historic Savannah Foundation responded to a crisis in Monterey Square, and the fight continued on to the Victorian district, the Beach Institute area, and has now reached Broughton Street.

Meanwhile, Savannah's religious community had resisted the national trend to abandon old churches and build new ones in the suburbs. This helped save the historic districts. Preservation in Savannah's historic districts has rarely been a gentrification project. Savannah families that had continued to live in their inherited homes were joined by new friends and neighbors, who renovated worn-out tenements or returned to live in houses they had previously owned and leased.

Another key to saving Savannah have been the Mills B. Lane family and the Lane Foundation. Few other Southern cities have a family and foundation as committed to preservation as the Lanes of the two recent generations. Members of the family have bought and restored eighteenth- and nineteenth-century houses, primarily of frame construction, and the family as a group has

**Figure 3** Details in wrought and cast iron can be enjoyed along West Jones Street. The Historic Savannah Foundation made possible the return of this street to its 1850s appearance. *Photograph by Goeff DeLorm, courtesy Savannah College of Art and Design*

initiated numerous projects for Historic Savannah and has financed other projects that the city and Historic Savannah Foundation have carried out

The late Jim Williams contributed with his far-reaching individual efforts. An antiques dealer who appeared on the Savannah scene in the late 1950s, he has had a considerable impact on the city through the purchase, renovation, and sale or rental of almost a score of notable houses and up to forty buildings essential to the historic scene across the city. During a 25-year period, from small frame cottages in the Old Fort area to Armstrong College at Bull and Gaston streets and his final home on Monterey Square, Jim Williams helped to change the face of Savannah.

I met Jim about 30 years ago at a party he hosted one afternoon at his recently moved and restored Hampton Lillibridge house on Washington Square. Good fortune had found the tall, handsome young man when he made a $600,000 profit on the sale of Cabbage Island, a little sand spit he had bought on a lark for $5000. At the time he was putting the money into the preservation of Savannah's historic houses in fringe areas. The little frame restoration on St. Julian Street was just the second of many buildings, some of them monumental undertakings, that he restored.

More recently, interaction among individuals and groups has served the preservation movement, broadening the base of interest in living in historic Savannah. The City of Savannah and the Savannah College of Art and Design have had an enormous impact on Savannah's rebirth. Others include strong African-American communities, notably one led by W. W. Law, a civil rights activist whose preservation efforts have benefited the entire community. He knows that buildings and the stories of their inhabitants are fine tools for education among the African-American community, as well as in cross-cultural communication.

Lee Adler's work in downtown Savannah has been visible since 1958. In the first decade, as he worked through the Historic Savannah Foundation, his creative thinking saved the Mary Marshall Row across from Colonial Cemetery. Alerted by the overnight demolition of the carriage buildings behind the row, the Historic Savannah Foundation, with the help of Lee Adler and a small group of business owners, acquired for $45,000 the land on which the houses stood. Then they offered the demolisher $9000, a profit on the Savannah gray bricks worth $6000 at the time.

When Armstrong College threatened to tear down the historic properties it owned in Monterey Ward to establish a lackluster campus, the Historic Savannah Foundation and a coalition of leaders, including Lee Adler, the Lane family, the late Walter C. Hartridge, Jim Williams, and others, moved to circumvent that misdirected plan and save the landmark Italianate and Beaux Arts mansions.

In 1970, Lee Adler set up the Savannah Landmark Rehabilitation Project. Its aim was to save the 78-block, 160-acre late Victorian district south of Oglethorpe's original settlement without displacing its occupants. The challenges of Savannah Landmark paralleled those that faced Oglethorpe and the Georgia Trustees in their efforts toward constructive philanthropy. Savannah Landmark proved that renovation of existing building inventory is more cost-effective than new federal housing projects. Low-interest loans and city, state, and federal participation at various levels were overseen by Savannah architectural historian and city planner Beth Reiter. Georgia's Jimmy Carter and his Habitat for Humanity became involved, both renovating old houses and building infill of appropriate scale. The National Housing Partnership then joined the effort. One key to renovation in the Victorian district was Lee Adler's networking, involving organizations across the city, state, and nation with people in Savannah.

Preservation continues in the Victorian districts, thanks in part to the students and faculty of the Savannah College of Art and Design. They rent the rehabilitated buildings and some stay on in the Victorian districts to buy derelict but aesthetically appealing historic properties to renovate. It's an uphill battle, and it looks as if the percentage of success with charitable grants in the Victorian districts of Savannah is about the same as Oglethorpe's success with the same approach between 1733 and 1753.

Since its establishment in 1979, the Savannah College of Art and Design (SCAD) has boosted the viability of historic Savannah in numerous ways. The college opened with one historic building, the Romanesque-style Savannah Volunteer Guards Armory at the corner of Bull and Charlton streets. By the fall of 1996, it had a collection of about forty buildings throughout Savannah, providing neighborhood anchors and uses for the large vacant institutional buildings across the historic city (Figure 4).

SCAD developed a new approach to the concept of "City College." It is both European and original. It not only has an urban campus; their campus is, in effect, historic Savannah, both the downtown historic district and the Victorian districts to the south. Marlborough Packard, chair of historic preservation for SCAD, puts it this way: "We don't want to tear down anything. And we don't want to build any new buildings." The city takes care of the streets and other infrastructure that normally would be left to the college to maintain, freeing the school to devote its time and money to the purchase and renovation of abandoned landmarks. Their Savannah Design Collaborative and full-time construction crew develop and oversee the renovations.

Students Sam Ross and Mike Sullivan summed it up: "We live in and walk through and attend class in spaces that are like what we've studied in class," said Sam. "The scale and proportion of Savannah's plan and buildings reflect everything the textbooks teach about an ideal environment," added Michael. These students and their peers learn to live and to look in one of the South's most habitable and visually pleasing cities.

**Figure 4**    340–344 Bull Street; photograph, 1946. The Savannah Volunteer Guards had William Gibbons Preston design their new headquarters in the Richardson Romanesque style in 1893. It became the first headquarters of the Savannah School of Art and Design eighteen years ago, now one of about forty buildings occupied by SCAD across the historic districts. *Cordray–Foltz Collection, courtesy Georgia Historical Society.*

The rehabilitation of the Central of Georgia Railroad complex has spurred the revitalization of the western edge of historic Savannah. The Coastal Heritage Society and the city of Savannah understood the importance of Savannah's unique railyard with its roundhouse, stack, and buildings, clustered on the site of the 1779 siege of Savannah when the French and patriots tried to eject the British from the city. Savannah Revolutionary Battlefield Park is a projected $80 million project that includes the 5-acre site.

Another hero of preservation in the western corridor of Savannah is W. W. Law, who sees this area as the heart of African-American Savannah. Law has caused the community to realize the potential of the various African-American churches, museums, neighborhoods, insurance companies, banks, and other institutions as cross-cultural opportunities. Law, who pursued preservation as a priority after serving as president of the Georgia NAACP and launching the Savannah chapter of the Association for the Study of Afro-American Life and History, treasures buildings more for the stories they tell and the lessons they embody and for the people who built, worked, and lived in them than for their aesthetics or architectural appeal. Savannah's built environment is a beneficiary of his viewpoint and efforts.

Thanks to the efforts of all of these people, Savannah is no longer the "beautiful lady with a dirty face" that Lady Astor once described in 1946. Strong, as a southern belle should be, Savannah has survived two devastating fires, yellow fever epidemics, and lengthy occupations by two enemies. Romantic as native son Johnny Mercer's "Moon River" but tough as "Hard-Hearted Hannah," Savannah has prevailed with an "accentuate the positive" attitude—first of Georgia's Trustees and 200 years later of its concerned citizens.

# 2

---

# FOUR MARYS AND MORE: WOMEN DEVELOPERS AND PRESERVERS

The stalwart women of Savannah during the siege of Savannah in 1779 and Sherman's occupation in 1864–1865 are subjects for table talk and history books. Sherman himself commented that it was a good thing that determined southern women were not on the front lines. Otherwise, he suggested, the war would have lasted for years longer. Such stories of women's accomplishments and attitudes are not apocryphal in Savannah. A number of nineteenth- and twentieth-century Savannah women were leaders in real estate development, in community service, and in cultural contributions.

Four women named Mary loom large in Savannah's development and architectural history: one Creek–English woman named Mary Musgrove owned more real estate in mid-eighteenth century Georgia than any one man or woman of the Trustee period (Figure 1). An Anglo-American Savannahian, Mary Marshall, was a bona fide mid-nineteenth-century developer. Mary Telfair, the notable nineteenth-century benefactress of Savannah institutions, inherited wealth and position and used them to benefit her city. In the 1940s, Mary Hillyer conceived and supervised restoration of the historic Trustees Garden area, thus spearheading restoration of the entire Old Fort area and the squares on the eastern side of the city.

Working at the same time as Mary Marshall, Eliza Ann Jewett developed real estate in Jasper Ward (Madison Square) and Lafayette Ward (Lafayette Square). In the next generation, Juliette Gordon Low committed her money and talent not just to interior decoration and art, in which she excelled, but to the betterment of women's lives across the nation and the world. Women's roles in Savannah development continued. Among the many women who

9

**Figure 1** "Mary Musgrove Bosomworth Inciting the Indians to Violence, (1750s)," wood engraving from Hezekiah Butterworth's *Zigzag Journeys in the Western States of America* (London: Dean and Son, about 1885). This romanticized scene shows Mary defending her title to the coastal islands. The text explains, "Led by the princess in her royal trappings and Thomas Bosomworth in his canonical robes, two hundred Indian braves marched into the seaport city [Savannah], where they remained for a fortnight threatening the authorities and intimidating residents." *Courtesy V. & J. Duncan Antique Maps and Prints.*

fought to preserve historic Savannah at its critical point in the 1950s, Stella Henderson, Anna Hunter, and Alida Harper Fowlkes purchased and restored historic properties. Some women like Mary Lane Morrison fought to save Savannah with the printed page and education; others became architects and contractors. In the age-old women's way, some worked through others—their husbands and family, and the city, state, and federal governments—in a coordinating effort that brought about preservation. It began soon after 1733 and continues today with hopes for a bright future for Savannah.

The tradition of the Indian woman as guide and diplomat, representing the white man to the Native Americans, is gaining recognition. Mary Musgrove and James Edward Oglethorpe in Georgia join Pocahontas and John Smith in Virginia, Hernando Cortes and his Aztec advisor and mistress Malinche in Mexico, and the Shoshone woman Sacajawea and Meriwether Lewis and William Clark in the west.

Mary Musgrove, half Creek Indian and half English, was the only woman of her time in Georgia to receive a salary—£100 a year for her translation services. Coosaponakesee, as Mary was called among the Creeks, translated at the first meeting of Oglethorpe and Tomochichi, chief of the Yamacraw division of the Creeks. With Mary's help, Oglethorpe gained their loyalty. Together they brought the Lower and Upper Creeks to Savannah. With Mary's assistance, Oglethorpe made trade and treaty agreements with the tribes of the Southeast.

Before Oglethorpe's arrival, Mary Musgrove, a niece of the Creek Chief Brim and a native of Coweta, the Creek capital 300 miles upcountry from Savannah on the Chattahoochee River, had married an English fur trader, John Musgrove, and she lived with him and her four sons running a trading post among the Yamacraw Indians. John Musgrove died within three years of Oglethorpe's arrival, and her sons died between 1733 and 1736. John Wesley's journal of November 1736 remarks: "I buried Mrs. Musgrove's only [then living] son." Oglethorpe delayed his trip to England so that he could attend the funeral.

During the Oglethorpe period, Mary Musgrove may have been the only woman to own land despite then-current Trustee regulations that prohibited women from receiving land grants or inheriting real property. Nonetheless, she received a grant of land of 500 acres in September 1735. Lord Egmont wrote about the grant and Mary. "She took her land. She is the best Interpreter in the Trustees' service and in good circumstances." Egmont's reasoning was that Musgrove's son "will enjoy it . . . and in the meantime Mary, his [Musgrove's] widow, enjoys it, and it has good improvements. The place is called Grantham." In addition to owning Grantham, Mary had a substantial Indian trading post upcountry called Cowpens and a tithing lot in the city. She kept eight English indentures to help her run her lucrative trading business.

Soon after Egmont's journal entry, Mary infuriated the class-conscious English by marrying one of her indentures, Jacob Matthews, who became a captain in the Rangers before his death in 1742.

In the following years, English courts confirmed Mary's ownership of three of the great coastal islands, Ossabaw, St. Catherines, and Sapelo. Admittedly, this grant was proved with the self-interested help of her third husband, Thomas Bosomworth, a minister in the service of the colony and a one-time commissioner of Indian Affairs.

Mary Musgrove had negotiated with her Creek cousin, Chief Malatchee, to sell her for a trifle the islands that had always been part of the vast Creek-claimed coastal lands. When the Trustees altered their regulations to allow slavery and ownership of land with transfer and mortgage rights in 1749, she had to defend her ownership rights before the Crown. Crown Colony Governor James Wright, whom she knew well, helped her negotiate a settlement by which she received 2050 pounds from the sale of two of the islands. She retained title to St. Catherines' 25,000 acres, where she developed a plantation. Mary Musgrove died and was buried on St. Catherines in the late 1760s.

Today, St. Catherines and Ossabaw have reverted to the natural state of Mary's time. Where slaves once worked to cultivate rice and cotton, wind now blows through sand and grass and the sea penetrates marshes once diked for rice growing.

Sapelo became a Spalding family sea island long-staple cotton plantation, with some sugar and rice growing on the side, from 1802 until 1925. Out-of-state ownership of Sapelo by the Coffin family in 1925, then by R. J. Reynolds, Jr., ended in 1978 when Sapelo was sold to the state. It is now managed by the Georgia Department of Natural Resources. The only private landowners on the island are the descendants of former slaves who worked cotton for the Spaldings. They inhabit a little community called Hog Hammock.

A century after the self-styled Creek Indian Empress met Oglethorpe, another woman named Mary imprinted Savannah. Mary Magdalen Leaver, an only child, was born in 1783 to Gabriel and Mary Schick Leaver. Her English father, a cabinetmaker and well-to-do Savannah citizen, bought property on Broughton Street and other key locations in Savannah that became the cornerstone of his daughter's future fortune when he died at 38.

Mary Leaver married Savannah banker James Marshall, originally from St. Augustine, Florida, in 1800, at age 16. Childless at age 56, Mary Marshall adopted a poor Irish immigrant, Margaret, five years before her husband's death in 1845. Margaret, after marriage at 15 to the son of the British consul at New York in 1855, divorced in 1860 and died in 1866.

Mary Marshall, in her eighties, raised her 8-year-old granddaughter, Mary Marshall Barclay, at her mansion, **47 West Broad Street** (demolished). She died when her heir was 19-years-old and the ward of J. J. Waring in Savannah.

Active in the Society for the Relief of Poor Widows with Dependent Children, she was also patroness of the Marshall Fire Hose Company. She presented plans by builders Scudder and Thomson to the city for Savannah's female asylum (Figure 2). In the event that her granddaughter had no heirs, she bequeathed her West Broad Street mansion to Christ Episcopal Church.

Mary Marshall owned eight slaves and one carriage, with a total worth of $200,810 soon after her father's death. With her inherited base of six properties, she bought real estate heavily, sometimes building on lots and sometimes buying the extant buildings. By 1864 she owned part of Tyler Cotton Press. Her forty properties included houses, stores, stables, and a hotel. The Marshall Hotel and the Mary Marshall Row of four-story rowhouses across from Colonial Cemetery on East Oglethorpe Avenue (Figure 3) remain as examples of her entrepreneurial success.

Eliza Ann Jewett may not have had the energy or the amazing life accorded Mary Marshall nor Mary's notorious superstitions, but she, too, prospered with her real estate acquisitions in mid-nineteenth-century Savannah.

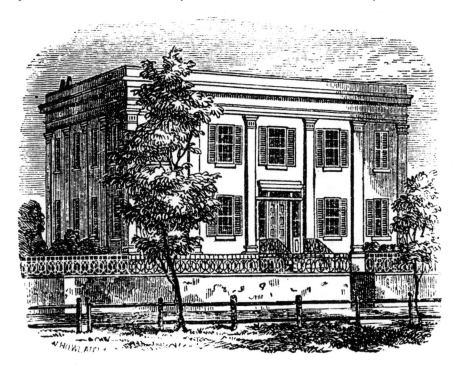

**Figure 2** Female orphan asylum, signed on plate "W. Howland"; from *Historical Record of the City of Savannah* (Savannah: J. H. Estill Morning News Steam Power Press, 1860). Mary Marshall, benefactress of Savannah and real estate developer, supported this institution. Her own daughter and heir was an impoverished Irish child. She presented plans to the city by Scudder and Thomson for a new building in the 1850s. In 1888, however, the orphans moved into the old Wetter mansion on Broad Street, near the Marshall mansion. The asylum, the female extension of Bethesda, moved to Savannah in 1810. *Courtesy V. & J. Duncan Antique Maps and Prints.*

**Figure 3**  Mary Marshall Row,
230–244 East Oglethorpe Avenue,
1855–1856. *Photograph by Goeff
DeLorm, courtesy Savannah College
of Art and Design.*

The widow Eliza Ann Jewett's Greek revival house on Madison Square at **326 Bull Street** (Figure 4; see p. 144) is well known. Behind that property is Jewett Row, one of Savannah's mid-nineteenth-century landmarks. By the time she built properties on Jones Street, a picture of a major real estate developer emerges.

Eliza Ann was born in 1779. Her first husband died early in their marriage and their daughter, Eliza Ann Bowles, married Francis Champion of Savannah, which may have brought the widow Bowles to Savannah. In 1817 she married Jasper W. Jewett at the First Baptist Church in Savannah. Mr. Jewett died two years later, leaving two infant daughters. The twice-widowed woman had her Bull Street townhouse built between 1834 and 1843. In 1842–1843 she had a pair of townhouses built at **20–22 West Harris Street** (Figure 5; see p. 146). But her most active years in real estate development occurred when she was past the age of 70. In 1847 the townhouse at

**Figure 4**   Eliza Ann Jewett house, 326 Bull Street on Madison Square, built in 1842. *Photograph by Goeff DeLorm, courtesy Savannah College of Art and Design.*

**Figure 5**   West Jones Street stoop in the Greek revival style, introduced to the area by Eliza Ann Jewett. *Photograph by Keith Cardwell, courtesy Savannah College of Art and Design.*

Figure 6 *Eliza Ann Jewett is responsible for the Greek revival look of Jones Street. Photograph by Keith Cardwell, courtesy Savannah College of Art and Design.*

**16 East Jones Street** was built for her, followed by five paired brick houses in Madison and Lafayette wards (Figure 6).

Eliza Ann Jewett died in 1856. The funeral for the 77-year-old widow was at her house on Madison Square. Eliza Ann Jewett is not known to have inherited great wealth, but she understood the value of real estate in Savannah during its golden age, between 1840 and the Civil War. Her contributions to the Greek revival appearance of Savannah are evident today.

Mary Telfair, as opposed to Eliza Jewett, was a Savannah heiress who knew how to enjoy her wealth and how to spend it for the benefit of her city. The last of the Telfairs, a family that had come to Savannah during the Crown colony days, Mary Telfair was born in 1791 in Augusta, where her father, Edward Telfair, was governor. Her mother, Sarah Gibbons Telfair (Figure 7), was a South Carolinian and her father had emigrated from Scotland and arrived at Savannah in 1766. By 1803, Edward Telfair had six children, the three eldest boys all studying at Princeton.

Her brother Alexander and her sister Margaret also figure in Savannah's community welfare. Through the 1804 bequest of their uncle, William Gibbons, the three owned half of the present site of the Telfair house, and by 1818 Alexander Telfair commissioned English architect William Jay to build his family home (Figure 8).

In 1825 Telfair held a Masonic banquet for visiting hero General Lafayette. His sister, Mary Telfair, who lived with him and their sister Margaret in the house, had a sardonic view of Lafayette's triumphal return to the United States. She wrote her friend Mary Few in New York: "I really think the hard service of the revolution light compared to his present campaign [raising money].... I feel a tender interest for his health, for I am sure he will be feted to death. Here [in Savannah]. They mean to outshine New York."

Alexander Telfair died in 1832 in Winchester, Virginia, as the family was returning to Georgia from a summer up north. He left much of his fortune and his mansion to his two sisters, Mary and Margaret, who had lived with him there since they were in their twenties.

**Figure 7**  Sarah Martin Gibbons, artist unknown, late eighteenth century. Mary Telfair's mother was from Charleston, but Thomas Gibbons moved to Savannah, where he made a fortune and built a mansion on West Broad Street (demolished) as well as Gibbons Range. *Courtesy Telfair Museum of Art, bequest of Mary Telfair, 1875.*

**Figure 8**  Telfair Museum of Art. Photograph, 1995, by Daniel L. Grantham, Jr. *Courtesy Telfair Museum of Art.*

**Figure 9**  Mary Telfair in her residence on Telfair Square. *Courtesy Telfair Museum of Art.*

The middle-aged but wealthy and well-connected Telfair sisters sailed for Europe in 1841 (Figure 9). They returned with William Brown Hodgson as husband for Margaret. A student of Berber languages who had served the American consular service at Algiers and Tunis, Hodgson used his talents and frame of reference in the service of Savannah. The establishment of Forsyth Park to the south of the city, for example, was his idea as early as 1851.

Mary Telfair died June 2, 1875. Through her will she provided Savannah with institutions running the gamut of cultural, religious, and social needs.

Because of her fortune and largesse, the city has the first continually open art museum in the South, launched in 1885 in the family home after suitable additions had been finished. She established the Telfair Hospital for Women, which served the indigent at **17 East Park Avenue** in a building designed by architects Fay and Eichberg in 1886 (Figures 10 and 11). After use as the maternity section of the Candler Hospital, it closed in 1980. The Georgia Historical Society building, named Hodgson Hall after her brother-in-law, was

**Figure 10**   Front elevation of the Telfair Hospital; photogravure from Charles Edgeworth Jones, *Art Work of Savannah and Augusta* (Chicago: Gravure Illustration Company, 1902). *Courtesy V. & J. Duncan Antique Maps and Prints.*

**Figure 11**   Rear elevation of the Telfair Hospital, photogravure from the "Annual Report, Telfair Hospital for Women, 30th Year," Savannah, 1916. *Courtesy V. & J. Duncan Antique Maps and Prints.*

the completion of her deceased sister's interest in the project. Her will also included a bequest for improvements to the nearby Independent Presbyterian Church.

Biographer Charles J. Johnson, Jr.'s analysis of Mary Telfair's "common-place book" and letters reveals an early feminist and a well-traveled, well-read woman. She was a good friend of notable figures throughout the country such as Thomas Paine, Albert Gallatin, and Nicholas Biddle.

Her name wasn't Mary, but Juliette Gordon Low, founder of the Girl Scouts of America, also belonged to one of Savannah's distinguished families. Juliette's grandfather, William Washington Gordon I (1796–1842), the first Georgian to graduate from West Point, founded Georgia's first railroad system in 1833.

Born in 1860 to W. W. Gordon II and Eleanor Kinzie Gordon, Juliette grew up in the Wayne–Gordon house at **10 East Oglethorpe Avenue** (Figure 12; see pp. 110–111). Her grandfather had purchased the house in 1831 from Savannah Mayor James Moore Wayne, the uncle of Mrs. W. W. Gordon I, upon Wayne's appointment to the Supreme Court of the United States by Andrew Jackson. Juliette was educated at boarding schools in Virginia and New York.

Juliette married William Mackay Low, son of millionaire Andrew Low, a British shipping magnate residing in Savannah on Lafayette Square (see pp. 147–149). The couple were married in 1886 at Christ Church with the wed-

**Figure 12** Wayne–Gordon house, Juliette Gordon Low birthplace, 10 Oglethorpe Avenue at Bull Street. Attributed to architect William Jay, 1820. *Courtesy Georgia Historical Society.*

**Figure 13** Juliette Gordon Low, founder of the Girl Scouts of the U.S.A. *Courtesy Juliette Gordon Low Girl Scout National Center.*

ding breakfast at the Gordon house, renovated and redecorated for the occasion. Juliette moved with her husband to Great Britain, where they circulated among a series of London townhouses, Wellesbourne house in Warwickshire, and Lude in Scotland.

After her husband's death, Juliette met Sir Robert Baden-Powell, a military hero who had established the Boy Scouts in England. She returned to Savannah in 1912 and contacted her cousin, Nina Pape, owner and principal of a local girls' school, saying, "Come right over. I have something for all the girls of Savannah and all America and all the world" (Figure 13).

In 1913 the American Girl Scouts were inaugurated in Savannah, meeting often in the carriage house behind the Andrew Low residence, where she lived. Juliette Low published the first handbook, *How Girls Can Help Their Country: A Handbook for Girl Scouts.* Her goal was to prepare girls for life by developing their career skills and by encouraging their participation in competitive sports. Before her death at her home on Lafayette Square in 1927, she had seen the Girl Scouting movement grow from 18 Savannah girls to 168,000 members nationally. Her birthplace in Savannah is a museum house established in 1953 by the Girl Scouts of the U.S.A. The carriage house behind the Low house on Lafayette Square is a Girl Scout building commemorating the first meeting of the organization. Juliette Gordon Low was an apt painter, sculptor, and designer; however, she left a far more important legacy to the nation: friendship and education of young women around the world through Girl Scouting.

Mary Hillyer and the Savannah Gas Company renovated the original Trustees Garden area, offering fifty-five dwelling units, twelve business locations and a school when it was finished in the 1940s. Trustees Garden, established by the Georgia Trustees from their London office, had been laid out on a 10-acre site along the river bluff on the east side of Oglethorpe's settlement at its founding. Inspired by the Chelsea Botanic Gardens, it had fallen into disuse in the late 1730s even before Oglethorpe's final 1743 departure. In 1748 Governor John Reynolds was granted the land which he made into a residential area (see pp. 85–88). The riverfront where it was located became a teeming nineteenth century commercial center. The garden site was replaced by taverns where dozens of languages from across the world could be heard. These became Irish tenements. Dot Lambert remembers as a child in the 1930s that the sure way to a good meal was to wander into a tenement in the Trustees Garden area if there was a wreath on the door. This meant a big Irish wake with lots of food.

Restoration of the Trustees Garden area was, in 1945, a creative and unusual undertaking. Southern ladies had heretofore spearheaded moves to save particular historic estates. For example, Mrs. Sidney Lanier, the Georgia poet's daughter-in-law, worked to save Mount Vernon. But seldom, at that time, had there been interest in urban preservation of old or historic buildings.

Mrs. Marmaduke Floyd had kept alive interest in the Trustees Garden, but all the buildings on the site were slated for demolition and redevelopment when Hansell Hillyer and his associates acquired the Savannah Gas Company in 1945. In an early example of corporately-financed preservation, the gas company, instead of demolishing its property, entered into an extensive preservation project conceived by Mary Hillyer of New Orleans and executed by her and her husband, Hansell Hillyer, the gas company president.

Anchor to the project was the Pirates House. This tavern was the site of Robert Louis Stevenson's episode in *Treasure Island*. Captain Flint died there, shouting with his last breath, "Darby, bring aft the rum." And Long John Silver, Stevenson's fictitious character, said, "I was with Flint when he died at Savannah."

The three-man executive committee of the South Atlantic Gas Company —Hansell Hillyer, Fred Wessels, Sr., and Alex A. Lawrence—went along with the seven-year project, grudgingly at times. Attorney Lawrence conceded, "As a businessman, the nicest thing I can say about the Village is that it's in black ink. With a fixed net investment of approximately $325,000, its gross rentals have already passed a rate of $40,000 a year." That was before it was finished. The Hillyers moved into their area, showing their commitment to the concept of preservation of Historic Savannah.

Michael Middleton called his book on city planning *Man Made The Town* (London: Bodley Head, 1987), but the author didn't finish the point. Women, at least in Savannah, were pivotal in the development of the city from the 1730s and played a focal role in saving the city in the 1950s, the years of crisis (Figure 14).

**Figure 14**  Catherine Littlefield Greene Miller; attributed to James Frothingham, 1805–1814. Caty Green, Revolutionary War General Nathanael Greene's widow, invited Eli Whitney to Mulberry Grove, her plantation 3 miles from Savannah, where he perfected the cotton gin. Mrs. Greene also built Dungeness at Cumberland Island, the foundations of which are beneath the Carnegie house ruins. *Courtesy Telfair Museum of Art, museum purchase, 1947.*

After 1955, seven women of Savannah initiated an all-out effort to save all that previous generations had built in Savannah, on Oglethorpe's ancient plan. This volunteer effort by energetic and well-educated Savannah women reflects Savannah's long history of constructive charity and civic work initiated in the eighteenth century by Selina, Countess of Huntingdon and benefactress of Bethesda Orphanage, at the behest of George Whitefield, its founder. Katherine Judkins Clark and Jane Wright worked hard against the demolition of the city market and the Davenport house and both were fundamental to the success of the Richardson–Owens–Thomas house. Artist–journalist Anna Colquitt Hunter used her journalistic ability to aid the cause, and she was among the first to renovate a space in a River Street warehouse for living quarters. Besides her work for Historic Savannah, Dorothy Ripley Roebling, with her husband Robert Roebling, is responsible for the Skidaway Island State Park. Elinor Adler Dillard continued the Adler family tradition of civic responsibility, as has Lee Adler. Lucy Barrow McIntire began the interest in preservation taken up by her granddaughter Cornelia McIntire Hartridge, and she won the prestigious Oglethorpe award doing it. Nola McEvoy Roos provided continuity to the efforts that resulted in saving and restoring the Davenport house. Adrienne Roberts nurtured the battle parks project.

Alida Harper (Mrs. Hunter McGuire Fowlkes), a rugged individualist and antiques dealer who saved and renovated eight major Savannah houses, including the Pink House on Reynolds Square and the Eliza Ann Jewett house on Madison Square, bought the Champion–McAlpin house on Orleans Square in 1939 and bequeathed it to the Georgia chapter of the Society of the Cincinnati. Stella Henderson preferred small early houses and she restored **131 Houston Street** and moved the little house at **536 East State Street** (see p. 94) to its present location.

Elfrida DeRenne (Mrs. Craig Barrow) of Wormsloe donated her portion of the Scarbrough house ownership to the Historic Savannah Foundation to thrust this magnificent William Jay–designed house into the forefront of salvaging the West Broad Street corridor. A decade later, when the Coastal Heritage Society went to work on the street that has become Martin Luther King Jr. Boulevard, she thus became an agent for saving the railroad complex.

Wormsloe Foundation and the women of the Junior League financed the first edition of the Historic Savannah Foundation inventory, which identified and documented historic buildings, providing incentive and credibility to the preservation movement. A name that appears quietly, in small print, is that of Mary Lane Morrison, who worked for preservation through print, as did Muriel Barrow Bell and as does Emmaline King Cooper today.

At first these volunteers and the organizations they belonged to, like the Trustees Garden Club, had the responsibility for the preservation movement, but it soon permeated the business community and city government. The preservation effort saved Savannah by salvaging the Trustees' and nineteenth-century architects' gifts: the city's plan, its squares, and its buildings. A viable historic city is the best gift a community can give to itself and to civilization.

The succeeding generations of women involved in the preservation movement understand that and the ranks have expanded to museum curators and directors, church women who have become professional volunteers, and to women architects and contractors, but most of all to women exhibiting civic responsibility while they live, work, and raise their families in the old city.

Emma Morel Adler, for example, has continued the tradition of working through the printed word; she has published preservation information and provided exhibition materials at Massie School (see p. 44) that have educated youths and potential property owners of Savannah. Her main thrust is to place

**Figure 15**  Mary Bryan Morel and her children, by Henry Benbridge, 1744–1812. Savannah remained English oriented after the Revolution despite the advent of a number of French refugees from St. Domingue, from the French Revolution and Terror, some of whom had been supporters of Napoleon. Marriage among the colonial families' descendants continues to this day. The resulting close-knit society has common aims and aspirations, belong to the same few churches, including Christ Church, St. John's Episcopal, and the Independent Presbyterian Church, as well as to the Oglethorpe Club, which represents about 400 interconnected families or new ones that are civic minded as well as socially oriented. *Courtesy Telfair Museum of Art, gift of Caroline Lamar Woodbridge.*

Savannah's plan and public buildings on UNESCO's World Heritage List. Beth Reiter, both volunteer and professional preservationist, has made inventories throughout the city and has served with both private and public institutions, heading up preservation projects (see pp. 218, 220).

"Live in a Landmark," a project led by the Historic Savannah Foundation targeting the Beach Institute area (see pp. 102–106), continues the spirit of the women who saved neighborhoods. Susan Riley Myers is among the volunteers who match abandoned houses to renovators and arrange renovation with existing owners. With her energy and knowledge she is fighting demolition by neglect and she coordinates city participation with sidewalk preservation, lighting, and cleanup.

Author William Cowper was too early with his pronouncement truth that "God made the country and Man made the town." He should have added that women saved the southern cities (Figure 15). Having been made, cities demand to be saved, remolded, and rethought continually.

# 3

## 250 YEARS OF ARCHITECTURE AND HISTORY ENJOYED BY FAMOUS VISITORS

For over 250 years, celebrities have visited Savannah, starting with the city's founder, James Edward Oglethorpe, in 1733, to President Taft almost 200 years later. They saw Savannah at different stages—from a village of fewer than 300 people to a port of more than 100,000 by the turn of the twentieth century.

Oglethorpe saw early Colonial Savannah, gone now except for the basic city plan. In 1791, President Washington saw the little frame town that had been built up during the Crown colony period. President Monroe enjoyed Savannah's sophisticated Regency architecture in 1820. Ornithologist John James Audubon stayed in the fancy new Regency hotel on Bay Street in 1832 and saw a new Federal-style city. By the time novelist William Makepeace Thackeray arrived in 1856, he observed a Greek revival mercantile city with a flourishing port, thanks to cotton (Figure 1). Jefferson Davis visited old friends in 1886 on Monterey Square in time to see an Italianate city. President Taft hit town in 1912, when the Second Empire baroque, Richardson Romanesque, and Beaux Arts architecture had invaded Savannah from the north.

Oglethorpe was not only an energetic on-site activist, but he was an educated and inquisitive Englishman, well traveled and possessing an astounding multinational frame of reference. Among his friends and colleagues were William Pitt, prime minister during Oglethorpe's later years in England, biographer James Boswell, and the great Dr. Samuel Johnson. Playwright Oliver Goldsmith was a familiar, and Alexander Pope immortalized Oglethorpe in a

**Figure 1** Francis Sorrel house, 6 West Harris Street. *Photograph by Goeff DeLorm, courtesy Savannah College of Art and Design.*

poem he wrote. Savannah's founder and administrator knew and liked John Adams and corresponded with Benjamin Franklin, Georgia's one-time agent in London.

Oglethorpe died at age 88 in Cranham, east of London, in 1785 at age 86, a credit to a family known for centuries for its service to the Crown. The perfect man for his century, he had been a military hero, member of Parliament, urban planner, bibliophile, and founder of the Trust Colony of Georgia.

Oglethorpe first came to Savannah at age 36, a founding member of the Trust to establish Georgia. Three trips later, in 1743, he sailed away from

Savannah for the last time. However, he never gave up on his perception of what Georgia and its people should be, a trusteeship directed by enlightened liberals, a colony of Protestants granted freedom of religion in an egalitarian, slaveless society. He returned to England to fight for Savannah, to raise money for the city, and to seek suitable settlers for the colony. There he failed to mention that his two sisters, the Marquise de Mézières and the Marquise des Marches, held vast holdings in French Catholic Louisiana, enemy to Georgia.

He had designed Savannah, brought the first settlers and protected them, and afterward left his little rental cottage on Bay Street for a final departure to England. There the Jacobite-bred Oglethorpe fought for the Crown at Colloden and tried to preserve his colony through Parliament. He also married an English heiress, Elizabeth Wright. (Did he still have his campaign tent with the yellow damask curtains he had pitched throughout the first years in Savannah?) He had brought it with him from the siege of Belgrade, where he fought with Prince Eugene to establish his status as a loyal Protestant.

When Oglethorpe left Savannah in 1743 for the last time, Bay, Broughton, and South Broad streets were 175 feet wide, and adjacent lots were filling up with buildings. Then, as today, the original six squares measured 270 by 315 feet. They had public ovens, wells, fences, a few straggly trees, and some garden plots. The squares served as meeting places as well as stockades for cattle in case of military uprising.

The trust lots of his six wards were not yet developed with public buildings. The Filature had failed as a silk processing plant, but it succeeded as a sort of city hall until it burned in 1840. Christ Church occupied a trust lot, and other churches were planned. Parliament and the Trustees paid for the other buildings on the trust or public lots, including the Strangers' House (a hotel), the parsonage house, warehouses, public store, guardhouse, quarters for visiting officials, the Filature, and military quarters.

The tithing lots extending from the squares had about 150 of the simple wood cottages that Oglethorpe designed for them, each 22 by 16 feet with a loft above and a yard to the rear with a split-rail fence. They probably had little shed dormers and large side yards, later filled in with townhouses. In 1751, two years after the planters won their demand for slaves, the population of the entire colony had grown to at least 2000, including the slaves. At that time Savannah was, in fact, the colony, except for the upcountry outposts and the plantations.

When George Washington visited Savannah in 1791, he saw the result of the colonial years, when the prospect of large land holdings had brought mercantile establishments and settlers to fill Oglethorpe's six wards. Most of the wooden buildings in the little town burned three years later in a great fire. However, there remain today some important buildings that reflect the post-colonial era, including James Habersham, Jr.'s house at **23 Abercorn Street** (see p. 84) on Reynolds Square.

Habersham had the house built in 1789, not five years after the last of the British loyalists had sailed away. The Habershams were Savannah's richest merchants, James' and Joseph's father having come to Savannah with Oglethorpe on his second voyage. By 1740 the family was doing just what the Crown wanted them to do, exporting goods from Savannah to the mother country. Now they were continuing the practice, sending rice and lumber to England, a credit to George Washington's United States.

Washington saw the 1760–1767 Christian Camphor cottage, then at the city limits, now **122 East Oglethorpe Avenue** (see p. 114). He just missed the Hampton Lillibridge house of 1797, then at **310 East Bryan Street,** now moved to St. Julian Street (see p. 93), but he saw houses that looked much like it. House plans were opening up, rooms enlarging, and refinements of detail were beginning to occur. Dormers were capped with pediments.

Savannah was just squeaking by when George Washington visited, not a successful place, with a population under 3000, not including about 2000 slaves. In 1796 a fire destroyed 229 houses, leaving only 171 houses standing.

President James Monroe arrived just before 1820 to see a transformed, thriving Federal-style port city. He saw Savannah at its most prosperous moment, perhaps, in history. Eli Whitney's cotton gins had already brought new seeds of wealth to Savannah with the export of bale after bale of clean cotton ready for the textile mills of England.

Builder Isaiah Davenport had moved to town from Rhode Island and had finished his Federal brick house at **324 East State Street** on Columbia Square (see p. 42). The Independent Presbyterian Church had just been completed; Monroe might have agreed with William Dean Howells' judgment that it was "the spiritualization of the financial moment." This assessment would have pleased the hard-working Presbyterians who financed the Federal-style church, designed by a notable Rhode Island architect, John Holden Greene, who won a competition for the commission (Figure 2; see p. 130).

Monroe also saw Regency Savannah in all its glory when the buildings designed by William Jay of Bath, England, were new. At that time the City Hotel on Bay Street, perhaps a Jay design and at least influenced by him, was under construction. Monroe might have attended the theater Jay designed at **222 Bull Street** on Chippewa Square (see p. 133). The Virginian was wined and dined by the new owners of Jay houses. William Scarbrough's house at **411 West Broad Street** (Martin Luther King Jr. Boulevard; see p. 116) was a tribute to the merchant prince, bankrupt in two years because of overextension in the development of the SS *Savannah*, the first steam-powered vessel to cross the Atlantic. Banker Richard Richardson was filling his house (Owens–Thomas house) at **124 Abercorn Street** (see p. 80) with furniture imported from London. The ship that brought it also brought two new gigs and a chaise, in which Monroe probably rode. James Moore Wayne, then

**Figure 2**  Independent Presbyterian Church, Crane and E. E. Soderholtz, Boston; photographic print, 1895. Built in the English restoration style in 1817 after designs by Rhode Island architect John Holden Greene, this church is as close to Regency England as Savannah's extant institutional buildings get. *Courtesy V. & J. Duncan Antique Maps and Prints.*

mayor, was just building his Regency house at the corner of Bull and South Broad streets (**10 East Oglethorpe Avenue;** see p. 110).

Monroe saw some Jay houses that we cannot enjoy because they were demolished after World War I. The Archibald S. Bulloch house on Orleans Square was designed by Jay about 1820. The Habersham family bought the house and lived there for three generations before it was razed a century later in 1916 to make way for a city auditorium (now the Civic Center). The Bulloch house was a presentation in domes and circles much more elegant and exciting than William Thornton's Tudor Place and the Octagon House in Washington, D.C., which Monroe knew well. Across the street at the corner of Hull and Barnard streets, Jay designed a house for Robert Habersham, long demolished. Monroe also saw the Jay-designed Bank of the United States (Figure 3). The president could see that William Jay had created a new Savannah singlehandedly. He could not have known that Savannah's most sophisticated houses had already been built.

Monroe saw Savannah just in time. The following year the great fire of 1820 destroyed 463 houses, causing an estimated loss of $4 million. Then a yellow fever epidemic hit the city. Ten years later the city had recovered, and by 1830 the population had built up to 5215.

John James Audubon came to Savannah in 1832 and set up at the City Hotel on Bay Street. The artist contacted Savannah merchant William Gaston to serve as local agent for his *Birds of America*. Among the subscribers, at $1000 a set, for a projected 420 folios were Alexander Telfair (what did Mary Telfair do with them?), John Mongin, Thomas Young, Thomas King, and Thomas Metcalf. Audubon probably had dinner with Telfair at his elegant Regency house, also designed by Jay, now the Telfair Academy of Arts and Sciences, and with John Mongin in his post-colonial 1797 house on Warren Square, now at **24 Habersham Street** (see p. 89). Although three of the subscribers died during Gaston's work with Audubon, Gaston was able to collect the full amount owed Audubon from their estates, an estimable feat.

**Figure 3** William Jay's Bank of the United States at the corner of Drayton and St. Julian streets on Reynolds Square; now demolished. This blue and white transferware Staffordshire compote and saucer depict one of architect William Jay's elegant Savannah commercial buildings, new when President Monroe visited Savannah. *Courtesy V. & J. Duncan Antique Maps and Prints.*

**Figure 4**  Samuel Bryant house, 122 West Oglethorpe Avenue. The 1822 brick entrance illustrates the restrained attenuated architecture of the Federal period. Frame houses and a few brick ones repeated this modest entrance with its conservative Adamesque overlight. Sometimes delicate carving accompanied sidelight frames. *Photograph by Goeff DeLorm, courtesy Savannah College of Art and Design.*

Thomas Young, who died just after Audubon left, was a Scottish bachelor who had come to Savannah when he inherited his uncle's Rae's Hall plantation four miles upriver. [Patriot Samuel Elbert (1740–1788) had married heiress Elizabeth Rae of Rae's Hall.] In addition to paying Audubon, his estate presented $5000 bequests to each of Savannah's four charitable institutions. Evidently, the spirit of Oglethorpe and the Trustees lived on.

Audubon saw Federal-style Savannah (Figure 4). The four squares laid out on the east side of the little town, along Habersham and Houston Streets, were filling with wooden two-story Federal houses and one-story center-hall cottages. An astute observer, he probably noticed the beginnings of the Savannah custom of paired houses, or doubles. As Audubon had come to Savannah from Philadelphia, he could observe how the neighborhood looked more like New England than other southern places. He probably met John Ash, the architect–builder responsible for early paired or double houses in the city. The Scudders were busy when he was there, building houses and commercial buildings between their port and river engineering projects. Thomas Gibbons's block of brick commercial buildings at **102–116 West Congress Street** (see p. 76) were built about 1820. They appear in Cerveau's 1837 view of Savannah. Audubon's Savannah totaled 7000 inhabitants, one-half of whom were African-Americans.

English novelist William Makepeace Thackeray invoked the town's tranquil English atmosphere in the *Feast of St. Valentine* after his 1856 visit with fellow Britain Andrew Low. He observed the fleets of merchantmen taking in cargo from the warehouses barricaded with cotton bales. He described Factors Walk, where cotton factors or commission merchants inspected and bid on baled cotton stacked below. Sampling, grading, and storage took place in vast brick buildings that architect Charles Cluskey had built for the cotton factors, brokers, and merchants at the river's edge. There was Stoddard's Range, brand new then, accessible from the decorative cast iron walks and bridges on Bay Street and from the new riverside cobblestone walk. The new Greek revival U.S. Customs House at **1–5 East Bay Street** (see p. 65), designed by John Norris in 1858, was shown to all visitors (Figure 5).

Thackeray was delighted to be away from the ceaseless racket of northern hotels. Most of all he was delighted with his free accommodations at the house of his friend Andrew Low of A. Low and Company, cotton brokers. The Low house on Lafayette Square was new then, designed in the Greek revival style by architect John S. Norris without the Italianate roof eaves and brackets that were added later (see p. 44). Undoubtedly, Thackeray visited Mr. Battersby — like Low, an English cotton broker, who lived in the West Indian–style house with piazza entrance across the street at **119 East Charlton Street** (see pp. 148–149).

Thackeray saw Greek revival Savannah at its finest. Rowhouses were filling block after block. They were built of Savannah gray brick, made at Henry McAlpin's plantation, the Hermitage (Figures 6 and 7). Architect Charles Cluskey's beautiful paired houses with their triple windows at **14 and 18 West Harris Street** on Madison Square had been built for the Kerr sisters in 1843. They show simple Greek revival at its best (see pp. 146–147).

**Figure 5** The U.S. Customs House, 1–5 East Bay Street. Thackeray saw architect John Norris's just finished Greek revival masterpiece. *Photograph by Keith Cardwell, Savannah College of Art and Design.*

**Figure 6** Hermitage master house, as it appeared in a 1920 photograph. Henry McAlpin is responsible for the bricks, ironwork, and lumber of most of the houses built in Savannah between 1819 and his death in 1851. His Hermitage plantation was America's first industrial park. The Scotsman worked closely with English architect William Jay and with Irish architect Charles B. Cluskey, who designed Savannah's finest antebellum houses. His own fine Greek revival plantation at the Hermitage just outside the city was taken down by Henry Ford in the early twentieth century for the bricks. *Courtesy V. & J. Duncan Antique Maps and Prints.*

**Figure 7** Slave quarters at Hermitage plantation; photograph, about 1900, Foltz Studio. Agriculture and industry went side by side at the Hermitage. Slaves worked the fields, the brickworks, and the iron foundry side by side. They were also knowledgeable in the running of rice mills, sugar works, and early cotton gins on the plantations. *Courtesy V. & J. Duncan Antique Maps and Prints.*

**Figure 8** Mary Marshall Row, 230–244 East Oglethorpe Avenue. Mary Marshall was just finishing her rowhouses when Thackeray was in town. *Photograph by Goeff DeLorm, courtesy Savannah College of Art and Design.*

**Figure 9** Francis Sorrel house, 6 West Harris Street. Charles Cluskey had finished this Greek revival mansion in 1841. *Photograph by Goeff DeLorm, courtesy Savannah College of Art and Design.*

Mary Marshall had completed Mary Marshall Row on South Broad (**230–244 East Oglethorpe Avenue;** see p. 114) and her Marshall Hotel at **107 East Broughton Street** (Figure 8; see p. 108). Francis Sorrel, of French St. Domingue, had settled into his own Greek revival center-hall mansion at **6 West Harris Street** (see p. 146), the highlight of Madison Square since 1841 (Figure 9). Did Thackeray know that the inspiration came in Biddle and Havilland's 1837 *Young Carpenters' Assistant*, published in Boston (W. Norman)?

On Madison Square, Thackeray probably visited Charles Green, a wealthy English cotton merchant, like Andrew Low. John Norris had designed both the Low and Green houses. Green's house on Madison Square was built in the Gothic revival style, complete with oriels, battlements, projecting bays, clustered columns, and molded drip stones (see pp. 144–145).

One of the main features of Thackeray's visit could well have been a walk to the new park, which was being called Hodgson's then, after Margaret Telfair's husband, William Brown Hodgson, who had conceived it in 1851 (see p. 18). Thackeray could have seen the new Central of Georgia brick railroad complex going up across West Broad Street (Martin Luther King Jr. Boulevard). The bridges, stack, work sheds, and buildings exhibited fine brickwork designs of German-American Augustus Schwaab.

A surprise visitor in 1886 to the Hugh Comer house on Monterey Square was the former president of the Confederate States of America, Jefferson Davis (Figure 10). Before the Civil War, Davis had a history that would make him welcome in any Savannah house. Davis's father, an upcountry Georgian, had joined the Continentals to fight in the American Revolution at the seige of Savannah. Jefferson Davis fit into the mold of citizen-soldier even before the Confederate states were a dream. A West Point graduate, he had fought in the popular war against Mexico with a number of Savannah soldiers, and he had served as Secretary of War as well as U.S. Senator from Mississippi before the Civil War.

Davis and his entourage were making a great swing through the South, much in the manner of General Lafayette before him. Money had been raised by southerners who did not want the memory of the Confederacy to die. They were building up the Myth of the Lost Cause.

**Figure 10**  2 East Taylor Street on Monterey Square. Hugh A. Comer hosted Jefferson Davis in his new Italianate house. *Photograph by Goeff DeLorm, courtesy Savannah College of Art and Design.*

**Figure 11**   This monumental house at 330 Abercorn Street, over 10,000 square feet, built in 1873, was part of the street scene during Jefferson Davis's visit. Mayor Samuel P. Hamilton probably entertained him here. *Cordray–Foltz Collection, courtesy Georgia Historical Society.*

Crowds gathered on Monterey Square to welcome the symbol of the fallen Confederate states. Mayor Samuel P. Hamilton may have entertained him at **330 Abercorn Street** (see pp. 148–149) in his Second Empire baroque extravaganza on Lafayette Square (Figure 11).

Davis saw Italianate mansions built since the war. General Hugh W. Mercer, General Noble Hardee (Figure 12), and Mr. Comer had built homes on Monterey Square in the pretentious, romantic style that swept the South, worthy of Sir Walter Scott's novels and Robert Burns's poetry.

In 1909, President William Howard Taft came to Savannah to have dinner with his classmate at Yale, William Washington Gordon II, at the family home at Oglethorpe and Bull streets (see p 110). Gordon had served with the Georgia Hussars in the Confederate Army and became a U.S. Army Brigadier General in the Spanish-American War a full forty years later. Home again, he was prepared to order heavy Chippendale-style chairs in anticipation of the arrival of the notoriously ponderous Taft. The chairs remain in place today in the Gordon house dining room—out of scale, as was Taft.

Taft saw a booming post-Reconstruction city of more than 50,000 people when he addressd the Hibernian Society on the occasion of its centennial. Architect Detlef Lienau, a founder of the American Institute of Architects, had introduced the Second Empire baroque style to the city and local builders were applying vivacious relief surfaces to the older staid Greek revival buildings and others (Figure 13).

**Figure 12** Italianate à la mode is the feeling of this fanciful facade at 3 West Gordon Street on Monterey Square across from where Davis was staying. Its owner, General Noble Hardee, knew the former Confederate president. *Photograph by Scot Hinson.*

**Figure 13** 12–14 East Taylor Street. President Taft arrived in Savannah to see New York–style applications of decorations to older homes, such as this Second Empire baroque extravaganza. *Photograph by Clement Speiden.*

**Figure 14**   225 East Hall Street. President Taft could have enjoyed the new and elegant homes lining East Hall Street beside Forsyth Park. He would have been familiar with the Richardson Romnesque style initiated by the Harvard-educated Richardson and taken up by architect William G. Preston in this house for MIT-educated Savannahian George H. Baldwin. *Photographs by Keith Cardwell, courtesy Savannah College of Art and Design.*

**Figure 15** Taft would have been the first of the famous visitors to see this woodwork wedding cake in the streetcar suburb at 1921 Bull Street. *Photograph by Keith Cardwell, courtesy Savannah College of Art and Design.*

William Gibbons Preston, brought to Savannah in 1889 to design the new Chatham County Courthouse on Wright Square at **124 Bull Street** (see p. 74), had stayed on to develop the area beyond Gaston Street with Richardson Romanesque mansions (Figure 14). He was joined by Alfred S. Eichberg, who built the same kinds of buildings.

The old city was losing its Athenian, Greek Temple ambiance as the churches were renovated in a more picturesque style. Temple Mikve Israel and Wesley Monumental Church had been built on trust lots on the newest southside squares in the newest revival style to hit Savannah — Gothic.

Had he taken the streetcar to the new suburbs, Taft would have seen a building boom of frame working-class houses on all the streets south of Forsyth Park. Late Victorian vernacular buildings, as well as a plethora of pattern-book eclectic houses, mostly rental, construction costing under $5000, were covering the south of town beyond Forsyth Park (Figure 15).

The burned-out Independent Presbyterian Church had been rebuilt at Bull Street near Chippewa Square using the original plans of the Federal period, and handsome adjunct buildings in the same general style anchored the neighborhood. William Dean Howells wrote about the church in *Harper's* magazine in 1919, "Whoever would appreciate its beauty must go at once to Savannah, and forget, for one beatific moment in its presence, the walls of Tiepolo and the ceilings of Veronese."

Now you can be the famous visitor to Savannah, where you can get a composite glimpse of what each of these worthy visitors and many others saw in their own time. Gathered together chronologically, Savannah's museums, museum houses, churches, and historic sites provide quite a lesson in American history and in aesthetics.

**Savannah History Museum,** Visitors Center, 303 Martin Luther King Jr. Boulevard, 238-1779. The Coastal Heritage Society presents the history of Savannah, along with a movie, in a restored railroad complex.

**Savannah Revolutionary Battlefield Park,** 303 Martin Luther King Jr. Boulevard, 238-1779. Sharing the handsome Central of Georgia Railroad Building headquarters with the Savannah Visitors' Center, Battlefield Park is a projected $80 million project to include a 5-acre site, part of the 1779 siege of Savannah. In 1779 the French forces of the Comte d'Estaing joined the Continentals led by General Benjamin Lincoln in an abortive effort to take Savannah from the British.

**Chamber of Commerce Visitors' Center,** 303 Martin Luther King Jr. Boulevard, 944-0455. Be sure to visit the information center and look at the movie. Take one of the many bus tours of Savannah that originate here.

**Historic Railroad Shops,** Coastal Heritage Society, Martin Luther King Jr. Boulevard at 601 West Harris Street, 651-6823. The Central of Georgia Railroad roundhouse, the stack, railroad sheds, and work buildings remain, thirteen brick structures creating a complex of national importance. You can even see the latrines at the bottom of the coal stack and have lunch in a railroad car.

**Davenport house,** 324 East State Street, 236-8097, Richard D. Betterly, curator. This building was the site of the first headquarters of the Historic Savannah Foundation and was the first building saved by the group in the mid 1950s.

The house now appears as it would have during the early years of Davenport's occupancy in the 1820s. Davenport was a builder whose fancy plasterwork adorns the parlor, where he is said to have received potential clients.

**Owens–Thomas house of the Telfair Museum of Art,** 124 Abercorn Street, on Oglethorpe Square, 233-9743, Olivia Alison, curator. The Owens–Thomas house is probably the finest example of English Regency architecture in America. Its sophisticated spatial arrangements, a unique stairway along with some original furniture in the main house plus the only stable-slave quarter you can visit in Savannah, make the house museum a favorite stop. The house is named after the second private owner, George Welshman Owens, and his granddaughter Margaret Thomas, who left it to the Telfair Academy of Arts and Sciences in 1951 (see p. 77). However, banker and entrepreneur Richard Richardson had the English architect William Jay design the house and brought the architect to Savannah to supervise construction and furnishing of the house. Soon after it was finished, Richardson lost the house in a bankruptcy takeover by his own bank, the Bank of the United States, ironically also a Jay design secured under the aegis of the young architect's patron and relative by marriage, Richardson. The Bank of the United States owned the house for eight years while Richardson moved on to New Orleans in a bid to recoup his considerable fortune (see pp. 80–83). Miss Thomas's grandfather, George Welshman Owens, bought it for $10,000 in 1830, so that the Owens–Thomas house reveals almost 180 years of continuous ownership by two families.

Similarly, the Green–Meldrim house was kept up by two families. The Telfair house had just one residing family, as did the Wayne–Gordon–Low museum house (Juliette Gordon Low's birthplace) and the Andrew Low house. The Scarbrough house lost much by its use as a school, although it had just two owning families. The Davenport house, too, had few owners, but suffered the decline of partitioning of space and boardinghouse use before its restoration. A comparison of Savannah's museum houses with that knowledge in mind can prove interesting.

**Telfair Academy of Arts and Sciences,** 121 Barnard Street on Telfair Square, 232-1177, Diane Lesko, director. Designed and built in 1818 by William Jay, this was the home of Alexander Telfair and his sisters, Margaret and Mary (see p. 77).

The Regency furniture, most imported from New York and Philadelphia, is of international importance, as are the American Impressionist paintings acquired by the Telfair Academy of Arts and Sciences early in the twentieth century. The paintings are housed in a large wing added in 1883 according to Mary Telfair's will, after designs by Detlef Lienau, a Beaux Arts–trained architect active in New York. The Telfair is the oldest public art museum in the South.

American Impressionist painter Gari Melchers is largely responsible for the Telfair Museum art collection. Melchers was connected to Savannah through his wife, Corinne Lawton Mackall, niece of the Telfair board president, A. R. Lawton. When the first director, Carl Brandt, died in 1905, Melchers became purchasing agent and art advisor. His official capacity ended in 1916, but his influence continued until the late 1920s. As a result, the Academy purchased a number of American and European Impressionist paintings directly from the artists at reasonable prices.

The museum board generally authorized an expenditure of about $1500 a year. This base was augmented by gifts from board members and Savannah citizens. The collections include paintings by Frederick Carl Freiseke and Childe Hassam. Melchers recognized the talent of Robert Henri, Frank Brangwyn, and Joseph Pennell and purchased their works. During the years before Americans were accepted as valid impressionist painters, the Telfair was a resource for students of American Impressionism.

The Telfair has wisely collected women artists, such as Lila Cabot Perry and Jane Stuart, daughter of Gilbert Stuart. The collection includes works by local artists Anna C. Hunter, Myrtle Jones, Mary Hoore Aiken, and Henrietta Waring and Elizabeth O'Neill Verner (1883–1979) of Charleston, who made etchings of Savannah scenes in 1926. Portraits of Savannah women, including miniatures by Carol Aus of three generations of Cunningham women, were donated to the Telfair collection.

**Scarbrough house,** 41 Martin Luther King Jr. Boulevard, 232-1511. Completed for William Scarbrough after designs of William Jay in 1818, the elegant Regency mansion was left empty after the owner lost all his money about 1821 in the financial debacle accompanying the successful sailing of the *SS Savannah* with steam to England. Although the project was successful and ultimately brought great wealth to Savannah, the investors overextended themselves and lost a great deal of money.

Scarbrough's son-in-law moved into the house in the 1830s. The Jones–DeRenne family came into ownership of the house, and from 1878 to 1972 Scarbrough house operated as a public school for children of African-American descent, donated for that cause by the owners. In a twist of fate, the house reverted to DeRenne heirs' ownership when the school closed and the house came into ownership of the Historic Savannah Foundation through the leadership of Elfrida DeRenne Barrow. The foundation had it restored and stabilized (see pp. 116–118).

Now housing the Ships of the Sea Museum, Scarbrough house is an essential adjunct to an understanding of the port.

**Andrew Low house of the National Society of the Colonial Dames of America in the State of Georgia,** 329 Abercorn Street on Lafayette Square, 233-6854, Betty Arnold, administrator (see pp. 147–149). A visit to the Low house illustrates the good taste and careful research of the Colonial Dames in presenting the interior in the style of the 1840s. You will also enjoy the residential neighborhood, filled with houses of the same period as the Low house.

**Green–Meldrim house,** 14 West Macon Street on Madison Square, 233-3845, Joanne Hardwick, curator. Open Thursdays and Fridays and after St. John's Episcopal Church services on Sunday mornings (see pp. 144–145). One of Savannah's most lavish interiors, this elegant Gothic revival house designed by the adaptable architect John S. Norris had had just two owners when St. John's Episcopal Church acquired the property. Volunteer staff is devoted to its preservation and presentation.

**Juliette Gordon Low house,** 142 Bull Street at Oglethorpe Avenue, 233-4501, Fran Harold, director, and Stephen Bohlin-Davis, curator (see pp. 20, 110). Now a property of the Girl Scouts of the U.S.A., this house represents far more than the birthplace and residence of the founder of the Girl Scouts. The house was designed for future Supreme Court Justice James Moore Wayne about 1820, perhaps by the English Regency architect and Savannah resident William Jay. It is interpreted in the Aesthetic period,

as it was arranged by the time of the wedding of Juliette Gordon to William Mackay Low in 1886. Sophisticated but comfortable, the house makes a warm impression as the visitor learns about late-nineteenth-century design contrasted with early-nineteenth-century architecture and about southern history as well as Juliette Gordon Low and the Girl Scouts movement.

**Massie Heritage Interpretation Center,** 207 East Gordon Street on Calhoun Square, 651-7022. This Greek revival building was designed and built by John S. Norris in 1855 according to Peter Massie's will. The facility was dedicated for the education of poor children and is the only remaining building of Georgia's original chartered school system. Now a resource center for living history, its outstanding exhibitions reveal Savannah's architectural history.

**Temple Mickve Israel,** 20 East Gordon Street, Monterey Square (see pp. 151–152). All but three families on the ship filled with Jews financed by a London synagogue, which Oglethorpe permitted to anchor in Savannah harbor in 1734, were of Portuguese and Spanish background. These Sephardic Jews did not realize how close they would be to the Spanish New World with its imported Inquisition. Having been jailed and persecuted for their religion, and forced to live as *conversos* (Catholic converts in Europe), they found themselves just a day's sail from Spanish St. Augustine. They were afraid, and in the early years many went north, leaving two Ashkenazim families that had sailed with them, the Sheftalls and the Minises, whose descendants remain in Savannah today.

The third-oldest Jewish congregation in what is now the United States worships in a congenial neo-Gothic revival synagogue. Through the German influence of the Sheftalls and the Minises, along with other German Jews who joined the Sephardic community through the century, what was Sephardic has become Reform. Respect for the past, adaptation to the prevailing society, preservation of a sense of history, and reverence for intellectual pursuit give Mickve Israel its sophisticated and comfortable southern character. The museum there is instructive about the Sephardic community that arrived in Savannah in 1734.

**207 East Charlton Street on Lafayette Square,** 233-6014. Georgia short-story writer, O. Henry Book Awardee, and three-time National Short Story Award winner Flannery O'Connor grew up in this narrow mid-nineteenth century stuccoed brick townhouse. O'Connor's short stories depict with sardonic wit and acuity the foibles of Georgian country life. Among her better known stories are *Wise Blood, A Good Man is Hard To Find,* and *The Violent Bear It Away* (New York: New American Library, 1964). The house is open from Friday through Sunday, 1–4 P.M., and for occasional readings.

**Georgia Historical Society,** 501 Whitaker Street at Gaston Street, Forsyth Park, 651-2128. No trip to Savannah is complete without a visit to the Historical Society in its home given to Savannah by the Telfair sisters in memory of Margaret Telfair's husband. Hodgson Hall was built in 1874–1875. Mrs. Lilla Hawes, long-time director, is gone, but her memory lingers, as do the stories she told to researchers. When Bill Abbot was pouring over colonial governors' letters, she rushed over to help him, apologizing, "I was just talking on the phone to Miss Johnson. She's a descendant of Sir Patrick Houston of the colonial period. I asked her why she didn't answer the phone when I had rung her up earlier in the morning. She never leaves before noon, you know. She said, 'Oh, Lilla, had I realized it was you ringing up I would have answered, but I wasn't quite dressed just then, you know.'"

**Beach Institute,** 502 East Harris Street, 234-8000. Headquarters for the Freedman's Bureau in Savannah in 1865, the handsome vernacular classic-style building was built by teachers of the American Missionary Association on land paid for by Alfred Beach, editor of *Scientific American.* It now houses the African-American Arts Center.

**King–Tisdell cottage,** 514 East Huntingdon Street, Beach Institute Area, 234-8000 (see p. 106). An 1896 late Victorian cottage is now a black cultural museum. The Negro Heritage Trail Tour begins here.

**Ralph Mark Gilbert Civil Rights Museum,** 460 Martin Luther King Jr. Boulevard, corner of Alice Street, 231-8900. Savannah's newest museum serves as a catalyst for educating the public about the heritage of African-Americans in Savannah. The museum is housed in the Guaranty Life Insurance Company building, a black-owned institution since its founding.

**Fort Jackson,** Three miles east of Savannah on President Street extended, Coastal Heritage Society Landmark. The site where the present fort stands was used in the 1740s for Oglethorpe's troops. The oldest standing brickwork fort in Georgia, Fort Jackson on the Savannah River, dates from 1809, built in time to defend Savannah against the British in the War of 1812. Robert Gunn was the architect selected to restore Fort Jackson after state bidding. The Scottish Heritage Society holds annual events there, including Scottish games.

**Fort Pulaski,** 15 miles on Highway 80 East en route to Tybee; National Park Service, 786-5787 (Figure 16). The most impressive of Savannah's brick forts was begun in 1829 and finished in the 1840s. Robert E. Lee's first assignment out of West Point was to work as engineer on the well-sited fort at the mouth of the Savannah River (Figure 17).

**Figure 16**   Fort Pulaski. *Photograph by Clement Speiden.*

The five-sided fort enclosing a 2½-acre parade ground rises to accommodate two tiers of guns and cannon inside a moat and portcullis. During the Civil War, Lee, then a Confederate general, considered Fort Pulaski to be impregnable, but Union forces bombarded it, using experimental rifled cannons from Tybee, more than a mile away, and within one hour Pulaski fell. These rifled cannons proved to have greater accuracy and longer range than those of conventional smooth-bore guns, opening gaps in walls over 7 feet thick. The surrender of Fort Pulaski under C. H. Olmstead of Savannah radically affected the design for all future military fortifications.

Today the fort is a national monument, along with 537 surrounding acres run by the National Park Service. It provides a good opportunity to see both military history, and the marshland growth and the savannahs at the river's mouth. Combine the trip with lunch at Williams Seafood or Goodfriend's Galley a few miles west of the fort on the other side of the bridge.

**Tybee Lighthouse and Museum,** U.S. 80 East, 786-5801. Have fun looking at this old-time museum, and learn the history of Martello towers, a type of round defense structure brought back to England by Admiral Nelson, who had seen them along the coast of northern Corsica. Walk along Officers' Quarters Row and have some Jamaican food outside at the Northbeach Grill on Van Horne Drive.

The first Tybee light, a small beacon, was built on Tybee under Oglethorpe's direction in 1734. The first 60-foot section of the present lighthouse dates to 1773, the top built in 1867. Fort Screven was built in 1875, in time to be manned during the Spanish-American War, in which Savannah played an

**Figure 17**   Robert E. Lee, as a young officer; steel engraving, New York, D. Appleton, 1875. Savannah's Fort Pulaski was his first assignment after West Point. *Courtesy V. & J. Duncan Antique Maps and Prints.*

**Figure 18** Library at Wormsloe plantation, Isle of Hope; postcard, about 1920. *Courtesy V. & J. Duncan Antique Maps and Prints.*

enthusiastic role as a quarantine station and embarcation point, also sending volunteer troops in large numbers. General George C. Marshall was one of its last commandants. Now you'll see houses nestled among the earthworks of the long-outdated fort.

**Wormsloe Historic Site,** 7601 Skidaway Road, National Park Service, 353-3023 (Figures 18 and 19). You cannot see the nineteenth-century house, a replacement of Noble Jones's Trustee period home, because Jones's descendants still live there. But most people take guests to Wormsloe to enjoy the allée of live oaks and a stroll along the river, with a look at the tabby ruins of the first fortified plantation in Georgia. An interpretive center offers a good selection of books for sale.

**AFRICAN-AMERICAN CULTURE AND HISTORY**

A new awareness pervades Savannah of the role that African-Americans have played in the history of Savannah and the nation. The African-American churches vividly contribute to the understanding of Savannah's architecture and culture. The African-American Baptist church is a concrete reflection of the African-American effect on southern culture. The steadfast efforts of their large and active congregations and of their leaders transformed life in this country.

**Figure 19** Noble Wimberly Jones; from *A History of Savannah and South Georgia* by William Harden (Chicago and New York: Lewis Publishing Company, 1913). Noble Jones and his wife and son Wimberly, a child, arrived with Oglethorpe on the first ship to Savannah, 1733. The family established Georgia's first fortified plantation at Savannah, and the family lives on the site today. *Courtesy V. & J. Duncan Antique Maps and Prints.*

Savannah's Catholics have been historically aggressive in their efforts to include the African-American community in their educational and cultural efforts. Benedictine monks and an order of African-American nuns offered educational opportunity to African-Americans here, an effort paralleled only in New Orleans. Among the results: a Supreme Court Justice, Clarence Thomas, educated in Savannah's Catholic schools. The churches and schools of these pioneers and those of the African-Methodist-Episcopalian church (St. Paul's School for Boys) and the Episcopalian church are testimony to their influence in Savannah.

**First African Baptist Church,** 23 Montgomery Street on Franklin Square. George Liele, a Virginia-born slave, was sold during the Royal Crown period of Georgia to Henry Sharpe of Kiokee, Georgia. Liele was baptized at his master's Baptist church. Subsequently, in 1777, Liele was freed to preach the gospel to slaves at plantations along the Savannah River. He formed the First Colored Church of Savannah about 1778 and was ordained as its first pastor. This became the First African Baptist Church in 1822, the oldest continuously active, autonomously developed African-American church in North America.

The Baptist congregation bought the property on Franklin Square in 1832, but the present church dates from 1859, built by members of the congregation, mostly slaves. Andrew Marshall, one-time driver for Richard Richardson of the Owens–Thomas house, was the pastor responsible for the building's construction. The church's third pastor, Marshall was a slave for 50 of his 100 years. The stained glass windows were installed in 1885. The original bell tower was blown away by a hurricane early in the twentieth century. During the Civil War, the church housed runaway slaves in a 4-foot-high space under the sanctuary floorboards.

**Second African Baptist Church,** 123 Houston Street on Green Square. The Reverend Andrew Bryan, Georgia's first native African-American religious leader, was ordained in 1788 after baptism by Reverend George Liele. Andrew Bryan was a slave at Jonathan Bryan's Brampton plantation. After being freed, he founded the Second African Baptist Church in 1802. Located in a white neighborhood, the church was encouraged by the Savannah First Baptist Church, and the trust lot was granted by the city and Chatham County in exchange for rent paid by the members.

The present church dates from 1925. General William Tecumseh Sherman, Savannah's conquerer during the Civil War, read the Emancipation Proclamation in the original wood church of 1802 and promised the freedmen "40 acres and a mule." Dr. Martin Luther King, Jr. preached his "I Have A Dream" sermon in the present church, an address later made famous during King's march on Washington, D.C., in 1963.

**First Bryan Baptist Church,** 575 West Bryan Street. The first church on this site, once a Yamacraw Indian village, dates from 1794. The Reverend Andrew Bryan bought the property for "thirty pounds sterling." The deed, dated September 4, 1793, indicates that this may be the oldest property in the United States owned continually by African-Americans. Bryan, who at first could not read or write, purchased a literate black man to conduct school in the church in the 1790s.

Slavery and its aftermath can be observed most dramatically along the sea islands of Georgia and South Carolina. Imagine communities of up to 500 slaves living in a series of remote rice or cotton plantations. Five generations of such slave communities worked many of the coastal island plantations until they were freed during the Civil War, often to become tenants on the same plantations, their descendants living nearby into the present day.

Envision the first generation of those sea island slaves, born in Africa, collected by slavers from diverse tribes representing a variety of religious and ethnic groups. Gathered aboard ship to sail to Georgia, many were unloaded at the sea islands, where they and their descendants for generations lived without setting foot on the mainland or seeing a town or village. Some never encountered people from off the plantation except perhaps visitors to the master house. For example, in one of Pierce Butler's plantations at St. Simons Island, 145 slave families, numbering from two to ten members apiece, inhabited spaces in the master house or overseer's house, outbuildings including a hospital, and dozens of separate slave quarters.

Occasionally, slaves from the British West Indies arrived to add to the frame of reference, language variety, and the gene pool of the original Africans. Without education, training in judgment, or experience beyond the "task" they were trained to execute, these people developed a method of communication using English as a base and retaining various native words. Above all, they retained the inflections, rhythms, and the order of words as they remembered them in Africa. They passed on the English that the first generation of slaves had learned in the eighteenth and early nineteenth centuries, without the modifications that occurred among mobile and schooled populations. This dialect is known as Geechee because it developed on rice plantations along the Ogeechee River south of Savannah.

**Figure 20** 1011 Lincoln Street. Victorian District street garden fashioned of shells, fake flowers, and ceramics mixed with a few local shrubs, trees, and flowers. *Photograph by Keith Cardwell.*

Slaves at Butler's Island recalled the difference in their condition from one generation of ownership to another. They considered times better in the second generation than the third. They knew they were better off when the owner of the plantation was in residence than during the residence of the overseer, Roswell King. Yet they confessed to more bearable lives under the efficient overseership of Roswell King and his son than that of intervening inefficient and uninterested overseers.

In one sale in Savannah in 1859, the only time he ever sold slaves in a group, Pierce Butler sold at Tenbroeck Race Course 460 "Negroes" trained in "long cotton and rice." The sale was accompanied by a catalog, and the newspaper reported that the sale averaged "$716 a head," for a total of $300,205. Butler, ashamed of his debts and the sale of his grandfather's "people," gave each of the departing slaves four quarters.

These slaves were hauled to Savannah by schooner or rowing craft from Pierce Butler's rice and cotton plantations at Butler's Island and Hampton on St. Simons Island. Three days of rain accompanied the sale, and the slaves referred to the experience for generations to come as "the weeping time."

As they were camped on the grounds of the slave pens in Savannah, they saw for the first time an urban environment, numbers of white persons, and groups of other slaves. At the same time that their familiar way of life and their families were being ripped apart, their exposure to urban life was beginning. Some entered a dwelling raised off a dirt floor for the first time. They saw clothes other than the expected "nigger cloth" woven especially for the plantation trade and doled out to them twice a year.

Descendants of Butler's Hampton plantation slaves on St. Simons Island, like those of the carefully run James Hamilton Couper's St. Simons plantation and of the Spaldings at Sapelo and other one-time Coastal Island slave holders, live in the Savannah area today (Figure 20). When they filtered into Savannah after the Civil War, they did not find a sophisticated freed black community, as found in New Orleans, or Charleston, or in Petersburg and Richmond, Virginia. In Savannah there had been two secret schools for blacks, one run by a free woman of color, Jane DeVeaux; state legislation in the 1830s had made it illegal to teach blacks to read or write. But for the most part their support came from the African-American Baptist church, the anchor for black adaptation to post–coastal island life. Government agencies such as the Freedman's Bureau and missionary societies augmented the church, which was the agency for change, education and welfare.

The fate of the coastal islands themselves has varied. Agriculture has all but disappeared. Some islands fell into the hands of wealthy industrialists who used them for game preserves, retreats, or active farming. Some owners or their descendants have arranged for the state or for private foundations to allow the islands to revert to their natural state. This is never inexpensive because it involves population manipulation, land management, and lots of money. You may take a ferry, for example, to Sapelo or St. Catherines islands. Access to Ossabaw Island is by phone to the Ossabaw Foundation. Call Trey Coursey to verify, at 912-233-5104. Except for a few architectural remnants in tabby or brick, you would not be able to imagine the lives of five generations of slaves, entire communities of Africans who tilled the land, worked in the dikes, fished and shrimped the waters, and dredged oysters for both tabby making and sustenance. The quarters they lived in for generations and the graves beside which they held services to mark their passing have disappeared. Only an occasional ripple in the lowland indicates where they labored so hard to clear the land and care for the fields.

Naturalist John Muir came to Savannah in 1867, just after the Civil War. His prime interest, though, was in the coastal islands, as it was for John James Audubon, and the naturalists and ornithologists Mark Catesby and William Bartram before him. You can take a ferry from Darien to Sapelo with its Estaurine Research Reserve, replacing the generations of Spalding family plantations there, followed by ownership by the Hudson Motor Company executive Howard Coffin and then the tobacco magnate R. J. Reynolds.

Ossabaw has a master house built for the H. N. Torrey family at the turn of the century by Henrik Wallin, who built the George Ferguson Armstrong mansion on Bull and Gaston streets in Savannah (see pp. 157–158). Writers are familiar with the house and grounds from the period in the 1950s when it was a writers' retreat. Now the owners are in a public–private partnership to establish a nature reserve. Ossabaw illustrates that the interim period of wealthy northern ownership after the plantation generations has worked well with the effort to return the island to its pre-plantation appearance. It takes money, planning, and hard work to let nature take over. Nature doesn't happen naturally these days.

To recall the Austrian Salzburger experience in coastal Georgia, go to Ebenezer with its Georgia Salzburger Museum and the Jerusalem Evangelical Lutheran Church and cemetery. The Puritans of Midway left a legacy that you may see in the church, museum, and cemetery at Midway, where you may go to Seabrook Village, an African-American living history museum.

Go to Hofwyl–Broadfield plantation south of Darien on the Altahama River to see what happened to the old rice plantations after the Civil War. Ophelia and Miriam Dent bequeathed to the public the plantation their family had owned since 1809 when their great-grandfather, William Brailsford, and his wife, Maria Heyward, both of Charleston, bought the plantation then called Broadface and renamed it. They took up rice planting near the place called Sutherlands Bluff. It passed through William Brailsford's daughter to the Troup family of nearby Darien and then into the Dent family by marriage. The two maiden ladies, Ophelia and Miriam Dent, who gave it to the public, left 150 years of rice-planting lore, every piece of English and American silver, and much else, down to the tatting and hand-embroidered sheets of four generations.

Don't be deceived as to the quality of the Brailford–Troup–Dent possessions by the modest house. The master house burned long ago and this small overseer's house was used by the spinsters. Ophelia Dent was a friend of the DuPonts and the Coffins, who had bought nearby estates, and they took her to Europe with them from time to time; these northerners understood "quality" when they saw it, they say in Georgia. After all, the Dent sisters and their mother Miriam Cohen Dent had saved a failing family plantation and freed it from generations of debt. This was accomplished through the judgment and accounting ability of Miriam Dent and the unceasing efforts of her daughters Ophelia and Miriam Dent, who turned the rice plantation into a dairy farm.

At St. Simons Island you can see the remnants of General Oglethorpe's Fort Frederica in tabby construction. The island was the site of the battle of Bloody Marsh, in which Oglethorpe, more or less by accident, came upon the Spaniards from St. Augustine at rest and unsuspecting. He dealt them such a blow on St. Simons that they never again threatened Georgia. Don't miss the Museum of Coastal History. It's hard to imagine the nineteenth century when the scholarly Hamilton–Couper family ran an extensive and examplary rice plantation here for two generations, not far from one of Pierce Butler's absentee ownership plantations.

The visitors center at Darien is particularly helpful. Imagine when the little village, laid out by Oglethorpe in 1734 and settled by the Scots Highlanders, was vying with Savannah in the 1880s for numbers of ships to haul away the vast fields of timber being stripped from the forests and swamps and sent down the Altahama River (Figure 21).

Cumberland Island, the southernmost and largest of Georgia's barrier islands, is accessible from St. Mary's. The 45-minute ferry boat ride on the *Cumberland Queen* takes you to the island named in 1734 by Toonahowi, Yamacrow chief, Tomochichi's heir and adopted son. When Oglethorpe took the 12-year-old Yamacraw with his parents and their entourage to London in 1734, his young contemporary William Augustus, the Duke of Cumberland, befriended him. Toonahowi named the island Cumberland after his English friend.

Catherine Greene, General Nathanael Greene's widow, built a grand mansion called Dungeness, named after Oglethorpe's hunting lodge on Cumberland Island, near Fort William. Mrs. Greene's Dungeness, completed in 1803, had tabby walls 6 feet thick at the base and 16 fireplaces in four stories. Dungeness was inherited by her daughter, Louisa Catherine Shaw, but it was stripped and looted during the Civil War and burned during Reconstruction. Its replacement was begun by Thomas Carnegie, younger brother of the famous financier Andrew Carnegie. When he died, his widow, Lucy Coleman Carnegie, continued the project in flamboyant style. The new and magnificent Dungeness burned in 1959 on the foundations of its burned predecessor. The place is a good spot for studying tabby ruins, and notice the

**Figure 21** Visit of Oglethorpe to the Highland Colony (Darien); wood engraving by Edmund Olliet from *The Youth's History of the U.S.* by Edward S. Ellis (New York: Cassell Publishing Company, about 1880). Oglethorpe was pleased with the Scots' progress and their adaptation to the Trustees' plan for Georgia. He also was a partisan for Stuart interests. *Courtesy V. & J. Duncan Antique Maps and Prints.*

two-story tabby house, the Greene's gardener's house, built about 1800. Follow the ruins to the ocean and pass by the cemetery of the Greene family. If you're lucky, you'll see a wild horse among the ruins. Part of the island is privately owned and other areas are controlled by the National Park Service. Greyfield, an estate used as an exclusive hotel, provides the only overnight accomodations on Cumberland Island aside from camping.

Side trips to Bluffton, South Carolina, and Guyton, Georgia, once summer retreats from the heat and mosquitoes and illness of Savannah and the islands, will enhance your understanding of the area. Bluffton, South Carolina, 24 miles from Savannah, is a quaint village on the May River. The board-and-batten

Episcopal Church of the Cross is beautifully situated on the banks of the May River. You will find frame summer cottages with screen porches raised on brick piers, the house of choice for the Southern climate for two centuries.

Guyton in Effingham County on the Georgia side is situated between the Savannah and Ogeechee rivers. Locals call it a sand hill town, the farm village where Juliette Gordon Low and some of her friends from Savannah retreated during the heat of summer and the yellow fever season. You'll see late Victorian tin-roofed farmhouses with galleries and screen porches. You'll notice that some houses are vernacular versions of the fancy late-nineteenth-century houses in Savannah, but in Guyton a garden grows beside each house and live oaks with their moss shade it all, except for a good corn patch in the back, bathed by the hot sun and humid air.

## WHEN TO VISIT SAVANNAH

The best time to visit Savannah is in February or the first week of March. The camellias are still in bloom and the azaleas have just come out. It's glorious, usually sweater-cool, and the city is about to burst into full bloom.

There's a reason, besides yellow fever, that everyone who could afford to do so left Savannah during the summer. Royal Governor Henry Ellis thought Savannah was the hottest place in the world west of the Seychelles.

Try the Georgia Heritage Celebration sometime in the first two weeks of February, sponsored by the Historic Savannah Foundation, 233-7787.

In March, the St. Patrick's Day celebration presents a good opportunity to see Savannah's squares at their peak. This is old-fashioned American fun, 1940s in feeling. Call the Savannah Waterfront Association, 234-0295.

The Annual Savannah Tour of Homes and Gardens is toward the end of March. Call their headquarters at 234-8054 to see about a four-day extravaganza.

Every April, the garden club sponsors the Hidden Gardens of Savannah Tour. Call 897-2177 or 238-0248.

Fort Pulaski Siege and Reduction Weekend commemorates the April 1862 battle that changed the history of military defense forever. Call Fort Pulaski National Monument, 786-5787.

It gets cool again in October, so you might enjoy just checking into an inn and enjoying the Savannah experience. Or wait until December and take the Annual Christmas Tour of Inns, an on-your-own walking or driving tour of at least fifteen inns decked out for Christmas. Call 1-800-444-2427.

Theater is doing well in Savannah and three of the historic early twentieth-century movie and performing arts theaters are being renovated, most notably the Lucas Theater. The Savannah Theater Company on the site of William Jay's 1820 theater at **222 Bull Street** (see p. 133) offers live theater, 233-7764. Call the Office of Cultural Affairs arts line at 912-233-ARTS for details on other musical and theater events.

One of Savannah's many hidden gardens. *Photograph by Scot Hinson.*

City Hall dome; unsigned pencil drawing by Christopher Murphy, Jr. *Courtesy V. & J. Duncan Antique Maps and Prints.*

# 4

## JEWELS
## IN THE CROWN:
## SAVANNAH'S SQUARES

M ore meetings have taken place on Savannah's behalf than for any other city in the New World. The meetings began about 1730 in London when 21 volunteer philanthropists planned Savannah as capital for a new British colony across the Atlantic Ocean. The meetings started again in the 1950s when volunteer preservationists worked to save the city that Georgia's Trustees projected from London 230 years earlier.

These meetings of the Georgia Trust or nonprofit corporation included 21 Trustees responsible for funding and regulating Savannah for 21 years. The Georgia Trustees, well-educated English noblemen, clergymen, and public officials came together because of their wide range of common interests. The catalyzing forces, however, were prison reform and the reform movement within the Anglican church. These men were reformers on one level or another. They represented both houses of Parliament: Oglethorpe was a member of the minority Tories, but his good friend, Lord Egmont, for example, represented the prevailing Whig party led by Sir Robert Walpole.

The aim of these gentlemen was different from that of any other colony in the New World: Spanish, French, or English. Raising money from benefaction, they sought to develop, through constructive charity, a society of small farmers, merchants, and soldiers, settled around Savannah and other to-be-established towns. These men would support themselves and their families without slave labor and without gathering large tracts of lands. The Trustees had in mind something positive: they were humanitarians. Georgia was not projected as a proprietorship financed by commercial interests and venture capital as were Virginia and the Carolinas.

Oglethorpe, as Trustee and military leader, sailed to Georgia with the first settlers when he was 36 years old, after having accomplished his foremost aim for society, the release of some 12,000 debtors from the prisons of London. He remained among the settlers but took three intermittent voyages back to England from 1733 to 1743. He laid out the town, set up and led Georgia's military defence, and spent almost £100,000 of his own fortune to keep Savannah viable.

Back in London the most indefatigable Trustee in his responsibility toward the colony was James Vernon, a commissioner of the excise and one-time envoy to the King of Denmark. He attended 394 meetings of the trust corporation, 176 of the Common Council, and 142 of committees, 712 meetings in all. In addition, he raised £18,000 of private money for the colony, and lobbied Parliament for the £137,000 it grudgingly contributed to Georgia before it finally took over in 1754 and sent a royal governor to a new Crown colony.

Although absent from London for years, Oglethorpe managed to attend 267 meetings and stood ninth in attendance among all Trustees. His zeal for the colony caused him to appear repeatedly before Parliament to raise money for what was considered Georgia's number one priority, defense. After all, a prime *raison d'être* for the colony in the minds of most was its position as a buffer between Spanish America and long-established Carolina to the north.

In a twist of irony in 1735 on his first return to London after establishing Savannah, Oglethorpe raised £25,800 in Parliament to fortify the border of Georgia from the threat of French Catholics at Mobile (founded 1706), Biloxi (founded 1717), and along the Gulf of Mexico. He announced to Parliament that the French colonials were looking east from the Mississippi. He should have known. His sister Eleanor, raised French Catholic at St. Germaine en Laye as a ward of the exiled English King James II and Queen Henrietta Mary, had married the Marquis de Mézières in 1707 and the two were heavy investors in Louisiana. In fact, his sister Fanny had married the Marquis des Marches in 1719 just as New Orleans was founded, and the two sisters, with their husbands, had acquired land grants of one half the acreage around Bay St. Louis on the Gulf coast. Additionally, the two Oglethorpe sisters had enriched themselves prodigiously on their own behalves from the sale of shares in the Mississippi Company, enough to fit out a ship and send 300 French colonists to Louisiana. Oglethorpe, their younger brother, having settled Savannah about a decade later, was raising money for a theoretical defense against the interests of his sisters.

In Savannah, the meetings continued: Oglethorpe met with founding settlers, Trust officials, and military personnel. He negotiated with the Yamacraw natives of the area for Savannah's location and with other Creek Indians for the tidewater lands of Georgia. He cemented relations with various southeastern tribes to augment trade and protection. His success at peaceful relations with the southeastern Indians lasted 100 years, until Andrew Jackson annihilated or ejected from their homeland these people that Oglethorpe had admired and protected.

Oglethorpe's other lasting contribution to Georgia remains visible today (Figure 1). His plan for Savannah has stood the test of time and growth from 140 persons around four squares in four wards to a city of over 150,000 that retains many of the elements that Oglethorpe and the other Trustees worked so hard to implant at Savannah.

The basic organizational unit in Savannah's plan was a ward. Oglethorpe established four of them in 1733, each centered by a square. On his second return to the colony in 1736, he added two more ward units. The southward march of the town of Savannah advanced through the nineteenth century in incremental units of wards within the east–west boundaries set by Oglethorpe and southward using up the city commons.

Each square had two lots on its east side and two on the west side called *trust lots,* reserved by the trustees for public buildings, churches, schools, and institutions. Residences were organized in the second basic unit, called a tithing block, consisting of ten lots, each lot measuring 60 by 90 feet, laid out on the north and south sides of each square. Four tithing blocks of ten lots each were divided by lanes, like English mews, so that there appear eight rectangular blocks (Figure 2).

Each tithing lot was accompanied by a nearby 5-acre garden lot and a farm of almost 45 acres outside the city commons. The city squares served as stockyards and as a safe retreat for inhabitants from outside the city in time of attack. The distribution of the set of 50-acre units, town lot, garden lot, and farm, took place on "the Strand," or riverfront, July 7, 1733.

After the land awards were made, the settlers began erecting frame cottages. Oglethorpe worked out an assembly line for cutting the timbers and building the identical cottages. Each measured 16 by 24 feet and was 8 feet high. Each cottage sat uniformly on its tithing lot with a garden to one side. Raised on logs 2 feet off the ground and floored with 1½-inch planks or rough deals, each was roofed with wood shingles and sided with feather-edged boards. Now, 250 years later, the tithing blocks are unchanged, but brick and frame townhouses and rowhouses fill them, each having 60 or fewer front feet.

Oglethorpe's use of Old English or Saxon lexicography for his ward system indicates that he was continuing a British concept. *Ward* is an Old English word, originally military, meaning to guard or to watch. *Garden* is a word that originally meant enclosure, from the same root as ward or guard. *Trust,* as a name for publicly owned lots, is a term popularized in early Middle English society, relative to land kept in trust for the inhabitants. *Tithe* is a biblical concept alluding to the contribution of one-tenth part. A tithing lot is one of ten lots on a tithing block, with 40 tithing lots on a square. In Oglethorpe's Savannah, a tithing com-

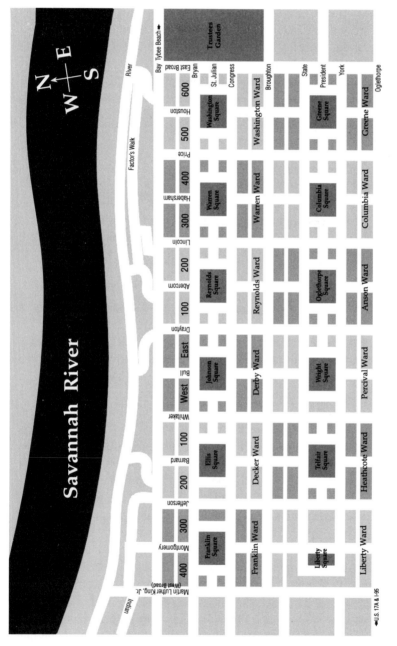

**Figure 2** Diagram of ward with square, trust lots, tithing lots, streets, and lanes. *Courtesy Savannah College of Art and Design.*

River Street to Oglethorpe Avenue

prised a company of ten lotholders or tithingmen, to be called up for military duty as needed. In some places in Europe a tithing was called a *decennary* after the Latin, or a *fribourg* among the Teutonic peoples.

Oglethorpe's reasoning behind the city plan, to provide an effective environment for the citizen-soldier and a fortified retreat for the farmer-soldier, reflects his own military training. He also had prints of the old Roman camp or castro system from Pietro Cataneo's 1567 publication that showed a grid street pattern with a system of multiple squares similar to those of Savannah.

Laura Palmer Bell of Savannah did research that related Savannah's plan to that of Peking as published during Oglethorpe's lifetime. We also know that Oglethorpe was profoundly influenced by his good friend Robert Castell, an English architect, whose book *The Villas of the Ancients Illustrated* was subscribed to by Oglethorpe. In fact, Oglethorpe wrote a treatise in the second edition of Castell's book, published after the author had died in Fleet Street prison, where he had been incarcerated as a debtor, unable to pay the expenses accrued from publishing and promoting his book.

Oglethorpe was satisfied with the plan he developed. He repeated it on a smaller scale at Darien (New Inverness) in 1735 for the Scots Highlanders and at New Ebenezer in 1736 for the Salzburgers on a larger scale.

Fort Frederica on St. Simons Island was Oglethorpe's fortress, used to defend Savannah from the Spaniards at St. Augustine. There, only the arrangement of the garden lots and the commons relates to Savannah's distribution of lands.

With Oglethorpe at Savannah, Vetruvius came to the New World in a way that the military engineers of France and Spain never conceived in Quebec, New Orleans, or St. Augustine. Most of the colonial cities of Central and South America were built within or onto earlier native American cities.

Savannah was planned before the people arrived. Although this could have been arranged by any number of the Lords Proprietor or in the charter colonies of the New World, it was not. Only Philadelphia was designed as a city, for William Penn, and then the populace was brought in 1683. Oglethorpe knew Penn, but whether the idea influenced him or not, James Oglethorpe followed suit fifty years later in 1733.

Certain Mennonite villages were planned ahead on paper, but it was not until the 1790s that Pierre l'Enfant was employed, at Thomas Jefferson's suggestion, to lay out a plan for Washington. L'Enfant had been an officer with the French in the siege of Savannah in 1779 and had been left for dead near the town limits. His new city between already settled Georgetown and Alexandria had a plan focused on the confluence of the Potomac and Anacostia rivers. In all three documented planned cities, Philadelphia, Savannah, and Washington, the primary resource and the parameters were rivers.

After Oglethorpe's departure in 1743, no new squares were developed until after the American Revolution. Additional wards to the east and west were established in the 1790s to 1801. The squares' names celebrate mililtary heroes and the new republic. After the War of 1812, Orleans and Chippewa squares were laid out beyond the original southern boundary, South Broad Street (Oglethorpe Avenue), and Liberty Street became the city limits. Pulaski, Lafayette, and Madison squares came along in the spurt of growth and prosperity of the 1830s. Monterey Square commemorates the war with Mexico, and William Crawford, a Georgia governor and Secretary of the Treasury under Madison and Monroe, was also honored. At the apex of the city's development, in the 1850s, final wards were laid out to the south, utilizing the last of the city commons to Gaston Street. During this time, religion, politics, and history were remembered in Whitefield, Calhoun, and Chatham squares. The pilot squares established by Oglethorpe set the standard for the units, followed by the city until 1851, when the creation of Forsyth Park ended Oglethorpe's ward system. With his fortuitous citizen-soldier plan for the city, Oglethorpe created *rus in urbe* 200 years before the landscape designers made it a goal. Savannah needs no suburbs.

From a planner's point of view, Oglethorpe's genius was the incremental potential of the plan. Wards could be laid out as needed in an urban, commercial-residential mix, so placed as to appear suburban in spatial relationships. The setting, with its squares, is tranquil and green, but the organization is tight and urban. The human-manipulated spaces contrast with the exuberance of the natural tropical growth.

The streets pierced with squares become chains, the squares their charms. Each segment of Savannah, the ward, is complete within itself but part of an interlocking whole. These interrelationships create tensions within the order.

Savannah today does not have one building dating from the time of Oglethorpe. Indeed, when the Trust colony was given over to the Crown in 1752, there were only two remaining family who had come over on the first ship with Oglethorpe, Noble Jones and his son. Their descendants continue to be active in Savannah's development today. However, the town retains houses built by descendants of Trustee-period settlers: Minises, Sheftalls, Habershams, Joneses, Telfairs, Wyllys, Morels, and others.

The last original cottage burned about 1845. Artist Fermin Cerveau painted it in his 1837 view of Savannah, at the corner of Bay and Bull streets, now the site of the U.S. Customs House. Just two pre-Revolutionary houses remain; one is the Christian Camphor cottage (1760–1767) at **122 South Broad Street** (East Oglethorpe Avenue), then the city limits. The other is the building associated with Lachlan McIntosh at **110 East Oglethorpe Avenue** (see p. 113).

One is hard pressed to find an eighteenth-century building in Savannah since two fires, in 1796 and 1820, burned hundreds of frame and brick houses of the colonial period. All the remaining houses that suggest the early period are frame. Ironically, bricks were shipped to Savannah in 1733 by the Trustees, and by early 1734 the German Salzburgers at Ebenezer had started a brickworks.

The wards that suggest the appearance of post-Revolutionary Savannah are on the northeast, the Old Fort Area, including Trustees Gardens. Warren, Washington, Columbia, and Greene squares, and the Beach Institute Area around Crawford Square, provide the post-Revolutionary eighteenth-century Savannah look. Modest frame housing, built there even until the 1870s, followed the types and styles of the eighteenth-century one-story cottages with their shed dormers and small openings. The Federal center-hall two-story houses, with their simple woodwork, plain cornices, and narrow entrances, recall the early days of the republic.

Start at the river and Bull Street, where the city began, and walk south to enjoy the squares that bisect Bull Street. Go around the squares among the Bull Street shaft that leads to Forsyth Park for a cross section of Savannah. The closer you are to the river, the more commercial the wards have become. Skyscrapers, Savannah style, replace the eighteenth- and nineteenth-century buildings on Johnson Square, the first to be laid out in 1733 by Oglethorpe. As you proceed south toward Monterey Square, the city becomes more residential and you may enjoy a lesson in architectural types and styles.

## BAY STREET AND THE RIVER

The Savannah River was the city's *raison d'être* (Figure 3). The site selected by Oglethorpe on the 40-foot-high bluff is considered the best port siting south of St. Mary's City, the first settlement of Lord Baltimore's Maryland. The rivalry between Savannah and Charleston stemmed from a spirited competition for "first port" status among shippers. Savannah, on the other hand, would be a place of opulence, according to John Pope, a Virginia traveler in 1789, as long as "commerce spread her canvas to the wind."

The waterfront grew helter-skelter, with wharves, taverns, and storage buildings strewn about the city-owned property. Then in 1803, New Franklin Ward was laid out, and the city property was sold "for the sole purpose of lighting the city with lamps." The ward covered the waterfront, called the "Strand," and what was called the "Bay," now Bay Street, bound by "Edward Telfair's lands to the east and W. Broad Street" (Martin Luther King Jr. Boulevard).

Ballast stones, left on the riverbanks by departing sailing ships, were used in 1845 to make ramps down the bluff (Figure 4). Cast iron bridges and catwalks were built to tie the varying levels together and make the stone and brick warehouses accessible. Architect Charles Cluskey built Greek revival "Embankment Stores" in 1854 along the stone ramps, creating elevations that were different levels on the river side than on the Bay Street side. The Factors Row buildings followed and the area continued to grow as the focus for a mercantile port city.

**Figure 3** City and harbor of Savannah, 1883; wood engraving by J. O. Davidson from *Harper's Weekly*, November 17, 1883, p. 729. View from West Broad Street shows Franklin Square with its water tower, rice mill on Bay Street, and the city exchange (now demolished). *Courtesy V. & J. Duncan Antique Maps and Prints.*

**Figure 4** Cobblestones brought from England as ships' ballast now pave the bluff at the Savannah River. Cotton and rice warehouses are testimony to the day when export was Savannah's key to fortune. *Photograph by Keith Cardwell, courtesy Savannah College of Art and Design.*

The granite and cast iron building fronts contrast with the ballast stone and brick and stucco-covered warehouses to create a medley of texture and shape along the riverfront. Massive walls made of ballast stones are punctuated with a progression of arches or rectangles. Occasionally, cast iron balconies add to the rich composition.

The cotton export business, with the attendant factors, brokers, graders, loaders, and shippers, consumed the bustling nineteenth-century waterfront. In times of drought and when the boll weevil descended, lumber and naval stores substituted for cotton. The port changed character after World War II, and the riverfront languished. Working with architect Robert Gunn, John Rousakis, 20 years the mayor until 1991, created a plaza or centerpiece to focus on River and Bay streets, to revitalize the area. Despite the controversial intrusion of the overscaled Hyatt Regency Hotel, a project of local developer Merritt W. Dixon III, the nineteenth-century riverfront holds up as Savannah's cynosure.

**Bay Steet at Bull Street** (Figure 5)

The central focus to the riverfront today is City Hall, designed in 1905 by Hyman W. Witcover. The vaulted dome topped by a round cupola rising above the fourth floor of the building presents an eclectic classicism to the city.

**1–5 East Bay Street** (Figure 6)

The south side of Bay Street is rich in buildings, most notable of which is the U.S. Customs House (Reynolds Ward; see p. 84). The Customs house is a monument to Savannah's importance as a port by 1848, when the federal govern-

**Figure 5** 204 West Bay Street. Riverfront architecture combining the available ballast stones from incoming ships with Savannah bricks offers texture and history at once. These sturdy riverfront warehouses were built by William Taylor in 1818 to accomodate the vast increase in cotton exports to Liverpool after Eli Whitney's cotton gin went into use. They've been used and reused, as cotton warehouses, for a ship chandler's busines, and later adapted as an artist's apartment and now a restaurant. *Photograph by Keith Caldwell, courtesy Savannah College of Art and Design.*

**Figure 6**  U.S. Customs House, 1–5 East Bay Street, designed and built by architect John S. Norris, 1848–1852. *Photograph by Goeff DeLorm, courtesy Savannah College of Art and Design.*

ment employed John S. Norris to design it. Norris's arrival here from Wilmington, North Carolina, where he had worked on public projects after leaving New York, signaled a rise in sophistication of Savannah's mid-nineteenth century residences and commercial buildings. Twenty-three buildings were designed by Norris.

**100 East Bay Street** (Figure 7)

The Savannah Cotton Exchange was designed by architect William Gibbons Preston in 1886. The central element with pilasters and spandrels decorated with terra-cotta relief is crowned with a fanciful terra-cotta-relief pediment. Again, eclecticism is the order of the day. Solidity is the theme: cotton was the most important aspect of Savannah and Georgia, the leading cotton producer of the country. Little did the merchants foresee the relentless advance of the boll weevil to make the building obsolete for its intended use by 1920.

**101 East Bay Street**

This neoclassical bank building in Reynolds Ward was designed in 1912 by Mowbray and Uffinger as the Hibernia Bank. Austere and masculine, it has a modified pediment, and the columns'

entases are exaggerated in the Doric order. The deep Doric frieze of triglylphs and metopes and the heavy free-standing Doric columns continue around the building. The bank is an appropriate twentieth-century version of Norris's nineteenth-century customs house.

**Figure 7**  Cotton exchange building, 100 East Bay Street at Drayton Street, decorated with bunting for a public celebration, 1930s. *Cordray–Foltz Collection, courtesy Georgia Historical Society.*

**Figure 8** Stoddard's Lower Range, Factors Walk, 208–230 East Bay Street, built in 1859 for John Stoddard. *W. C. Hartridge Collection, courtesy Georgia Historical Society.*

The New York firm of Mowbray and Uffinger had first arrived in Savannah in 1907 for the Citizens and Savings Bank commission by Mills B. Lane. They proceeded to design the house at **26 East Gaston Street** (see p. 159) for banker Lane in 1909. The handsome Georgian revival house with heavy central broken pediment is a facile rendition of the then-popular style. In 1911 they designed the Savannah Bank and Trust at **2–6 East Bryan Street** (see p. 72), and this bank in 1912. Mowbray was the son of an Englishman who made a fortune in industry in New York in the late-nineteenth century.

**208–230 East Bay Street** (Figure 8)
Merchant John Stoddard had these compositions in bricks and arches built in 1858–1859. The cast iron bridges or catwalks across which the factors walked to inspect the cotton stacked beneath are decorative aspects of the scene today (Figure 9).

**425 East Bay Street**
Built for John Eppinger in 1809 in Warren Ward, this two-story frame house continues the post-colonial tradition. It was moved from the corner of Jefferson and West Hull streets when the city auditorium was going up. The

house follows no established plan, having five bays with a side entrance. Two dormers, six-over-nine windows at the second level, and gable ends with an exterior brick chimney are clues to the early date. A first level front gallery is

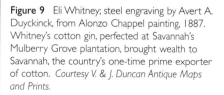

**Figure 9** Eli Whitney; steel engraving by Avert A. Duyckinck, from Alonzo Chappel painting, 1887. Whitney's cotton gin, perfected at Savannah's Mulberry Grove plantation, brought wealth to Savannah, the country's one-time prime exporter of cotton. *Courtesy V. & J. Duncan Antique Maps and Prints.*

covered by a shed roof supported by simple columns.

### 21–23 West Bay Street

The exterior of this simple four-story stucco-front commercial structure built as the City Hotel does not intimate the luxury of the interior. It is known that Eleazer Early had the hotel built about 1821, probably after architect William Jay's designs. The flat front facade once had iron balconies that crossed the facade at two levels, and a covered walkway guarded the hotel entrance. The first floor was fitted as commercial establishments to complement the hotel on each side of an expansive center lobby. A fine brick carriage house faces the lane. It should be restored with the City Hotel.

The old City Hotel's lush interior indicates a William Jay design and is the street's hidden masterpiece. Double stairways, retiring parlors with exquisite plasterwork, carefully carved mantels, and paneled doorways have been allowed to decay from water exposure

for years beneath a faulty roof. Even the crumbling walls cannot efface the sophistication of spatial relationships and proportion of the building's interior.

The City Hotel had a fine wine cellar in a basement that continued under the sidewalk. A number of duels among Savannahians, sea island planters, and upcountry cotton and lumber magnates were instigated in its bar. Some unsuccessful duelists' graves at the Colonial Cemetery tell the story.

### 112–130 West Bay Street (Figures 10 and 11)

George Jones and the Telfair Estate had architects Charles Sholl and Calvin Fay design these rows of two-story cast iron–front commercial buildings in 1852–1854. Note the full entablature with the recessed rectangles crowning the row above dentils.

### 202–206 West Bay Street (Figure 12)

These stone and brick warehouses and stores were built for William Taylor in 1818, rebuilt in part after a fire in 1885.

**Figure 10**  Peters Bottling Company, 118 West Bay Street, about 1940. The bottling company has taken advantage of advertising space offered through their own building surface. Graphics become part of the building design. *Cordray–Foltz Collection, courtesy Georgia Historical Society.*

**Figure 11**   Cast iron front at 114 West Bay Street, one of a row with bricks at the second level, 1852–1854. *Photograph by Keith Cardwell, courtesy Savannah College of Art and Design.*

**Figure 12**   202–206 West Bay Street. *Photographs by Keith Cardwell, courtesy Savannah College of Art and Design.*

**Figure 13** International Milling Company, 220–222 West Bay Street, about 1940. Advertising included vast painted surfaces of brick buildings. Graphics here provide an abstract and oversized entablature above a row of dentils. *Cordray–Foltz Collection, courtesy Georgia Historical Society.*

**220–222 West Bay Street** (Figure 13) Among the earlier buildings in the riverfront area, these warehouses with their arched openings present a one-story facade on Bay Street but also face the river with multiple stories. The brick buildings were built in 1821 for Matthew Johnston and others.

# OGLETHORPE'S
# SIX SQUARES, 1733–1746

## JOHNSON SQUARE AND DERBY WARD, 1733

The Nathanael Greene Monument is a William Strickland design of 1830. Derby Ward, laid out along Bull Street, was named after the Right Honorable James, Tenth Earl of Derby and Georgia Trustee. The square was named for Robert Johnson, the governor of South Carolina, who helped the Georgia colony.

This first ward laid out by Oglethorpe held the public stores and a public mill (Figure 14). One of the trust lots contained the Strangers' House, built at Trustees' expense, and another trust lot was reserved for the Church of England. Savannah's first forty houses were built in Derby Ward.

At old number 10 Tyrconel Tything, the first child born in the Georgia colony, on March 17, 1733, daughter of Thomas and Hannah Close, received the silver boat and spoon promised by Oglethorpe to the firstborn in the new colony. Her parents named her Georgia, of course. They were among the thirty-five families: forty-four men, twenty women, twenty-five boys, and seventeen girls, that arrived on the first ship. By January 1734 there were 259 people in Savannah, centered around this square.

Because of its proximity to the water, Johnson Square (Figure 15) became the heart of commercial Savannah, now filled with Savannah's early skyscrapers. It remains the favorite square of those people who enjoy the effects of the marble and stone building edges around the lush green square.

Because of the lanes intersecting tithing blocks, the early twentieth-century buildings, five and six stories in height, couldn't overrun the large trust lots or the tithing squares of 90 feet by 300 feet. Therefore, the proper scale of building to square has been maintained.

**Figure 14**  "Scene in the principal square of Savannah, on arrival of the news of the capture of Port Royal by the National Forces—indiscriminate flight of inhabitants to the interior." *Courtesy Georgia Historical Society.*

**Figure 15**  Dedication of the sundial, Johnson Square, Derby Ward. This ward, laid out in 1733 by the city's founder, remains a place for public ceremonies, here, in the 1930s. The street becomes a shaft of space with the monument to W. W. Gordon in Wright Square to the south. *Courtesy Georgia Historical Society.*

**Figure 16** Christ Church, 28 Bull Street on Johnson Square; stereoview, about 1870. *Courtesy V. & J. Duncan Antique Maps and Prints.*

**28 Bull Street** (Figure 16)

This trust lot was the site Oglethorpe set aside for the colony's first church. The mother church of Georgia held its first Anglican service in Savannah on February 12, 1733. Christ Church, Episcopal, the fourth church on the site, dates from 1838, with an interior rebuilding in 1897 after a fire.

The present building was designed by St. Simons Island planter and scholar James Hamilton Couper, a published expert in tabby construction. The Greek revival building exhibits Roman orders, with an interior seeking the simplicity of Christopher Wren. No colorful stained glass windows decorate the nave at Christ Church, outstanding in its stark simplicity. Corinthian columns and pilasters support the gallery balcony and flank the tall, narrow side windows.

The first Sunday School class in North America was held here under the direction of minister John Wesley, who also wrote the first hymnal published in British America at Christ Church. Wesley, who later established the Methodist church, came to the colony along with his brother Charles on Oglethorpe's second voyage. The

founder was an old friend of their father, also a reform minister.

**22 Bull Street**

Design for the Citizens and Southern National Bank brought architects Mowbray and Uffinger to Savannah in 1907. The neoclassical building continues the scale and style of Christ Church, almost a century later. A heavy parapet and deeply incised dentils beneath the extruding molded cornice lend strength and monumentality to the building. Set low to the ground, the building provides easy accessibility to the bank.

**2–6 East Bryan Street**

The same architects, Mowbray and Uffinger, designed the Savannah Bank and Trust Company in 1911. This nearby bank shows the versatility of the architects and the range of styles available to a business or bank in the early twentieth century. Designed in the traditional Greek tripartite scheme, the building appears as a column with its base, eight-story body, and capital. Thus it suits Savannah's classic theme.

**24–26 East Bryan Street**

This three-story, four-bay, plastered commercial building dates from 1824. The earliest building remaining near

Johnson Square, it should be restored to its simple, Federal-style appearance. Attributed to builder Amos Scudder, it was built for Mrs. Ann Hamilton.

## WRIGHT SQUARE AND PERCIVAL WARD, 1733

Wright Square, Savannah's second-oldest square, a project of constructive philanthropy by the Georgia Trustees, now has a monument to commemorate William Washington Gordon, giant of commerce and trade, founder and first president of the Central of Georgia Railroad Company (Figure 17). Van Brunt and Howe of Boston designed it, and Walter F. Peach of New York was the builder.

Percival Ward was named by Oglethorpe after the Right Honorable John, Lord Viscount Percival, Earl of Egmont, the Trustee most efficient at raising money from Parliament and most visible in his service to Savannah and Georgia. King George II made him Earl of Egmont the year that Oglethorpe settled Savannah, and appointed him president of the Trust colony of Georgia. Egmont resigned in protest from the Trust after ten years of service, when the Trust and Parliament were bowing to the clergy's and venture capitalists' demands for unlimited land holdings and slavery.

After Oglethorpe's time, the square was renamed for the third and most competent royal governor, Sir James Wright, who served from 1760 to the end of the American Revolution except for a short period when the patriots of Savannah exiled him before the British reclaimed their southernmost colony in 1779.

Wright's father had been chief justice of South Carolina. He himself had been attorney general of South Carolina and its agent in London when the Crown appointed him royal governor of the new Crown colony of Georgia. His governorship began on a sad note, his son having died at sea during Wright's voyage back to the colonies to assume his duties. Wright buried his son in Charleston in 1760, and his wife died while he was stationed in Savannah. However, another son represented the Crown's most fervent hopes for its colonists: He got rich! The South Carolina *Gazette* reported, "Married, Alexander Wright, Esquire, son of His Excellency, Governor of Georgia, to Miss Elizbeth Izard, [of Charleston] with a fortune of thirty thousand pounds, Sterling."

In Wright's day rice was a source of wealth and power. By the 1770s Wright had twelve plantations in Georgia, each having about 450 acres and 45 slaves, half of whom were adult men. He owned about 600 slaves overall. Lt. Governor John Graham bested Wright in respect to wealth, while merchant James Habersham trailed his affluence on his double-unit plantation.

**Figure 17**  Post Office at Wright Square and monument to W. W. Gordon, founder of the Central of Georgia Railroad. *Courtesy Georgia Historical Society.*

**Figure 18** Evangelical Lutheran Church, 122 Bull Street, before 1879, when it was rebuilt; stereoview. *Courtesy V. & J. Duncan Antique Maps and Prints.*

Although born in the colonies, Wright put king first and mother country before colony. What was good for England, he thought, in common with the Trustees before him, would be good for the colony. He held a fragile Georgia together during the early days of the upcountry Liberty Boys' efforts, saving Savannah from anarchy before the American Revolution.

**Figure 19** Chatham County Courthouse in the 1930s, 124 Bull Street. *Walter C. Hartridge Collection, courtesy Georgia Historical Society.*

**122 Bull Street** (Figure 18)

Evangelical Lutheran Church of the Ascension, 1879, designed by George B. Clarke, was established by Lutherans from Salzburg, Austria, brought by 1734 on the third ship sent by the Trustees. The Reverend Johann Martin Bolzius, a distinguished Lutheran exile, was their leader and minister. By 1771 they had bought this trust lot. George B. Clarke built the present building in 1875, using the walls of the 1844 Greek revival building and adding a second story. He patterned it after an example in Samuel Sloan's *The Model Architect* (Philadelpia: E.S. Jones, 1852). Tripar-tite both vertically and horizontally, the building holds together with the medieval-style corner turrets that repeat the shape of the central steeple.

Services were conducted in English from 1824, but German was spoken at the church well into the twentieth century. The Austrians or Salzburgers who started this church came closer than any settlers to embodying the plan of the Trustees, working their 45- to 500-acre farms efficiently without slave labor. They were temperance men for the most part and were so industrious that Oglethorpe's letters to the Trustees begged for more German-speaking Lutherans.

**124 Bull Street** (Figures 19 and 20)

Architect William Gibbons Preston, F.A.I.A. (1840–1910), came to Savannah

**Figure 20**   Wright Square. "Monthly auction sale of horses, cattle, government bonds, furniture, etc. at the Courthouse," from a sketch by James E. Taylor, about 1863. The Greek revival courthouse has been replaced by the late-nineteenth-century Preston-designed building. The squares were always gathering places full of public activity. *Courtesy Georgia Historical Society.*

to build the Chatham County Courthouse in 1889. This assignment initiated a local craze for Romanesque revival and the English Romantic revival styles of architecture. If you see a red brick, terracotta, and sandstone building with a large and complex footprint, as detailed as its roofline, chances are you are looking at a Preston building. Over time many funeral establishments, but some are still private homes, such as **225 East Hall Street** (see p. 176), built in 1888 for Lucy and George Baldwin, a businessman who had made a fortune in phosphates.

Preston's yellow brick courthouse displays the semicircular arches that provide rhythm. A foliated rinceau with sculptural ornamentation in terra-cotta adds texture and movement to the animated facade.

**Bull Street Between York and State Streets** (Figure 21)

Look carefully at the U.S. Post Office built in 1898 with William Aiken as supervising architect, and you will see

that its size was more than doubled in an addition supervised by James A. Wetmore in 1931. The grace and care used to enlarge this massive building of Georgia marble with granite base and terra-cotta ornamentation shows that both the federal government and cities can be sensitive to their architectural precedents.

**Figure 21**   Post Office, Bull Street between York and State Streets. *Photograph by Goeff DeLorm, courtesy Savannah College of Art and Design.*

**136–140 Bull Street**

John Schwarz built this four-story commercial building in 1890 after designs by Alfred S. Eichberg, architect, and it was remodeled in 1907 and 1913. He used shallow blind arches and paired windows popular with the Romanesque theme, prevalent around this square. The curved corner is a sophisticated touch and the corner building has two finished facades.

**21–25 East York Street**

These paired brick sidehall houses built for investor Esther Stewart, 1853–1856, are typical of the Greek revival period of Savannah architecture. One retains a particularly severe entrance above the high stoop.

**ELLIS SQUARE AND DECKER WARD**

Decker Ward, the third ward laid out by Oglethorpe, in 1733, honors Sir Matthew Decker (1697–1749) a Trustee and commissioner of fund collections for the Trustees, director and governor of the East India Company, and member of Parliament.

Ellis Square, strung along Barnard Street, was renamed after Sir Henry Ellis, second royal governor of Georgia. Ellis was a wealthy Englishman, born in Ireland, who had run away from home as a child to sail around the world as a seaman. A scientist and dilettante as well as a man of letters, Ellis was remembered as the governor who walked about Savannah with a thermometer hanging from the brim of his tricorn. When the temperature reached 104 degrees one day, he exclaimed that Savannah was the hottest place on earth short of the Seychelles. He should have known, since as a veteran of the Guinea trade, he had sailed throughout the West Indies and had explored Hudson Bay on a voyage he financed as a member of the Royal Society.

Although royal governor, Ellis thought more like Oglethorpe and the Trustees; he wanted to restrict land holding size. He sought a large population of small farms, run without slaves, realizing that immense coastal plantations made profitable by a large slave population could lead to a planter oligarchy.

The city market, established here in 1763, had a brick building designed by railroad architect Augustus Schwaab in the 1850s. It served Savannah until 1954, when its demolition sparked the movement that finally resulted in establishment of the Historic Savannah Foundation.

General John Charles Fremont (1813–1890) was born here at Barnard and Broughton streets (demolished) in 1812. The explorer and pathfinder to the west, officer in the U.S. Army during the Civil War, and first Republican presidential candidate in 1856 in a race against Buchanan, lived at 563 West Bay Street.

John Musgrove and his Creek–English wife, Mary, Oglethorpe's official translator, were assigned a lot in Decker Ward, as were Noble Jones and his son, Noble Wimberly Jones. The latter lots remained in ownership of descendants until the mid-twentieth century.

Most of the early Jewish families arriving in 1733 were granted lots in Decker Ward. Oglethorpe's grants to the Jewish settlers occurred only after he consulted lawyers in Charleston, who noted that since the charter forbade only grants to Catholics, the Jews qualified. Their appearance in Savannah, on the first ship to arrive after Oglethorpe's own voyage, had not been authorized by the Trustees in London. The Trustees had debated the request of three wealthy London merchants of the Bevis Marks congregation for passage of a Jewish group to Georgia at the expense of the Jewish community. However, by the time the Trustees had decided against allowing them to settle in Savannah, the persecuted Jews had already arrived.

**102–116 West Congress Street**

The Thomas Gibbons range of three-story commercial buildings were built in the 1820s, soon after the previous buildings on the block burned. Thomas Gibbons wrote his son William from New York to have new buildings put up immediately. A deep cornice with a series of moldings beneath a handsome parapet and first-floor pillars (where they are original) produce both monumentality and simplicity. They are seen on artist Fermin Cerveau's view of Savannah in 1837, but were probably renovated or rebuilt about 1851.

The Gibbons family came to Savannah from South Carolina during the Crown colony period. They prospered and their mansion, built in the 1820s on West Broad Street (Martin Luther King Jr. Boulevard) at Bay Street, was demolished and the magnificent entrance sent to the American Wing of the Metropolitan Museum of Art.

### 115–117 and 123 West Congress Street

The row of Italianate-style three-story commercial buildings at 115–117 date from 1857 and were built for Noah K. Barnum. The buildings at **123 West Congress Street,** built two years later as the Lovell and Lattimore store, feature cast iron hood moldings above segmental arched window openings. Historic Savannah Foundation saved them from demolition. Consequently, the street is lined with Italianate commercial buildings and the historic Thomas Gibbons block of 1820 across the street.

### TELFAIR SQUARE AND HEATHCOTE WARD

The fourth and last of the wards laid out in 1733 was named after George Heathcote, Trustee and benefactor of the colony. Its square, along Barnard Street, was called St. James Square by Oglethorpe, but renamed Telfair in 1883 in honor of the Telfair family, which had produced a Revolutionary patriot and governor along with great wealth and one of Savannah's most important mansions. Mary Telfair, the last of the name, used the family wealth to take care of the needs of Savannahians in all spheres: religious, cultural, and social (see pp. 16–20).

The Telfair progenitor in Georgia, Edward Telfair (1743–1807) flourished during the Crown colony period. He obtained vast land grants in Liberty County, upcountry near the later town of Louisville, south of Augusta. His export-business partner was Joseph Clay, a relative, who came from England to make a fortune in Savannah. Telfair married into the Thomas Gibbons family, formerly of South Carolina, thus enhancing both power and fortune. Eventually, he became governor of Georgia.

### 121 Barnard Street (Figures 22 and 23)

Telfair house was built for Alexander Telfair in 1820 using designs by William Jay. In the 1880s, a New York architect, foreign-born Detlef Lienau, designed a Renaissance revival–style addition. Architect Augustus Schwaab served as

**Figure 22** Telfair Academy of Arts and Sciences, about 1910; photograph by Adams Studio. *Courtesy V. & J. Duncan Antique Maps and Prints.*

**Figure 23**   Alexander Telfair, 1789–1832; minia-ture attributed to G. L. Saunders, 1774–1854. Mary Telfair's brother Alexander had William Jay design and build the Telfair house. The Princeton-educated governor's son had no children and left the house to his two surviving sisters, who lived with him. *Courtesy Telfair Museum of Art.*

contractor. The building opened as the Telfair Museum of Arts and Sciences in 1886 according to instructions in Mary Telfair's 1875 will.

Today, the dining room and the octagon room of the Jay-designed resi-dence are restored to their original appearance and furnished with Telfair-period furniture and decorative arts. Look for the original gilt-bronze oil chandelier in the reception room with its faux bois walls and multisided shape. A suite of curly maple neoclassical furni-ture includes two delicate meridiennes, a table, and seventeen side chairs. The Telfair collection of American Regency and Federal-style furniture is of interna-tional importance, and there is also a fine group of American Impressionist paintings.

**127 Barnard Street** (Figure 24)
Trinity Methodist Church was designed by John B. Hogg in 1848 in the Greek revival style. The building's relationship

in style to the Hogg-designed First Bryan Baptist Church at **575 West Bryan Street** (see p. 48) is notable, although the latter building dates from 1873. Both are characterized by columns in antis flanked by panels below a chaste pediment. The resulting facades create conservative examples of the Greek revival style.

In 1812 the predecessor of this church was established as Wesley Chapel at Oglethorpe Avenue and Lincoln Street (demolished). John Wesley had initiated at Christ Church College, Oxford, a "Holy Club" of young religious enthusiasts renowned for their "method" of teaching and interpreting gospel, for their changes in the ritual, and their penchant for hymn singing. After his short stint in Savannah, Wesley returned to England to be considered a founder of the Methodist church. A key-stone to the eventual success of Methodism in America was the appoint-ing and commissioning of lay preachers and circuit-riding evangelists (see pp. 11, 41).

**Barnard Street Between West State Street and West York Street**
The two tile-faced federal government buildings on the eastern trust lots of Telfair Square and the larger coordinat-ed building across the street have been a divisive issue in Savannah's civic life. The U.S. General Services Administra-tion organized the $21 million federal office complex on three city blocks fac-ing Telfair Square after concerned citi-zens failed to save the 1889 three-story red brick Helmly Building (Union Society) on part of the site.

Conceived as contemporary infill, appropriate in scale and design, the buildings were meant to perpetuate the viability and vitality of the city. They also represent a return to the concept of the original city plan whereby trust lots were used for public buildings.

These three buildings were the result of a design competition won by

**Figure 24** Methodist Episcopal Church, now Trinity Methodist Church; wood engraving, from *Historical Collections of Georgia,* by Rev. George White (New York: Pudney & Russell, 1854). *Courtesy V. & J. Duncan Antique Maps and Prints.*

architect Hugh Jacobsen. However, both money to keep Jacobsen on the job and federal regulations mandating that the tile cladding be manufactured in the United States caused the facade designs to be altered. Savannahians of all ages and education call them the bathroom buildings, and there is even talk of demolishing them.

The thoughtful designs in the dated, postmodern style address the scale and decorative details of the Regency Telfair building and the Greek revival Trinity United Methodist Church across the square. Jacobsen and his team continued a Savannah tradition by which sophisticated out-of-state architects, such as Jay of England, Preston of New York, and Beaux Arts–trained Lienau, was brought to Savannah for public commissions and stayed on to build similarly inspired buildings in multiples. These three government buildings, the focus of uneven sentiments and reputations are the result of much planning, much anguish, and more money.

**114 Barnard Street**

This two-story brick commercial building built for Henry Haym in 1889 must have been architect designed. Notice the paired windows with Gothic revival hood molds between pilasters. Bricks are used decoratively to make stringcourses, typical of the building date. The sophisticated building should have its first level restored.

**127–131 Whitaker Street**

A four-story brick commercial building of 1890, designed by architect Alfred S. Eichberg for Andrew Hanley, shows off its curtain wall at the third level with tripartite windows encased in wide arches.

**OGLETHORPE SQUARE AND ANSON WARD**

Oglethorpe Square and Anson Ward were laid out in 1742 during Oglethorpe's second sojourn to the city he founded. It was the sixth and final ward laid out during his stay in the colony. As admiral of the fleet, Lord George Anson (1692–1762) was assigned to protect the coast of the

**Figure 25** Owens–Thomas house, 124 Abercorn Street. *Courtesy Owens–Thomas House, Telfair Museum of Art.*

Carolinas and Georgia in the 1720s and 1730s. Remember that Lincoln Street honors General Benjamin Lincoln of the Continental Army, who was present at the unsuccessful siege of Savannah in 1779. Postrevolutionary sentiment rejected the colonial names of some streets. President Street was changed from its colonial name, King Street, and State Street was previously named Prince Street. Duke Street became Congress Street.

**124 Abercorn Street** (Figures 25 and 26) The Owens–Thomas house museum is one of Savannah's crowning glories, one of three extant Regency houses in Savannah designed by architect William Jay from Bath, England. Richard Richardson, a wealthy banker and cotton broker, born in Bermuda, recently arrived in Savannah, commissioned Jay, a 24-year-old relative of his wife's, to design his new house. Jay arrived from

**Figure 26** Side gallery of the Owens–Thomas house, 124 Abercorn Street. *Courtesy Owens–Thomas house, Telfair Museum of Art.*

England in December 1817 to supervise construction of Savannah's most sophisticated house, then and now.

Young Jay obviously took an astute look about his birthplace, Bath, as he was growing up, during the time the city was buzzing with gentry in their rented townhouses visiting the fashionable salons and pump rooms. This ambiance provided the perfect background for the young architect's education. Work in London with David Roper, a surveyor involved in John Nash's London projects, completed Jay's architectural vocabulary. Oglethorpe's squares and trust lots provided the perfect setting for Jay's architecture. Within five years he had transformed Savannah into a London-like city.

The Owens–Thomas house reflects Jay's innovative mind as well as his belief in things English, both for his designs and the materials that he used to build the house. A recently discovered shipping manifest reveals that the paint, brushes, and even the exterior finish stucco was sent from England along with 24,500 bricks. This "exterior finish English natural cement" was a forerunner of portland cement. It provides the finish over the tabby, made of lime leeched from burned oyster shells and mixed with crushed oyster shells, formed on the site for the first level of the house. This cement also covers the coquina, also known as Bermuda stone, from South Georgia or Florida, quarried and sent in blocks to the site to build the second level. From England too probably came the cast iron balcony, fashioned to resemble leaves, which was installed on the south elevation.

"Thirty-six cases of stone" in the manifest list referred to the coadestone column caps, front entrance balustrades, and other decorative details. Coadestone, a ceramic process in which a dough made of ground terra-cotta is fired as a clay body, was perfected in the eighteenth century at a Lambeth (South London) factory inherited and expand-ed by Eleanor Coade, widow of the inventor. Mrs. Coade's catalog featured 700 different designs between 1769 and 1821 when she died. Her coadestone products had become an element essential to the Georgian decorative scene. Jay imported it from manufacturer James Bubb of London, who went out of business in 1817, immediately after this order was made.

The ship's manifest indicates that all the house furnishings and even a chaise and two gigs were imported from England. Two containers of furniture, two cases of paintings, a case of wallpapers, and a case of statuary suitable to the house arrived at Savannah wharves. Jay or Richardson's business agent in London ordered these embellishments. Fortunately, the good taste of the period left little to chance. No records remain to reveal wlhether Mrs. Richardson participated in the selection or at what level.

Richardson lost the house soon after it was built because of financial reverses in the launching of the SS *Savannah*. George Welshman Owens bought it for just $10,000 in 1830 after eight years of ownership by the Bank of the United States. He and his descendants lived in the house until Miss Margaret Thomas, his granddaughter, bequeathed it to the Telfair Museum in 1951 (Figure 27).

Restoration of a historic house is never finished, and the Owens–Thomas complex is fortunate to include the finest remaining stable-slave quarters in the city as well as the tabby walls original to the garden site. These, together with the main house, offer many mysteries associated with history and construction. Unraveling the mysteries takes time, money, and patience. The Owens–Thomas house staff continually releases a subtle treasure trove of information as together with volunteers under the direction of the curator, Olivia Alison, they find ghost lines and old cistern contents. Recently, they studied the lead pipes that shunted water

**Figure 27**   Margaret Thomas, garden promenade. *Courtesy Owens–Thomas House, Telfair Museum of Art.*

from four different cisterns to bathtubs, water closets, showers, and lavatories in an intricate early plumbing system.

### 127–129 Abercorn Street

Developer Mary Marshall had these fine paired brick houses built in the Greek revival style on one of the ancient trust lots in 1859. Once a stoop with paired steps led to a pair of central raised entrances; now the entrances lead into what was once a full raised basement. The facade of the three-and-one-half-story brick building is articulated with two rows of dentils, somewhat unusual. Mary Marshall worked with architect Charles Cluskey, but he had gone to Washington to work on the capitol when these were built. Designs can be used again, however, and building by analogy was rampant in Savannah. With uniform lots and large numbers of rental houses going up during the decade of the 1850s, it was less expensive, easier, and common to have a series of rows built just alike in different wards, on different streets, or even on the same streets. A search for identical facades

and entrances is an interesting challenge for a walk in Savannah.

### 201–203 East York Street

These Greek revival paired brick houses were built for Henry J. Dickerson in 1853 using hard imported brick in common bond for the front elevation. The entrances were once identical.

### 205 East York Street

The 1855 Greek revival brick townhouse built for James G. Mills was saved by the Historic Savannah Foundation about 100 years after it was built. It is a detached sidehall townhouse much like its neigbors at **201–203 East York Street** with the same hard-brick facade. Sandstone pediments have been installed above the windows to match the band at the entrance level, and the house has a fine piazza on the east side.

### 211 East York Street (Figure 28)

Built for Jane Young in 1853, this three-and-one-half-story Greek revival townhouse has notable sidelights and an overlight at the entrance and hard bricks on the front elevation. It, too, is much like its neighbors. Notice the subtle differences among the group of similar Greek revival houses. One has full-length jib windows, another full-length six-over-nine sash windows at the first level, and yet another, short-sash six-over-six windows.

### 217–219 East York Street

The two-bay brick rowhouses without interior halls were built for John Feely in 1872. Despite the late date, they look Greek revival in style.

### 127–131 Lincoln Street

The fine step-gabled-end brick Greek revival paired houses were restored in 1986 for the President's Quarters Inn. Cotton factor and railroad magnate W. W. Gordon and his partner George Anderson had John Scudder build them in 1855. Scudder was a second-generation builder in Savannah who, with his brother Ephraim, a mason, worked on

**Figure 28**  2 I I East York Street. *Photograph by Goeff DeLorm, courtesy Savannah College of Art and Design.*

many Greek revival buildings. Amos, their father, came to Savannah from New Jersey.

General Alexander R. Lawton lived in the house facing East York Street in the 1870s and Robert E. Lee visited him and Mrs. Lawton here in 1870 on his last visit to Savannah. Judge William Law moved into the house facing East President Street.

### 133–141 Lincoln Street

These two-story late Italianate rowhouses form a set of paired houses, built in 1886 for Joseph Sognier by builder P. J. Fallon.

### REYNOLDS SQUARE AND REYNOLDS WARD

Reynolds was one of the two wards laid out along Abercorn Street in 1734 on Oglethorpe's return to Savannah from London. It was renamed after the first and least popular colonial governor, John Reynolds, who came to Savannah in 1754 when the Trustees relinquished the colony to the Crown. The center of colonial government, Reynolds Square held the House of Assembly, the site of the first reading of the Declaration of Independence in Georgia.

This ward has suffered from its location in the central business district. Yet it contains two of Savannah's major buildings, the eighteenth-century James

Habersham house and the early nineteenth century Oliver Sturges house, both redolent with Savannah history. One of Savannah's most important early buildings, the Filature for silk making, was located here. After silk making failed as an industry, the Filature was used as a meetinghouse; George Washington was honored here with a dance in 1791, where he commented on the hundred well-dressed ladies in attendance. The Filature served as city hall and meeting hall through fires and rebuilding until about 1845.

### 22 Abercorn Street

The Lucas Theater, built by C. K. Howell in 1921 for Savannah-born Colonel Arthur Lucas, is being restored in a public–private partnership to present to the city one of its most romantic and lush theater buildings. Originally designed for silent films and vaudeville shows, it was adjusted for the talkies in the 1930s. Until 1976, three generations of Savannahians attended movies with ladies dressed in their finest attire and men wearing the required jacket and tie. Four stories of concrete and steel are decorated in the Adamesque style using terra-cotta and Italian marble. A dome 40 feet in diameter was lit by 620 lights.

**Figure 29** James Habersham house, 23 Abercorn Street, 1789. *Courtesy Georgia Historical Society.*

**23 Abercorn Street** (Figure 29)

Habersham house (Pink House), an exciting Georgian house, was built for prominent merchant and founding-family member, James Habersham, Jr., in 1789, soon after the end of the Revolution. In 1804, architect William Jay's sister and brother-in-law, the Boltons, lived in the house. Between 1812 and 1865 the house was used by the Planters' Bank and First State Bank of Georgia. The portico and window lintels were added by the bank between 1812 and 1820 and the wing was built in the 1870s.

A young woman, Alida Harper, saved the house by opening a tea room in it in the 1930s, long before preservation of historic houses was stylish, and it continues today to be a fine restaurant. The formalized, symmetrical arrangement of parts, such as the then-new-style six-over-six windows, is enriched with classical detail reflecting the English Palladian revival. The center-hall floor plan was initiated in Georgian England and became the hallmark, much later, of the Greek revival house in the United States. This Georgian house is less vertical in appearance than the Federal houses that followed it. The roof pitch is lower and there is less distance between the bottom of the eaves and the tops of the second-story windows.

**27 Abercorn Street**

The Oliver Sturges house, dating from 1813, is the sidehall townhouse equivalent of the center-hall Pink House nearby. An elliptical fanlight adorns the entrance, and above the portico is an arched window in the Palladian manner above tripartite windows. These are signs of a late Georgian house. An octagonal room was added in the rear before 1819. The Sturges house twin, built for Benjamin Burroughs, once occupied the site of the adjacent inn. The early house is set back from the street, unusual in Savannah. The Sturges house is one of Savannah's most important houses from the architectural and historical viewpoints. Sturges was one of the planners for the Atlantic crossing of the steamship SS *Savannah*.

**18 Abercorn Street** (Figure 30)

The Leroy Myers Cigar building was designed by Henrik Wallin in 1911. This four-story stuccoed brick commercial building recalls Mediterranean precedents with its arches, overhanging eaves, and tower. It is now used by Christ Church as offices, a good adaptive use.

**Figure 30**  Reynolds Square, showing the cigar factory tower and streetcar tracks, about 1920. *Courtesy Georgia Historical Society.*

# OLD FORT AND
# TRUSTEES GARDEN AREA

## OLD FORT AREA

The Old Fort area, bounded by the Trustees Garden along East Broad Street, has the only remnants of the old city walls. Crown Colony Governor Ellis had military engineer William G. DeBrahm come to Savannah from Charleston in 1767 to design the city walls and defensive fortifications. DeBrahm stayed long enough to receive a tithing lot and have the walls built. He surrounded the town with a wall entered by six city gates, and he designed two bastioned towers for the south walls. The brick walls began to go down during the seige of Savannah, when the French and the Patriots battered the British-held city. They disappeared soon after the Revolution except for the brick walls that shore up the area that held Trustees Garden, known as Fort Wayne, after General Anthony Wayne, patriot and hero to the South during the Revolution.

## TRUSTEES GARDEN AREA

Trustees Garden (see pp. 22–23) was authorized by the Trustees in England before Oglethorpe sailed. He selected the site soon after his arrival. The Trustees hoped that the southernmost colony, which had the warmest climate, would provide mulberry trees and their worms for silk, grapes for wine, and medicinal herbs since one purpose of the colony was to relieve England of her dependency on other countries for imports. The cotton, first produced at Trustees Garden from seeds sent to the colony from the Chelsea Physic Garden in London, engendered cultivation of upland cotton in Georgia. The cotton trade ultimately enriched Savannah in the nineteenth century.

The 10-acre garden, stretching down the hillside to the banks of the Savannah River, was laid out within four months of the first ship's arrival. The Trustees at Georgia House in London raised money for the experimental garden. The Duke of Richmond, the Earl of Derby, Lord Peters, and the Apothecarys' Company, as well as Sir Hans Sloan, a physician, provided the necessary funds. Dr. William Houstoun, who had applied for the post of resident botanist for Georgia, sailed to the Spanish West Indies to collect specimens for the Trustees Garden in Savannah.

Unfortunately, the Trustees Garden was abandoned within four years, much to the disappointment of its fund-raisers in England. The site was developed as an adjunct to the riverfront, with taverns and nighttime places for slaves who had been hired out for wharf work. When the Irish arrived in vast numbers in the 1840s, rental houses were thrown up for them in the old Trustees Garden.

A century later, in the 1940s, the entire vicinity was slated for demolition by the Savannah Gas Company. Mrs. Hansell Hillyer perceived the historical importance of the site and the potential charm of the collection of buildings that remained, in derelict condition. Determined and talented, she was fortunate enough to enlist the help of her husband Hansell Hillyer and the board of directors of the Savannah Gas Company to begin a seven-year renovation project.

The Trustees Garden area is an important lesson in early historic preservation. It began in the 1940s and the commercial and residential buildings remain "cash cows." Pirates House and 45 South, popular restaurants, and numerous attractive shops fill Trustees Garden (see pp. 22–23).

**26 East Broad Street** (Figure 31)
Some insist that the little Herb Garden house is part of the original Trustee Garden, and it is claimed to be the oldest building in Georgia. Shrouded in romance and mystery, the site was inhabited as early as 1733.

**48 East Broad Street at Congress Street** (Figure 32)
Archibald Smith had this competent little Federal house built before 1830. Its setback position on the lot gives it a rural ambiance, unusual in Savannah.

**East Broughton Street Behind the Trustees Garden** (Figure 33)
The Kehoe Ironworks were built in the 1870s to make industrial cast iron and decorative ironwork.

**Figure 31**   Herb house, 26 East Broad Street. *Photograph by Goeff DeLorm, courtesy Savannah College of Art and Design.*

**Figure 32**   48 East Broad Street. *Photograph by Goeff DeLorm, courtesy Savannah College of Art and Design.*

**Figure 33**   Kehoe Ironworks, East Broughton Street. *Courtesy V. & J. Duncan Antique Maps and Prints.*

## WARREN SQUARE AND WARREN WARD

Warren Square and Warren Ward were laid out in 1790 along Habersham Street, taking a part of Oglethorpe's eastern common. This ward and Washington Ward to the east were the first extensions of the city after Oglethorpe's final departure. General Joseph Warren was a hero of Bunker Hill in the Revolutionary War and president of the Third Provincial Congress of Massachusetts. Historic Savannah Foundation spearheaded the St. Julian Street project in the 1960s to preserve the area and bring threatened houses to the old street.

**324–326 East Bryan Street** (Figure 34)
Frame Federal houses with gable ends, built as raised-basement semidetached double houses with centered entrances or an entrance at each end, may have set the style for scores of brick paired houses throughout the historic old city. These early paired houses or double houses were built for William Parker in 1806–1809, but were remodeled in 1895.

**404 East Bryan Street** (Figures 35 and 36)
Built for the John Eppinger family in 1821–1822, the frame house was moved from West Perry Street. It is a center-hall post-colonial house with

**Figure 34**   324–326 East Bryan Street. *Photograph by Goeff DeLorm, courtesy Savannah College of Art and Design.*

**Figure 35**   John Eppinger house, 404 East Bryan Street, before it was moved from 211 West Perry Street. *Walter C. Hartridge Collection, courtesy Georgia Historical Society.*

**Figure 36**    404 East Bryan Street. *Photograph by Goeff DeLorm, courtesy Savannah College of Art and Design.*

hints of Federal styling in the quarter-arch gable penetrations, the interior chimneys at each end and an arched entrance door. Peter W. Meldrim, later a judge, lived here as a young man during the Civil War years.

**22 Habersham Street**

This post-colonial two-story frame center-hall house was built for George Basil Spencer after 1790 and before 1804. The small dormers and the regular proportions are so conservative that they do not indicate that this was one of the more elaborate houses of its time. The Historic Savannah Foundation's Revolving Fund saved the house.

**24 Habersham Street**

John David Mongin, who owned a plantation at Dafuskie Island inherited from his wife's family, had this frame house built in 1797. The house, visited by General Lafayette in 1825, served as the rectory for Christ Episcopal Church and as a hospital for yellow fever victims during the epidemic of 1876.

The center-hall, two-story house built in the post-colonial style was moved here from a nearby southwest tithing lot of Warren Square. Besides a new portico and basement, the house presents the usual mysteries of old houses. Why are the windows at the second level all full length although there is no gallery onto which to walk? Like the tripartite windows in some Greek revival houses, this building practice is a custom in Savannah, but irregular elsewhere. Are the weatherboards too narrow? Did the house always have three dormers? Building watching in Warren and Washington squares can become a game.

**426 East St. Julian Street** (Figure 37)

This attractive, steep-gabled old-time cottage with its shed dormers and its exterior-end chimney is nicely set back from the street, with a picket fence. It, too, was moved, from Price Street, where it was built in 1845 for Henry F. Willink. During the Civil War Willink owned a Confederate shipyard, which

**Figure 37**   426 East St. Julian Street, front and rear elevations. *Photographs by Goeff DeLorm, courtesy Savannah College of Art and Design.*

built the SS *Savannah, Georgia, Macon* and *Milledgeville*, all Confederate Navy vessels.

The occupying Union forces charged him with aiding the enemy, which Willink freely admitted. This patriotic admission impressed the presiding naval officer so much that Willink was released.

## WASHINGTON SQUARE AND WASHINGTON WARD

Washington Square and Washington Ward were laid out in 1790 after the colonial period ended and the colony was part of an independent nation. During the colonial period the square was called Firehouse Square, after the firehouse in its middle. Small post-colonial wooden houses filled the tithing blocks on each side of the square. Mrs. Lindsey Henderson, Mrs. Hansell Hillyer, Jim Williams, Mr. and Mrs. Mills B. Lane, and later the Mills B. Lane Foundation worked hard to restore the area.

**12, 14, and 16 Price Street** (Figure 38)
The street scene begins with **16 Price Street**, featuring its gable end with dou-

**Figure 38**   12, 14, and 16 Price Street at East Bryan Street. *Photograph by Goeff DeLorm, courtesy Savannah college of Art and Design.*

ble kicks. The front section covers a double gallery, unusual in Savannah. This is a 1968 replica of a house built for William Williams before 1809. The corner setting displays the handsome profile of the center-hall house.

**14 Price Street,** a little brick carriage house remaining after the demolition of its master house built in 1866 for Joseph Sullivan, has been adapted as an apartment.

**12 Price Street,** a small center-hall house with a Federal narrow central entrance, has a gallery running across the front below a shed roof. It was built for D. D. Williams in 1816.

### 508–510–512 East Bryan Street
(Figure 39)

Margaret Prindible had these two-story rowhouses built in 1892 in the carpenter-Italianate style. The frame construction and small proportion cause them to fit well into the ward, which was almost a century old when the rowhouses were built. Low stoops indicate that the houses were built after the street was paved.

**Figure 39**   508–510–512 East Bryan Street. *Photograph by Goeff DeLorm, courtesy Savannah College of Art and Design.*

**Figure 40** 21 and 23 Houston Street with a view of Washington Square. *Photograph by Goeff DeLorm, courtesy Savannah College of Art and Design.*

**Figure 41** 26–28–30 Houston Street. *Photograph by Goeff DeLorm, courtesy Savannah College of Art and Design.*

**21 and 23 Houston Street** (Figure 40)
This house at **21 Houston Street** was built in 1852 for descendants of Frenchman Louis Mirault, a tailor, who died in 1828, after refugeeing here from Toussaint l'Overture's revolution in St. Domingue. The five-bay raised one-and-one-half-story cottage was moved from Troup Ward. Its six-over-nine windows, the wide weatherboards, and the dormers with peaked pediments would indicate an earlier date with later renovations after Mirault's ownership. Is this another mystery house, or is the house retardate style in a conservative city?

Built for Joachim Hartstene, **23 Houston Street** dates from 1803. The standard center-hall two-story. clapboard house in the Federal style with six-over-nine windows would be at home in New England or any one-time English colony. A simple rectangular overlight adorns the entrance. The house was rebuilt in 1964 using its original timbers, mantels, and flooring.

**26–28–30 Houston Street** (Figure 41)
Another set of carpenter-Italianate frame rowhouses date from 1887. Built for Catherine McCarthy, they represent an

**Figure 42**  31–33 Houston Street. *Photograph by Goeff DeLorm, courtesy Savannah College of Art and Design.*

unusual situation where a trust lot is used for inexpensive rowhouses. The houses are infill for earlier structures. Trust lots on Troup Square are used for similar Italianate rowhouses of brick.

**31–33 Houston Street** (Figure 42)
Architect Augustus Schwaab, a German-American architect responsible for the brick building complex for the Central of Georgia Railroad, designed this detached Italianate corner townhouse in 1875. Although built of brick, low to the ground, it has covered porticos exhibiting jigsaw work.

**507 East St. Julian Street**
Built for Hampton Lillibridge, this post-colonial house, dating from 1796, might be called vernacular-Georgian in style. Three stories, four unevenly spaced openings on two levels, a gambrel roof, and shed dormers all bespeak its eighteenth-century origin. The fine house was moved here from East Bryan Street, where the added captain's walk, outstanding woodwork, and paneling fit comfortably.

**510 East St. Julian Street**
Major Charles Odingsells, a South Carolina native, prosperous Skidaway

Island planter, and owner of Little Wassaw Island, had this first house on the tithing block built in 1797. Odingsells had been a Revolutionary War officer and was an active member of the Union Society. The one-story gable-ended house of clapboard epitomizes the cottage style. This one has a Federal-style center hall, flanked by two sash windows, six-over-nine, on each side. The house has a stoop and steps leading past a relatively low basement. The present porch is a nineteenth-century addition.

**GREENE SQUARE AND GREENE WARD**

Greene Square and Greene Ward were laid out along Houston Street after the Revolutionary War to honor Nathanael Greene, military hero of the southern front (Figure 43). The ward matches Columbia and Washington wards, laid out to reflect the revolutionary fervor of a new nation. Houston Street is bisected by only three squares, Washington, Greene, and Crawford, because unlike other north–south streets in historic Savannah, Houston Street does not continue south of Liberty Street.

**Figure 43** General Nathanael Greene; copper engraving, about 1784. The Rhode Island officer was awarded Mulberry Grove plantation by the grateful state of Georgia. He moved to Savannah with his family after the American Revolution, but soon died of heat stroke, leaving his widow, Catherine Littlefield Greene, a son, George, who departed for school in France with General Lafayette's son, and two daughters, Martha and Cornelia. Catherine later married plantation manager Phineas Miller, also a New Englander, and they moved to Dungeness, a mansion of tabby construction she built on Cumberland Island. *Courtesy V. & J. Duncan Antique Maps and Prints.*

Although Greene Square contains a house built by Isaiah Davenport on an eastern trust lot, it is another of the intimate little squares on the east side of town that were so shabby before the preservation movement began.

**502–512 East State Street** (Figure 44)
The estate of Edward C. Anderson had these two-story rowhouses built in 1890. Splayed bricks make segmental arches above the six-over-six windows. Full-length windows leading to a long

balcony at the second level provide some sophistication to these simple, low-to-the-ground rowhouses. Bracketed eaves and recessed entrances with sidelights and overlights reflect the Italianate style.

**536 East State Street** (Figure 45)
This tiny two-bay cottage with a brick chimney in one gable end was moved from Hull Street, where it was built for John Dorsett in 1845. An eighteenth-century visitor to Savannah commented that the wood houses were painted in either red or blue, which explains the red color used here in the renovation. In the nineteenth century calcimine blue paint was popular for inexpensive houses, carriage house interiors, and attics because it was cheap. This entrance overhang with its pediment was not the right choice in a renovation.

**542 East State Street**
Charlotte and William Wall built their vernacular cottage in 1818. The tall basement adds charm to the plain raised clapboard cottage, which features a set of dentils across the facade to create a cornice, repeated now in the front portico with its shed roof.

**117–119 Houston Street**
Henry Cunningham had these two-story clapboard paired houses built in 1810, one of the early examples of a paired or double house in the city. The brick chimneys are set within the gable ends. A 1901 renovation probably explains the roof eaves.

The house served as the first home for the Female Orphans Asylum after the girls' section broke off from the orphanage at Bethesda. The girls moved into this house in 1810, where they lived until 1838, when a new building was built at Bull and Charlton streets. In 1888 they bought the Wetter mansion at West Broad Street and Oglethorpe Avenue, where they stayed until 1929. This historic mansion was destroyed in 1959.

**Figure 44** Anderson Row, 502–512 East State Street. *Photograph by Goeff DeLorm, courtesy Savannah College of Art and Design.*

**Figure 45** 536 East State Street. *Photograph by Goeff DeLorm, courtesy Savannah College of Art and Design.*

**Figure 46**  124 Houston Street. *Photograph by Goeff DeLorm, courtesy Savannah College of Art and Design.*

**124 Houston Street** (Figure 46; see pp.97–98)
Built for Isaiah Davenport in 1814–1816 on a trust lot, the frame

house is one of all too few documented houses by the master builder commemorated with a museum in his own house. Much of his work must have burned in the 1820 fire that consumed hundreds of buildings.

**123 Houston Street** (see p.48)
The congregation for the Second African Baptist Church was formed in 1802 by Andrew Bryan. This church, built in 1925, replaced a wood and stone church dating from 1802, built by African-American Baptists on this trust lot.

**503 East President Street** (Figure 47)
Thomas Williams's house is an out-and-out Federal house, Savannah fashion, built between 1799 and 1808. The narrow front door with its chaste arched overlight is centered between two flanking six-over-nine lighted windows on each side. Gable ends emphasize the lack of depth of the house. Cornerboards and exterior-end brick chimneys, while simple, are well proportioned and make a good Federal-style composition. The paired dormers are widely spaced.

**Figure 47**  503 East President Street. *Photograph by Goeff DeLorm, courtesy Savannah College of Art and Design.*

**Figure 48**
Davenport house,
324 East State Street,
1821, prior
to restoration by the
Historic Savannah
Foundation.
*Cordray–Foltz
Collection, courtesy
Georgia Historical
Society.*

### 509 East President Street

It is rare to find a house where a gable end faces the street. But here it is, built for George Jones between 1799 and 1808. The little frame cottage with shed dormers recalls the earliest houses during the Oglethorpe period.

### 513 East York Street

This little two-story cottage with odd fenestration fits right in the clapboard neighborhood, but it is much later in date than it looks, built for the estate of Catherine DeVeaux in 1853. Inexpensive frame cottage were thrown up in the same vernacular type and style for generations.

The DeVeauxes were a family of free persons of color who stand out in Savannah's history in three generations. Jane DeVeaux, a generation earlier had a secret school to teach African-Americans to read and write during the period when it was illegal. Colonel John H. DeVeaux, a free man of color from St. Domingue, founded the *Colored Tribune* in 1875, later the *Savannah Tribune*.

### 517 East York Street

Greene Square abounds in picturesque and modest clapboard cottages such as this tiny three-bay example with a shed dormer on the tin roof. Most were built low to the ground with a rustic add-on porch or front gallery. Susannah R. Clarke had this one built between 1801 and 1806.

## COLUMBIA SQUARE AND COLUMBIA WARD

Columbia Square and Columbia Ward, laid out in 1799 along Habersham Street, were in terrible condition in the 1970s when Eudora and Wainwright Roebling renovated the square in memory of her parents, Augusta and Wymberly DeRenne. The fountain came from Wormsloe plantation, seat of the Jones and DeRenne families. Now the square looks all but complete except for the trust lot, with a one-story building replacement in poor proportion. One tithing lot has a row of infill townhouses in the middle of the block. Isaiah Davenport house is Columbia Square's crowning glory.

### 324 East State Street (Figure 48)

Isaiah Davenport, an alderman, bought the lot for £20 in 1812 from merchant

Edward Stebbins. As a contractor and builder, Davenport built his own house. He also built the tabby Martello tower near the lighthouse on Tybee, used for coastal defense after the War of 1812.

As early as 1817, Davenport's will was recorded leaving the house to his heirs, and in 1840 the heirs sold the house for $9000 to planter William E. Baynard. The house remained in the Baynard family until 1955, when its threatened demolition sparked the ire of painter-journalist Anna Hunter. Within a 24-hour period, Mrs. Hunter, working by telephone with women of similar interests, raised the money to save the house from demolition. This effort launched the development of the Historic Savannah Foundation, and between 1956 and 1960 the house was restored as a museum house and headquarters for the organization.

Built of brick and brownstone, the center-hall house, measuring 48 by 40 feet, with two rooms on each side of the

**Figure 49**   130 Habersham Street, 1884. *Photograph by Goeff DeLorm, courtesy Savannah College of Art and Design.*

wall, reflects the balance and symmetry that mark the Federal style. An elliptical arched entrance has a recessed door with an arched fanlight and sidelights. The handsome double-entry stairway must have set the standard for future graceful curving entry staircases leading to high stoops that dot the city in houses of all styles. The dormers are arched, too, and elongated with side pilasters and pediments, unusual in Savannah (see p. 42).

### 123 Habersham Street
The Kehoe house and inn, built for William Kehoe of Kehoe Ironworks, dates from 1893. Dewitt Bruyn was architect of the pretentious Queen Anne brick mansion. It exhibits most of the characteristics of the florid style; bay windows beneath a parapet; single, double, and triple windows; paired columns; a truncated turret; and a variegated roofline. Bruyn was active in Atlanta and worked in Savannah with Calvin Fay. He was a member of the Société Central d'Architecture of Belgium.

### 130 Habersham Street (Figure 49)
Iron foundry owner William Kehoe had this Italianate townhouse built about 1885, before he had his mansion built at **123 Habersham Street** in 1893.

### 134–136 Habersham Street
Sometime before 1809, Frederick Ball, a master carpenter, built this tall, skinny frame house for himself, using wide board siding and the simple and delicate precepts of the Federal style. The original fenestration has been restored. Ball came from New Jersey, where he was born in 1771. In Savannah he married Elizabeth Toxey, and he died in 1820.

### 402–404 East State Street
This Federal house was built about 1817 for Francis Stone, an alderman, hero of the 1854 yellow fever epidemic and one of the Trustees who built Trinity Methodist Church. The house was saved

**Figure 50**   Timothy Bonticou house, 416–418 East State Street. *Photograph by Goeff DeLorm, courtesy Savannah College of Art and Design.*

in 1927 by Fred Wessels, Sr., a pioneer in the preservation of Savannah's early architecture. In 1958 he leased it to Historic Savannah, and Mills B. Lane subsequently restored it. An enlargement in 1880 explains its unusual fenestration.

**416–418 East State Street** (Figure 50)
The unusual frame, hip-roofed house associated with Timothy Bonticou was built originally facing Broughton Lane at 419, one of the lanes dividing the tithing blocks between Broughton and State streets. To buy a back portion of the standard 60- by 90-foot lots was one way to obtain inexpensive lots. Recent title research by Historic Savannah Foundation dates this house to 1850 under the ownership of Henry Willink, who developed a number of houses in the neighborhood, probably for his shipyard workers.

**420 East State Street**
This tiny frame house is atypical, with a gable facing the front and a porch

beneath a single six-over-six sash window. The two rooms below and two rooms above served as a long-time home to Mrs. Laura Jones, whose name is associated with the house. Known as a Davenport tenement, it dates between 1799 and 1810. The Historic Savannah Foundation saved the house and moved it from Greene Square.

**422–424 East State Street**
Shipbuilder Henry Willink had these paired houses built in the Greek revival style in 1850. They appear to be earlier than 1850 because of the small size, just two stories plus full basement and an attic space with four front dormers. Straight gable ends and one chimney suggest the earlier Federal style.

**307–311 East York Street**
Three brick rowhouses were built in 1872 for Jerome H. Wilson in a simple style that continues the Greek revival motifs of forty years earlier. Even the iron balcony at the second level and the

dentil cornice recall the Greek revival style.

### 321 East York Street

This three-bay frame house with a central chimney and hip roof dates from 1818 and is an atypical house for Savannah. The house was built for Abraham Sheftall and was moved here from Elbert Square (destroyed). The Sheftall family arrived in Savannah on the second ship to land, in 1733, one of three German-speaking Jewish families among the Sephardic Jews from Portugal who sailed to Savannah from London under the sponsorship of the Bevis Marks congregation. The family has remained in Savannah since that time, providing a well-known officer of the Continental Army in the American Revolution. First-generation family members donated land along Oglethorpe Avenue for the first Jewish burial ground.

### 130–132 Lincoln Street (Figure 51)

These paired frame houses are early examples of the type, dating from 1821–1823, built in the Federal style for Steele White, a merchant who came to Savannah from Virginia. He died after a fall from a horse on March 23, 1823, just as the house was finished.

The hip roof and central chimney are unusual for vernacular frame Federal houses. Note the nine-over-nine sash windows and the fanlight over the entrances. The arrangement of bricks in a lattice pattern to protect the stoop area was a standard nineteenth-century custom. The paired houses replace an earlier building on the site, as do most in this ancient area of town, and the 1790s basement gave the name to the inn that has restored the property (see p. 212). The building has historic associations with Anna Powers.

### 134–136 Lincoln Street

This conservative early nineteenth-century frame two-story plus basement center-hall house looks like New England, with its gable ends and exterior brick chimneys. It was built for Joseph Gammon in 1843. Gammon was an investor in housing in the city.

### 424 East President Street (Figure 52)

This fine center-hall clapboard Federal house dates from 1810 and was built for Abraham Scribner, a merchant who had come to Savannah from New York. Born

**Figure 51**   Steele White house, 130–132 Lincoln Street. *Photograph by Goeff DeLorm, courtesy Savannah College of Art and Design.*

Figure 52  Abraham Scribner house, 424 East President Street. *Photograph by Goeff DeLorm, courtesy Savannah College of Art and Design.*

in 1785, he married Margaret W. Williams here in 1808, dying in 1817. Double stairways now lead to the central narrow arched entrance with the typical Federal overlight. Remodeling in 1899 saved the building from demolition.

## FRANKLIN SQUARE AND FRANKLIN WARD

Franklin Square and Franklin Ward were laid out on the western edge of town late in 1790 along Montgomery Street after the Revolutionary War in honor of Benjamin Franklin, one-time agent for Georgia in London. For years locals called it Water Tank Square because the old city water tank occupied it (Figure 53). Now the ward is filled with post–Civil War brick commercial buildings.

### 23 Montgomery Street (see p. 48)

The First African Baptist Church was organized in 1788, twelve years before the organization in Savannah of the first Baptist church for whites. Bryan's congregation is believed to have been the first in America organized by and for African-Americans. The Baptist church

Figure 53  Franklin Square from St. Julian Street showing the water tower, built in 1854, and First African Baptist Church before the steeple toppled in a hurricane of the 1890s; photograph from Charles Hart Olmstead's *Art Work of Savannah* (Chicago: W.H. Parish Publishing Co., 1893). *Courtesy V. & J. Duncan Antique Maps and Prints.*

appealed to African-Americans at a time when the Methodists were collecting potential Baptists from the white community.

### 401, 403, 405, and 407 West Congress Street

Augustus Walter had the three-story brick commercial buildings at 401 and 403 built in 1867 just after the Civil War. Their interesting cornice and chimney decoration reflect their building date. Walter added 405 to his row in 1870, adding the top floor later. The first level should be restored with granite or cast iron supports. The third set of three bays, 407, built in 1880, has segmental openings and is a three-bay townhouse.

### 409 West Congress Street

This storehouse built in 1872 for William Solte is two and one-half stories with openings beneath the eaves in the attic.

## BEACH INSTITUTE AREA

Today, the Beach Institute area on the eastern side of the historic district is a target for renovation of its abandoned small frame cottages, many of them built by and for African-Americans and owned by them today. The target area east of Troup Square is in Bartow and parts of Davis and Mercer wards, all without squares, bound by Liberty to Gwinnett streets and Price to East Broad streets. Interesting street scenes include the 500 blocks of East Jones Street and East Taylor Street, and Charlton Lane near East Broad Street (Figure 54).

The tools of historic preservation have become much more sophisticated since the Historic Savannah Foundation's establishment in the late 1950s. Here the foundation hopes to overcome the endemic problem of demolition by neglect by working with the city and the courts to speed up the process by which the city acquires an abandoned property in danger of demolition by neglect. Once the city acquires the property, the accrued fees, money due, tax liens, penalties, and fines on the property usually have mounted to more than the property is worth. Efforts are being made to have most of these fees waived to save a targeted building from demolition by neglect.

**Figure 54** 500 Block of East Taylor Street. This pair of entrances along a row of renovated 1890s brick rowhouses showing brick sidewalks and streetlights creates a picturesque street scene. *Photograph by Goeff DeLorm, courtesy Savannah College of Art and Design.*

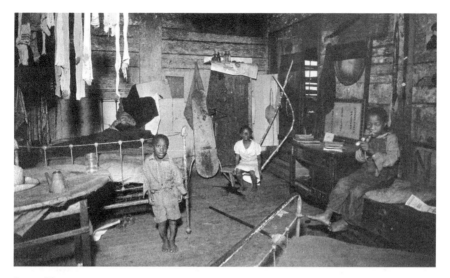

**Figure 55** Interior of an 1870s vernacular frame house like those being renovated in the Beach Institute area; photograph dating from the 1930s. *Cordray–Foltz Collection, courtesy Georgia Historical Society.*

The Savannah, Albany and Gulf Railroad built housing for its workers here beginning in 1853. When the railroad bought the old Oglethorpe period 4½-acre garden lots directly to the east of the railroad, other investors began building modest rental houses in the area (Figure 55). African-American laborers, seamstresses, cooks, coopers, porters, pattern makers, picture framers, and even messengers rented, bought, and built here between about 1867 and World War I.

The lots measured the traditional 90 feet in depth and the owners of lots sold the rear halves for building sites to finance their own houses on the remainder of each lot. Thus the lanes are rich in architecture and appear as street fronts with their modest cottages.

The small one-story single and double cottages, sometimes with shed dormers and wide beaded board covering, usually have six-over-six double-hung windows, gable ends, and brick chimneys. Most have working louvered shutters or simpler batten shutters. Four-panel doors are most common, although six-panel doors face the earlier examples. Box cornices abound with wood stoops with box columns or square posts. The singles and doubles of one or one-and-one-half stories recall in type and style eighteenth-century cottages. The two-story frame townhouses, by their simplicity and absence of decorative detail, recall the 1820s Federal houses of Savannah.

Vernacular Federal or Greek revival houses and examples may be found at **507–517 East Jones Street** (Figure 56), **521 East Harris Street, 509 East Charlton Street** (see pp. 122–169), and **525 East Harris Street.** Their interiors were well-proportioned and simple (Figure 57).

**Figure 56**  513–515 and 509–511 East Jones Street. One by one the vernacular Greek revival paired houses and rowhouses are being renovated for owner occupancy and rental use. *Photograph by Geoff DeLorm, courtesy Savannah College of Art and Design.*

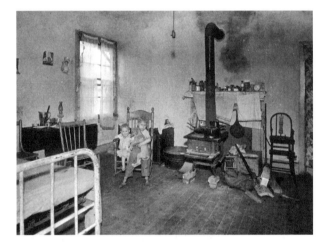

**Figure 57**  An interior from the 1930s in the Cordray–Foltz Collection. General proportions, wide floorboards, and a nine-tenth-century fireplace along with high base-boards and large sash windows indicate a mid-nine-teenth-century house, heated in the 1930s by a wood-burning stove resting on bricks. *Courtesy Georgia Historical Society.*

The other most frequently occurring style of building here is the carpenter-Italianate house. Boxlike frame two-story buildings with three bays and sidehalls or two bays and two rooms, they have shallow hip roofs and bracketed eaves. Simple sawn wood trim complements the brackets and comprises the Italianate factor. Four-panel doors are often surrounded by narrow overlights and sidelights. Good examples are at **422–428 Price Street, 440–448 Price Street, 524–526 East Jones Street** (Figure 58), and **522½ Gwinnett Street.**

**Figure 58**  524–526 East Jones Street. This carpenter-Italianate row of houses dating from 1885 merits renovation. *Photograph by Goeff DeLorm, courtesy Savannah College of Art and Design.*

### 512 East Taylor Street and Jones Lane, and 509 East Charlton Street
(Figure 59)

Recently, a Savannahian bought two frame one-story double cottages fronting Taylor Street and Jones Lane behind it. Raised on brick piers, the houses' construction is completely exposed. Built in the 1860s, the doubles have four rooms each. He will have a four-room main house and, across a patio, a four-room office–guest house. The front set of rooms has one remaining staircase to a garret. He also bought a nine-bay two-story frame building on Taylor Street that in renovation will return to its original configuration of three two-story rowhouses. The total purchase price was just over $30,000. Now the renovation costs continue to mount up.

**Figure 59**  Rear of lot at about 512 East Taylor Street. This double cottage in the vernacular Greek revival manner features a central chimney and six-over-six windows above its raised brick pillar foundations. Such cottages are presently undergoing restoration in the area. *Photograph by Goeff DeLorm, courtesy Savannah College of Art and Design.*

**502 East Harris Street** (see p. 45)

The American Missionary Association established the Beach Institute (now the African-American Cultural Center) in 1865 to educate newly freed black citizens.

**556 East Gordon Street**

Most African-Americans are Protestants, except in New Orleans, but Savannah has a strong enclave of African-American Catholics that increased in number during the second half of the nineteenth-century. Benedictine monks arrived from Europe in 1874, when the Bishop of Savannah recognized a need to establish a mission church, St. Benedict the Moor, named for the sixteenth-century monk from Palermo, Italy. By 1889 the Benedictines were able to build the extant monastery at 556 East Gordon Street. They were assisted by Mother Matilda Beasley, who had established an order of African-American nuns with a girls' orphanage in Savannah. Around 1907, nuns of this order, Handmaids of Mary, lived nearby on Gordon Lane.

**514 East Huntington Street**

The King–Tisdell cottage, the Museum of Black History (see pp. 48–50), is an 1896 late Victorian center-hall cottage. It was moved to the site under the leadership of civil rights leader W. W. Law. Named for local African-American citizens Eugene and Sarah King, and Mrs. King's second husband, Robert Tisdell, the building serves as a black cultural museum. African-American sculptor Ulysses Davis's (1913–1990) works are featured here and at the Beach Institute.

**500 Block East Taylor Street** (see Figure 54)

German-American Henry Luderman built this row of small two-story rowhouses in 1893. Entrances are retardate in style but quite interesting. The building facades were altered in renovation. When the row was renovated, the owners had to install their own street lighting and the sidewalks.

## STREETS OF SAVANNAH

**BROUGHTON STREET**

Broughton Street saw its finest hour after it had become the commercial retail center of Savannah between 1880 and the Depression (Figure 60). By the turn of the twentieth century, the old buildings that remained had been remodeled into stores, and new commercial buildings had gone up (Figures 61 and 62). However, even today, the

**Figure 60** The Lightning Express, oxcart with wood wheels at Broughton and Drayton streets; albumen stereo-view, about 1880. *Courtesy V. & J. Duncan Antique Maps and Prints.*

**Figure 61** View from East Broughton Street. In 1934 Broughton Street provided a full urban service environment, filled with amenities and visual pleasures: here a large clock, lamps on cast iron posts, awnings, and signs. Access was guaranteed by streetcars with their tracks. Parking meters had not appeared, but each parking space was delineated in white. The commercial strip stretched, full of vitality, from East Broad Street to West Broad Street (Martin Luther King Jr. Boulevard). *Cordray–Foltz Collection, courtesy Georgia Historical Society.*

**Figure 62** 1 East Broughton Street at Bull Street. Adler's Department Store was a major attraction to downtown Savannah in 1935. Leopold Adler knew how to engage his clients. Interaction between the building and the street is evident everywhere. Bay windows for display project from the building front. Awnings, wide glass windows, and inviting recessed doors are part of the scheme to show that the store must be visited. Adler also had signs painted over the brick building surface, the cheapest and most prominent advertising. The signage becomes a sculptural and decorative part of the overall design. *Cordray–Foltz Collection, courtesy Georgia Historical Society.*

**Figure 63** 408–410 West Broughton Street, about 1940. *Cordray–Foltz Collection, courtesy Georgia Historical Society.*

building watcher can find carriage houses at the back ends of most of the building lots. These face the lanes, and the spaces between the main building and the carriage houses are often filled in. These are traces of the one-time residential character of the street.

Facing Broughton Street, post–World War II panels deface the facades of fine nineteenth-century buildings. These could be removed to reveal Broughton Street as it should be. The street could revert back to the nineteenth-century style, where residents lived above the stores below.

**408–410 West Broughton Street**
(Figure 63)
Simon Byck is said to have had this unusual three-bay stucco-front three-and-one-half-story building built. Notice the carriage house to the rear on the lane.

**322 West Broughton Street** (Figure 64)
The old Franck building is clouded in mystery. What first seems to be a standard 1850s Savannah-style Greek revival commercial building is enhanced with a mezzanine level with cast iron supports. The unusual arrangement shown in the 1934 photograph should be restored.

**107 East Broughton Street** (Figure 65)
The Marshall Hotel next to Levy's Jewelry Store remains hidden behind a 1950s-type commercial facade. The Greek revival 62-room hotel was built

**Figure 64** Franck Corporation, 322 West Broughton Street, about 1940. *Cordray–Foltz Collection, courtesy Georgia Historical Society.*

**Figure 65** Mary Marshall's Hotel, 100 block of East Broughton Street. *Courtesy Georgia Historical Society.*

**Figure 66** 410–416 East Broughton Street. *Photograph by Scot Hinson.*

for real estate developer Mary Marshall in the 1850s. Two restaurants that seated ninety, a men's cigar smoking room, and women's retiring parlors were among the amenities, which included bedrooms and suites with fine Greek revival mantels, molding, and sliding doors.

Hotel guests came from England to negotiate cotton futures from the sea island plantations and upcountry cotton farms. The cladding that mutilates this fine building should be torn away to expose the original facade.

### 322–324 East Broughton Street

This exciting post-colonial frame house was built about 1790 for John McPherson Berrien, Savannah's first Collector of Customs, later U.S. Attorney General under Andrew

Jackson, and U.S. Senator from Georgia. Berrien's father was George Washington's adjutant and native of Princeton, New Jersey, where his family home is a museum house. Washington made his farewell address during his 1791 visit to Savannah from the now-missing porch of the Berrien house.

This fine house was elevated to make it suitable for commercial use in 1917. This center-hall house of two-and-one-half stories, built in the eighteenth-century Georgian style, merits restoration both for aesthetic and historical reasons.

### 410–416 East Broughton Street
(Figure 66)

Look above the elevated first level to see a post-colonial-style house complete with steep gable ends and a pair of widely spaced dormers above eight openings. Built before 1809 for John Deubell, this house merits attention. Deubell was a native of Elpenroth, Germany, where he was born in 1766. He became a merchant in Savannah, elected to the city council in 1807. He died eight years later in 1815 and is buried in Colonial Cemetery.

**530 East Broughton Street** (Figure 67)
John Rourke, an ornamental cast iron manufacturer, had this sidehall townhouse built in the late Italianate style in 1884 on a street fast becoming commercial. The cast iron galleries, wrapping around two elevations on two levels, are lavish for Savannah. Evidently, he was showcasing his cast iron.

**548 East Broughton Street**
A conservative Greek revival institutional building, the Abrahams house was designed by architect John S. Norris in 1858. He came to Savannah to design and build the U.S. Customs House and

**Figure 67**  John Rourke house, 530 East Broughton Street. *Photograph by Scot Hinson.*

stayed on to build in the Greek revival and Italianate styles all over Savannah. It is now part of the SCAD complex.

**OGLETHORPE AVENUE**
Oglethorpe Avenue, once South Broad Street, marked the city limits until the post-colonial expansion. The first Jewish burying ground in Savannah was on part of the commons, now the Oglethorpe Avenue median, granted to one of the three German-speaking or Ashkenazim families on the 1733 ship.

Today the thoroughfare, with its wide tree-lined median, is bordered with handsome houses dating from the colonial and Federal periods through the nineteenth century. They include the earliest extant colonial-period residence in town. The avenue is richest, however, in Federal paired houses, rowhouses, and townhouses. Start walking on the west side of town and go all the way to the Colonial Cemetery—you'll get a cross section of Savannah architecture (Figures 68 and 69).

**24 West Oglethorpe Avenue**
The Independent Presbyterian Church, a sophisticated Federal building designed by John Holden Greene of Rhode Island, was built at the enormous cost of $120,000 and dedicated in 1819 with President James Monroe in attendance. The three Presbyterian trustees in charge of its financing and construction, Joseph Bryan, Josiah Telfair, and Barach Gibbons, numbered among the wealthiest men in the city. The congregation had been organized in 1755 for members of the Church of Scotland (see p. 31).

**10 East Oglethorpe Avenue** (Figure 70; see pp. 20, 44)
The James Moore Wayne house built between 1818 and 1820 is attributed to architect William Jay. Mayor Wayne was elected to the U.S. Congress, then appointed to the Supreme Court of the United States. Consequently, the portico and interior were not finished until the

**Figure 68** Greek revival cast iron decoration on an Oglethorpe Avenue fence.

late 1820s. In 1831, Judge Wayne sold the house to his niece, Sarah Stites, and her husband, William Washington Gordon I, whose family retained it until 1953, when the Girl Scouts of the U.S.A. purchased it. The top floor and the rear addition were added in 1886 for William Washington Gordon II by Detlef Lienau of New York City, a founder of the American Institute of Architects.

Now the Girl Scout National Center, the house is interpreted as it would have appeared in 1884 when Juliette Gordon, founder of the Girl Scout movement in America, was married to William Mackay Low. The Aesthetic-period interior was arranged by Eleanor Kinzie Gordon, a wealthy Chicago native, and by her daughter, Juliette Gordon.

**Figure 69** 103–111 East Oglethorpe Avenue. *W.C. Hartridge Collection, courtesy Georgia Historical Society.*

**Figure 70** James Moore Wayne; steel engraving, etched on plate, "by Albert Rosenthal, Philadelphia," 1899. Wayne had the house at 10 W. Oglethorpe Avenue built about 1820, selling it to his niece, Mrs. William Washington Gordon I, when he moved to Washington, first as a congressman, then as Supreme Court Justice. *Courtesy V. & J. Duncan Antique Maps and Prints.*

**Figure 71**  John Hunter houses, 105 East Oglethorpe Avenue. *Photograph by Goeff DeLorm, courtesy Savannah College of Art and Design.*

**Figure 72**  Lufburrow houses, 107–109 East Oglethorpe Avenue. *Photograph by Goeff DeLorm, courtesy Savannah College of Art and Design.*

### 14 East Oglethorpe Avenue

Built for George Anderson in 1853, this house was enlarged by architect William G. Preston in 1892 and is now the Ballastone Inn. Nina Anderson Pape, founder and headmistress of the Pape School, lived here. The forerunner of Savannah Country Day School, established in the 1950s, Miss Pape's school continued the tradition of her predecessor, Emmelyn Hartridge Battersby, who was called Vassarlyn, as her girls were always accepted at Vassar. Juliette Gordon Low's cousin, Miss Pape encouraged sixteen of her young students to join America's first Girl Scout troop.

### 101–105 East Oglethorpe Avenue
(Figure 71)

These paired three-story brick houses are said to date from 1821, when they were built for John Hunter, a Savannah merchant who married Margaret Glen and died in 1825. The houses have a Greek revival look today. Additions and changes were made in 1892.

Confederate General Joseph Johnston lived here after the Civil War, and for decades afterward authors Malcolm and Muriel Bell lived here.

### 107–109 East Oglethorpe Avenue
(Figure 72)

Builder Mathew Lufburrow built these paired houses in the Federal style in 1820 with Thomas Clark (1789–1845). Clark, a builder, came to Savannah from Union County, New Jersey, and bought this lot in 1819. Handsome elliptical entrances recessed behind Ionic columns and the six-over-six windows reveal the date of the houses, one of which has had a story added.

### 113 East Oglethorpe Avenue (Figure 73)

It takes a hard look to find John Haupt's 1819 Federal house among the later additions. It was elevated in 1867, and the side gallery was added in 1884. But much more happened, such as a bracketed cornice and an added entrance. It was the home of Dr. and Mrs. A. J. Waring, Jr., and remains in the family today.

**Figure 73** John Haupt house, 113 East Oglethorpe Avenue. *Photograph by Goeff DeLorm, courtesy Savannah College of Art and Design.*

### 110 East Oglethorpe Avenue

John Eppinger, Sr., brickmaker and bricklayer, built a brick public house, perhaps the oldest brick house in Savannah. Documented on the lot in 1783, it must have been built before the Revolution, by 1764. The settlement of John Eppinger, Sr.'s will about 1784 listed this lot with brick dwelling house awarded to his three sons and the adjacent house to his daughter Winifred, Mrs. James Roberts. General Lachlan McIntosh bought the house after the fiery patriot killed Button Gwinnet, Declaration of Independence signer, in a duel. McIntosh felt it prudent to leave Savannah and he fought under George Washington in the Revolution. His plantation on the Altamaha River was plundered by Tories, but McIntosh reclaimed it after the Revolution, and George Washington visited the plantation house in 1791.

### 116 East Oglethorpe Avenue (Figure 74)

John F. and Marmaduke Hamilton had this townhouse with its curving cast

**Figure 74** John and Marmaduke Hamilton house, 116 East Oglethorpe Avenue. The stoop usually intrudes onto city sidewalks in Savannah. The result is interaction between private and public domains. Visually, the curved entrance with cast iron newel posts and the protruding bay window, an air-right intrusion, are picturesque and they add sculptural effect to the flat-front brick house. *Photograph by Goeff DeLorm, courtesy Savannah College of Art and Design.*

Figure 75  122 East Oglethorpe Avenue. *Photograph by Goeff DeLorm, courtesy Savannah College of Art and Design.*

iron entrance railing built in 1869. Except for its bay, it looks Greek revival, showing the continuing conservatism after the Civil War.

**122 East Oglethorpe Avenue** (Figure 75) Christian Camphor built this little cottage during the early Crown colony period in the 1760s. Its steep gable roof is a key to its age, along with its little dormers and uneven fenestration.

**228 East Oglethorpe Avenue** (Figure 76) Built in 1855 for Oscar T. H. Dibble, the two-bay Greek revival townhouse features tripartite windows. In 1853, Margaret Dibble had **107–109 East Jones Street** built, also with tripartite windows. Dibble came to Savannah from New York, where he was born in 1811. He died in Columbus, Georgia, in 1860.

**230–244 East Oglethorpe Avenue** (Figure 77)
Mary Marshall Row, a group of Greek

Figure 76  Oscar Dibble house, 228 East Oglethorpe Avenue. *Photograph by Goeff DeLorm, courtesy Savannah College of Art and Design.*

**Figure 77** Mary Marshall Row, 230–244 East Oglethorpe Avenue. *Photograph by Goeff DeLorm, Courtesy Savannah College of Art and Design.*

revival townhouses built in 1854 by Charles Cluskey for Mary Marshall are among the most handsome in the city, and their interiors have been carefully restored. The service buildings were taken down for their bricks. The buildings would have been demolished except for last-minute efforts of a group of businesspeople led by Lee Adler, after being alerted by women preservationists.

Georgia poet Conrad Aiken lived with his parents in one of these houses until his eleventh year, when he found them dead by murder and suicide. He returned with his third wife Mary in 1962 to live in 230 Oglethorpe Avenue. He remembered the neighborhood as ideal for a young boy to grow up in.

### 314 East Oglethorpe Avenue (Figure 78)

Built in 1809 for Thomas W. Rodman, this house has been wrapped in galleries in the plantation style and was enlarged in 1911.

**Figure 78** Thomas Rodman house, 314 East Oglethorpe Avenue. *Photograph by Goeff DeLorm, courtesy Savannah College of Art and Design.*

**322 East Oglethorpe Avenue** (Figure 79)

Built before 1809 for William J. Spencer, the house's 1884 enlargement has obscured its Federal-style origins.

**323 East Oglethorpe Avenue** (Figures 80 and 81)

The police barracks, designed by J. H. Boggs in the Italianate style, border the old Colonial Cemetery, now used as a public park.

## WEST BROAD STREET

West Broad Street marked the city limits during Oglethorpe's day. By 1787 the west side was developed in a strip consuming the hamlet of Ewensburg and Yamacraw, once the site of Tomochichi's settlement and once claimed by Mary Musgrove. The city granted much of it to the Central of Georgia Railroad starting in 1831. Their brick buildings anchor and decorate the thoroughfare, now known as Martin Luther King Jr. Boulevard.

Early nineteenth-century brick mansions once held forth on West Broad Street. The Gibbons, Marshall, and Wetter mansions have all been demolished. Symbol of the grandeur that once reigned here is the house William and Julia Scarbrough had architect William Jay design and build for them in 1819.

**41 West Broad Street (Martin Luther King Jr. Boulevard)** (Figure 82)

The Regency mansion was designed and built in 1818 for William Scarbrough, president of the Savannah Steamship Company, which financed and built the first transatlantic steamship, the *SS Savannah.* Scarbrough had bought the lot in 1803, and William Jay, a young architect from Bath, England, designed the sophisticated residence for one of Savannah's leading mercantile families. President Monroe visited Scarbrough's house in 1819.

Scarbrough was ruined within two years of building the house, and he lost it in bankruptcy in 1820. By 1827 the house had been willed by then-owner Robert Isaac to Mrs. William Taylor, Charlotte de Berniére Scarbrough, Scarbrough's daughter.

This last magnificent residence on old West Broad Street is a metaphor for

**Figure 79**   William J. Spencer house, 322 East Oglethorpe Avenue. *Photograph by Goeff DeLorm, courtesy Savannah College of Art and Design.*

**Figure 80** Colonial Cemetery and Police Barracks, 323 East Oglethorpe Avenue. The barracks were designed by J. H. Boggs in 1869–1870 in the Italianate style. *Photograph by Clement Speiden.*

**Figure 81** Edward G. Malbone; stipple engraving, about 1815–1820. The miniaturist was born in Charleston but worked in Savannah, where he died, buried at Colonial Cemetery. *Courtesy V. & J. Duncan Antique Maps and Prints.*

**Figure 82** William Scarbrough house, 41 West Broad Street (Martin Luther King Jr. Boulevard), about 1900, showing the third floor added for the mansion's use as a school for African-American students. *Courtesy Georgia Historical Society.*

the spirit of Savannah. William Jay made this the most austere of his Savannah designs, with a portico of the archaic Greek Doric order. Severe symmetry is achieved with the Roman-style windows that flank the entrance. Thermal windows and a skylight light the two-story hall, where four fluted Doric columns support a gallery. Jay's hallmark included distinctive room shapes, rooms with semicircular ends, screens of columns, and niches for stat-

**Figure 83**    109 West Broad Street (Martin Luther King Jr. Boulevard). *Courtesy Georgia Historical Society.*

uary, all of which can be seen in the house.

From 1870 to 1876, the Bishop of Savannah ran the house as a boys' orphanage. In 1878 the Scarbrough house became the first public school in Savannah, and one of the first in the south, for African-Americans. For eighty-four years it was the West Broad Street School, until its closing in 1962.

The mansion was made available for this extended public use by George Wymberly Jones DeRenne of the Noble Jones family, who bought the house in 1878 and gave it to the board of education for a "School for Negro Boys." According to the legal arrangements, the school reverted back to DeRenne heirs when the board of education closed the school. Elfrida DeRenne (Mrs. Craig Barrow), of Wormsloe plantation, gave her share of the building to the Historic Savannah Foundation in 1966. The foundation ran the Scarbrough house as a museum from 1972 until it turned its energies to the Broughton Street com-

mercial district. The house reopens in Spring 1997 as Ships of the Sea Museum.

**109 Martin Luther King Jr. Boulevard**
(Figure 83)
The art deco Greyhound Bus Station illustrates that the street had become a transportation artery by the 1940s.

**227 Martin Luther King Jr. Boulevard**
The Central of Georgia Railroad administration building, dating from 1856 after Schwaab's designs, has a Doric hexastyle portico with pilasters between bays and a full entablature with widely spaced triglyphs around both portico and building. This neoclassical late-nineteenth-century railroad building serves as an anchor for the boulevard.

**233 Martin Luther King Jr. Boulevard**
(Figure 84)
The Central of Georgia Railroad had Calvin Fay and Alfred S. Eichberg design this handsome building in 1888 in the nationally popular eclectic style.

**Figure 84**   233 West Broad Street (Martin Luther King Jr. Boulevard). *Cordray–Foltz Collection, courtesy Georgia Historical Society.*

**Figure 85**   Central of Georgia Railroad yard. *Photograph by Goeff DeLorm, courtesy Savannah College of Art and Design.*

**301 Martin Luther King Jr. Boulevard**
(Figures 85 and 86; see p. 42)
Augustus Schwaab was the architect in 1860 for the Central of Georgia Railroad complex, completed in 1876. The passenger terminal is now the Chamber of Commerce office, the Savannah Visitors' Center, and the Savannah History Museum of the Coastal Heritage Society.

The Coastal Heritage Society was established in 1974 by William C. Fleetwood, Jr., Frances Wilson Smith, and John Hall. The organization's accomplishments under executive director Scott Smith include the restoration of Fort Jackson by Robert Gunn of Meyerhoff and Gunn, architects and engineers.

**Figure 86**  Central of Georgia Railroad work sheds. *Photograph by Goeff DeLorm, courtesy Savannah College of Art and Design.*

**Figure 87**  Central of Georgia Railroad stack and latrines. *Photograph by Goeff DeLorm, courtesy Savannah College of Art and Design.*

The large brick railroad complex constitutes one of the oldest railroad facilities in the country. The train shed is the earliest remaining example of tri-composite truss construction in the United States. The Classical and Romanesque motifs of architect Augustus Schwaab are presented in brick with granite trim and include marble and metal cornices (Figure 87).

The arcaded brick shed has iron detailing with exposed wood, cast iron, and wrought iron trusses. The sheds have an open clerestory type of construction, with ventilators running the length of the roof ridge.

Augustus Schwaab, the railroad complex architect, designed the demolished city market that stood on Ellis Square, and he also designed the brick railroad bridges behind the Central of Georgia Railroad complex. On the east side of town he designed the Savannah, Albany and Gulf Railroad building, using Scudder and Hamlet as builders. The cotton warehouse on West Gordon Street on the site of the old Bradley mill was designed by him in 1884. Among the residences he designed is the Lawrence Dunn house at **31–33 Houston Street** in 1875 (Washington Ward), a detached three-bay townhouse with side porches, in the Italianate style. He also designed the handsome paired houses at **7–9 West Gordon Street** in Monterey Ward, built in the Italianate style in 1884 for Anson and Lazurus Mohr. The German-American architect was active in the Georgia Historical Society, the Schutzenverein, a society of Germans, and the Gejsel-Schait Rifle Company.

### 575 West Bryan Street

First Bryan Baptist Church, 1873, designed by John B. Hogg (see p. 48).

**Figure 1** Entrance to walled garden, 17–19 East Gordon Street. *Photograph by Goeff DeLorm, courtesy Savannah College of Art and Design.*

# 5

## SQUARES: OUTDOOR LIVING ROOMS

South of Oglethorpe Avenue, the one-time city limits, you find the heavily residential squares that developed during the golden age of Savannah (Figure 1). Greek revival was the idiom, and cotton, the economic backbone of the city, brought in the means to build large new mansions for wealthy residents and blocks of investment rowhouses for rental. Savannah became a brick city for merchants who were flourishing from the cotton trade in the late 1840s and 1850s, and builders used the oversized rough-face Savannah gray bricks from Henry McAlpin's Hermitage plantation kilns. Charles Blaney Cluskey, an Irish-born architect who arrived in Savannah in 1838, carried with him architectural plan and pattern books and ideas about Greek revival architecture. He began to use the Savannah grays that came from the McAlpin plantation, where he made arrangements to live. Having seen Georgian Dublin, he was wedded to the three-bay brick sidehall townhouse and he may well have introduced the tripartite window system to Savannah. Many of the Greek revival houses he designed have them, and some of the houses with such windows built before his 1847 departure might be attributed to him.

Cluskey set the house type with the townhouses, detached or in paired houses and rowhouses, that characterize Savannah today by their repetition in large numbers. After Cluskey left to go to Washington in 1847 to work on additions to the capitol, Savannah's builders were set in their ways just as the oversized Savannah gray bricks were set in common bond, occasionally in American bond, and sometimes stuccoed. But there was never interest in fancy Savannah houses or fancy brickwork on them until architects from New York brought late-century eclectic architecture styles to Savannah. The only nod to national fashion was the use of hard-baked Baltimore or Philadelphia bricks for use on front elevations. These more expensive bricks were available by the 1850s, when ships began bringing them in.

Active builders who used the Greek revival plan and restrained mode of decoration were the Scudder brothers; Mathew Lufburrow; Calvin N. Otis and Calvin Fay, both of Buffalo, New York; Englishman Charles Sholl; and George H. Ash, builder John H. Ash's son.

Row after row of the flat-front sidehall English-plan houses went up with simple dentil cornices wrapping around a low hip roof or fronting a row. The high raised stoop projecting into the sidewalk with single or double stairways having balusters of wood or cast iron provided the uniform characteristic of the Savannah version of such houses.

A portico might have pilasters or columns on each side of a door with sidelights and an overlight, or sometimes an entrance was recessed with paneled reveals behind a columned or pilastered enframement. Inside, wide wooden frames around doors and windows decreased in diameter as they ascended to a trabeated molding at the top, called a Greek key surround, although the provenance is Egyptian as well. Occasionally, molded cornices and columned screens graced hallways and double parlors. Stairways rose from the hall front, returning at a landing. Applied wood-carved designs might decorate the sides of the risers. But all in all, the style inside and outside the Greek revival houses was restrained and conservative.

The Champion–McAlpin–Fowlkes house at **230 Barnard Street** (Figure 2) and the Hull–Barrow house behind it on Chippewa Square at 17 West McDonough Street (see p. 134), as well as the Sorrel–Weed house on Madison Square at **6 West Harris Street** (see p. 146), reflect the apex of the detached

**Figure 2**   City residence of the McAlpin family, 230 Barnard Street on Orleans Square, now Society of the Cincinnati of the State of Georgia. From *Art Work of Savannah* by Charles Hart Olmstead (Chicago: W. H. Parish Publishing Co., 1893). *Courtesy V. & J. Duncan Antique Maps and Prints.*

**Figure 3** Lafayette Square in the 1880s, showing the Battersby house and the Andrew Low house with children playing games in the square. *Courtesy Georgia Historical Society.*

Greek revival family home in Savannah. The Abraham Minis house at **204 East Jones Street** (see p. 150), and the Charleston-style Battersby house at **119 West Charlton Street** (Figure 3; see pp. 148–149) are also good examples. All are substantial center-hall houses with an English Georgian floor plan.

These mid-nineteenth-century houses went up around squares laid out by the city after the War of 1812: Orleans and Chippewa. After the economic good times of the 1830s, Lafayette, Madison, and Pulaski squares were established. By the 1850s, when Whitefield, Troup, Calhoun, and Chatham squares were laid out, the city had consumed the last of the commonly owned property that Oglethorpe had preserved. Forsyth Park, established in 1851, ended the ward and square system that had lasted 125 years.

Mary Adelaide Hartridge Green, homesick in Paris in the early years of the twentieth century, recalled life in Savannah during her childhood. The social life centered around the squares. During balmy evenings from March through October, she remembered, each square became a large salon with flowers in the center (Figure 4). The twang of mandolins strummed by teenage swains and singing voices wafted through the humid air, and the stars made a spangled lighting for these outdoor living rooms.

Clustered about the steps of their houses, young women in long skirts chatted in groups, listening to the sounds of the boys. After a pickup supper, their parents repaired to the piazzas above, off the double parlors of the hous-

**Figure 4** Alice under a banana tree; illustrates the tropical growth in Savannah's squares in the 1920s. *Courtesy Georgia Historical Society.*

es, to wait for the evening breezes to cool the interiors. They chatted to their neighbors in muted voices across narrow lots from piazza to piazza.

Young children were free to play and cavort on the squares with their hoops and balls. They ran in and out of the banana trees and elephant ears, hiding behind and among moss-draped oak trees. The tree branches provided both places to swing and hiding places. The children kicked balls among sweet shrubs, tea olive, and jasmine bushes. The whole environment was a public household.

The squares served as outdoor living rooms, crowded with shrubs and flowers, vegetation patterns that were reflected inside the houses with textiles, upholstery, drapery, tiles, and wallpapers. Hallmark of the Victorian period, when architecture began to ring these squares, was ebullience of decoration—materialism and consumerism gone wild—reflected in collections and objects from all over the world. A multitude of decorative arts inundated the Victorian aesthetic, extolled in magazines, pattern books, agricultural reviews, and texts. Profusion reigned inside the houses and outside in the squares, where the tropical climate encouraged palms and palmettos, live oak trees, and monkey grass. Moss hung from trees like the fringe hung from shawls over the interior grand pianos. Today that exuberance of growth is represented by clustered azaleas, crape myrtle, and the age-old live oaks.

In Mary Adelaide Green's day, street lamps, gazebos, and monuments and fountains were being installed as furniture for the outdoor parlors. These were replacing the original town wells, water towers, and other public facilities that characterized each square beginning in Oglethorpe's time.

The structure of rectangular public squares, surrounded by boxlike houses and side piazzas with similar-shaped carriage houses to the rear, provided geometric defining units around which the lush variety of objects and decoration could be organized. The architecture that borders the squares serve as edges to define the squares (Figures 5 and 6). Within these borders often lie private enclosed gardens, which continued the exhibition of objects such as

**Figure 5** This Taylor Street high stoop shows the usual height of stoops in Savannah and how the porticos and stoops penetrate the brick sidewalk space. *Photograph by Goeff DeLorm, courtesy Savannah College of Art and Design.*

**Figure 6** Brackets supporting and decorating a series of stoops on houses around a square create rhythms and patterns. *Photograph by Scot Hinson.*

**Figure 7** 329 Abercorn Street, showing children sitting on stone lions in this 1920s photograph. Notice the casual condition of the yard with the Savannah-style edgers and the wrought iron vine support. *Courtesy Georgia Historical Society.*

footscrapers and flowerbed border tiles with their scalloped edges and incised sunburst pattern particular to Savannah. These gardens, sometimes with parterres, sometimes more romantic and less structured (Figure 7), were small in scale and intimate in appearance, a contrast to the openness of the squares.

The squares make Savannah a series of villages in an urban setting. The mystery is whether to call Savannah 24 small villages, or the city with the most sophisticated and livable plan in North America.

The consciousness of exterior aesthetic extended beyond the squares to the cemeteries. The Colonial Cemetery had officially become a park and promenade in the 1890s. The new cemetery at Laurel Grove was established in 1845 as a place to be, to stroll, to rest among deceased friends and loved ones. Grave surrounds were set up as little houses with outdoor parlors for visitors (Figures 8 and 9).

**Figure 8**   Margaret Marshall, Mary Marshall's adopted daughter, died young after a turbulent and unhappy life, leaving behind a young daughter. The nineteenth-century grave at Laurel Grove Cemetery illustrates the custom of statuary and people, both in a visiting attitude. The *carte de visite* is all that is missing. *Photograph by Keith Cardwell, courtesy Savannah College of Art and Design.*

**Figure 9**   Screven family tomb in the Egyptian revival style at Laurel Grove cemetery. *Photograph by Keith Cardwell, courtesy Savannah College of Art and Design.*

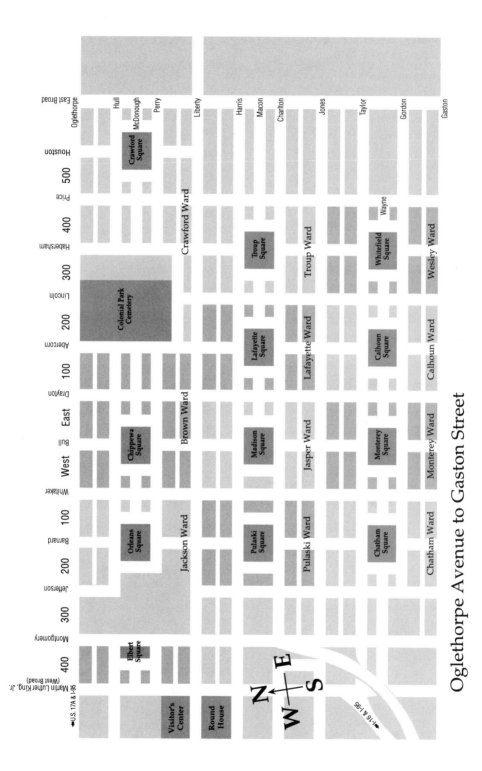

Oglethorpe Avenue to Gaston Street

## CRAWFORD SQUARE AND CRAWFORD WARD

Crawford Square and Crawford Ward, laid out in 1841 along Houston Street, honor William H. Crawford, a Georgia governor. Houston Street was named after John Houston, son of the important British Crown colony military leader and president of the King's Council, Sir Patrick, whose name was spelled "Houstoun" (1698–1762). Crawford Square was the last of the squares to be renovated, at a cost of $231,000, including a gazebo, replanting, and a basketball court. The architectural wood children's furniture was costly, and a drive by at any time of day indicates that it is underused, although the basketball court is in con- stant use. The centerpiece of the ward is the police barracks, bordering Colonial Cemetery, built in 1869–1870 after designs of J. H. Boggs. Italianate with fancy hood molds, large brackets beneath the eaves, segmental arched openings, and quoins, this is a fine civic building.

### 235–239 Habersham Street (Figures 10 and 11)

The county jail and police department, with its outstanding tower, a combina- tion of the Italianate style with exotic North African overtones, was designed in 1887 by the McDonald Brothers.

### 212 East Liberty Street

Double galleries with lacy cast iron decora- tion on this two-story frame house, car-

**Figure 10**  Crawford Ward's old county jail, designed in 1887 by the McDonald Brothers with its mosquelike tower. The twin spires of the Cathedral of St. John the Baptist in Lafayette Square rise up in the background. The old jail has been renovated as Habersham Hall of the Savannah College of Art and Design. *Photograph by Goeff DeLorm, courtesy Savannah College of Art and Design.*

**Figure 11**  Old county jail of 1887, designed by the McDonald Brothers, now Habersham Hall of the Savannah College of Art and Design. *Courtesy Savannah College of Art and Design.*

penter-Italianate in style, make it look like New Orleans. It was built for Laurence Connell in 1851 and remodeled in 1880.

### 214 East Liberty Street

You can see what **212 East Liberty Street** would look like without the galleries by looking at this house, built at the same time for the same owner, Laurence Connell. East Liberty Street here has a number of detached sidehall and center-hall houses built in groups by owners who lived in one and rented the house next door.

### 218–220 East Liberty Street

Crawford Ward has numerous paired brick townhouses dating from the 1840s through the 1880s, like these built in 1850 for George Willet.

### 402–412 East Liberty Street at Habersham Street (Figure 12)

These low-built brick townhouses in the Italianate manner date from 1882–1883, when they were built for Nicholas and Mary Jones. Projecting molded window cornices over segmental arched windows have little dentils that relate to those in the portico, a nice touch. See that the window above the portico is full length; there are some subtle amenities in this modest row.

**234–244 Price Street** (Figures 13 and 14) A set of two-bay rowhouses in the Greek revival style built in 1854 for Stewart Austin are modest but quite elegant. It is unusual for such early rowhouses to be built close to the ground without stoops.

## CHIPPEWA SQUARE AND BROWN WARD

Chippewa Square (Figure 15) and Brown Ward, established about 1815 bisecting Bull Street, commemorate the victory led by Major-General Jacob Jennings Brown in the battle of Chippewa in Canada, defeating the British. The central statue of Oglethorpe, designed by Daniel Chester French, was erected in 1910. The handsome monument with the palmetto leaves of Savannah has a base designed by Henry Bacon which is worth reading. Whitaker Street is the bounding avenue, one way running south.

**Figure 12** 402–412 East Liberty Street. *Photograph by Goeff DeLorm, courtesy Savannah College of Art and Design.*

**Figure 13**   Austin Row, 234–244 Price Street at Perry Street. *Photograph by Goeff DeLorm, courtesy Savannah College of Art and Design.*

**Figure 14**   The Coca-Cola sign covers the entire side elevation of Austin Row. *Photograph by Goeff DeLorm, courtesy Savannah College of Art and Design.*

**Figure 15**   Chippewa Square as it appeared in the 1930s. *Courtesy Georgia Historical Society.*

## 25 West Oglethorpe Avenue at Bull Street (Figure 16)

The Independent Presbyterian Church complex occupies tithing lots rather than a trust lot in an unusual situation for such an important and early religious structure (1817). Yet it is Brown Ward's crowning glory (see pp. 30–31).

## 222 Bull Street (Figure 17)

Architect William Jay built a theater in the trust lot in 1820. Although Jay's building burned, the spot has been used continuously as a theater. Jay's rather simple building should be rebuilt on the site.

## 17 West McDonough Street (Figure 18)

An anchor of Chippewa Square, this important Charles B. Cluskey house was built in 1844 for Moses Eastman, silversmith and patron of the Unitarian church, on the trust lot beside the Baptist church. Joseph Hull bought the house in 1893. Henrik Wallin was the architect in 1911 for the addition of the

**Figure 17** Drawing of the theater at 222 Bull Street between Hull Street and McDonough Street designed by William Jay between 1816 and 1819. A gallery had been added by 1882, and then the building burned. The site still houses a theater, and the building might be reconstructed. *Cordray–Foltz Collection, courtesy Georgia Historical Society.*

third floor. The house is associated with the Barrow family, and Fred Wessels purchased it in the 1950s for his insurance business offices.

## 230–232 Bull Street (Figure 19)

These Italianate-style paired stucco houses date from 1871, built for Julius Koox.

## 233 Bull Street

The First Baptist Church was designed by architect Elias Carter in 1833, with a 1922 renovation by Henrik Wallin. This restrained temple with its deep pediment, slender columns, and cool marble construction material is subdued for a Baptist church. It serves as a noteworthy anchor to Chippewa Square.

## 249–251 Bull Street (2–4 East Liberty Street)

The Second Empire style, characterized by a mansard roof, came late to Savannah. The Hamilton–Turner house at **330 Abercorn Street** (see p. 148) on Lafayette Square is the premier example. This similar house, with its center hall and heavy Italianate hood molds, is notable.

## 11 East Perry Street

This detached frame Federal townhouse dates from 1820, built for Hetty, Abbie,

**Figure 16** Independent Presbyterian Church, 25 West Oglethorpe Avenue. The tall Federal windows are a feature of this church. *Photograph by Clement Speiden.*

Figure 18   Eastman–Stoddard–Hull–Barrow house, 17 West McDonough Street. *Courtesy Georgia Historical Society.*

Figure 19   230–232 Bull Street. *Photograph by Goeff DeLorm, courtesy Savannah College of Art and Design.*

and Phillipa Minis. A hip roof distinguishes it from most Federal houses in Savannah. The notable feature is the outstanding entrance (the door has been mutilated); notice the delicate carving on the sidelights and elliptical fanlight above. It became known as the Florida House, a paying-guest boardinghouse where author Joel Chandler Harris stayed when he was assistant editor of the local newspaper (Figure 20). Christopher Murphy, Jr., the printmaker, owned the house for some time. Murphy is perhaps Savannah's most significant artist, along with the miniaturist Edward Malbone, a Charlestonian active in Savannah, a century earlier.

### 3 West Perry Street

This frame raised five-bay house built in 1831 for Joseph R. Thompson was remodeled with Italianate features in 1874, during its association with the Waring family.

### 15 West Perry Street

Despite associations with planter and merchant John Stoddard, who bought the containing lot in 1857, the Italianate house is recorded as built by William Hunter, who bought the lot in 1867. Notice the roofline. Could a sidehall townhouse, built by Stoddard, have been the base for an addition by Hunter creating a large center-hall mansion redecorated in the Italianate style? House watching and archival research combine to create more mysteries.

General Alexander Robert Lawton bought the house in 1867. The house should be named after this notable Savannahian. He was Quartermaster General of the Confederacy, but returned home to become the president of the American Bar Association and U.S. minister to Austria. After his death the house became a rooming house, then was empty for years before its restoration.

### 114 East McDonough Street (Figure 21)

The Federal-style brick T. P. Ravenel house, originally a detached townhouse,

**Figure 20** Joel Chandler Harris, engraving from *The History of the State of Georgia* (New York: I. W. Avery, 1881). Harris, author of the "Uncle Remus" stories, lived at the Federal-style Murphy house at 11 East Perry Street when he was an editor of the Savannah newspaper. He met his future wife there. *Courtesy V. & J. Duncan Antique Maps and Prints.*

**Figure 21** 114 East McDonough Street. *Photograph by Goeff DeLorm, courtesy Savannah College of Art and Design.*

was built by and for Mathew Lufburrow in 1831. Lufburrow was a master builder, long in Savannah when John S. Norris employed him as his construction foreman for the U.S. Customs House on Bay Street.

**124 East McDonough Street** (Figure 22) This fine but altered center-hall brick house in the Greek revival style dates from about 1861, built for Alfred Haywood, whose wealth came from ice, imported from the north in ships to tropical Savannah.

## ORLEANS SQUARE AND JACKSON WARD

Orleans Square commemorates the battle of New Orleans (Figure 23). Jackson Ward, laid out in 1815, is an early commemoration of the future president of the United States, General Andrew Jackson (1767–1845), hero of the battle of New Orleans. Jackson was very

popular in Georgia as the man who defeated the Creek Indians and who, as U.S. President, ordered the expulsion of the Cherokees out of Georgia in 1829-1837, thereby opening that area to settlement by the Anglo-Americans.

Bisected by Barnard Street, Orleans Square has been mutilated to the west by the Civic Center. Plans did not preserve the original city units used throughout the historic district. This overscaled

**Figure 22** 124 East McDonough Street. *Photograph by Goeff DeLorm, courtesy Savannah College of Art and Design.*

**Figure 23** Orleans Square before demolition of the Habersham and Bulloch houses on the site of, first, the city auditorium, then the Civic Center. *Courtesy Georgia Historical Society.*

building was designed so that the square lost its architectural edge, the trust lots were destroyed, and a street was obliterated. Despite this, the square radiates charm because of the Greek revival house at **230 Barnard Street,** the Champion–McAlpin–Fowlkes house.

## 230 Barnard Street (Figure 24)

Designed and built by architect Charles B. Cluskey in 1843, this monumental house is now owned by the Order of the Cincinnati. The building evokes force by its scale, its monumental Tower of the Winds columns, and the late Second Empire roof that was a late-nineteenth-century addition. Sophistication and monumentality pervade the interior.

## 114–116 West Hull Street

These paired brick Federal houses are the only two remaining houses on the tithing block on Hull Street backed by Oglethorpe Lane. The delicate, dormered masterpieces were built by John H. Ash in 1817. Author and architectural historian Walter Charlton Hartridge lived in 116 West Hull Street (see pp. ii–ix).

## 105–107 West Perry Street (Figure 25)

Architect DeWitt Bruyn designed these paired brick houses for John Martin and A. J. Miller, and they were built in 1872 and 1873 with a mansard roof. They exhibit fine Italianate detailing and round–headed recessed entrances as well as sophisticated corner pilasters. Bruyn had come to Savannah by 1860 to assist John S. Norris. He remodeled and designed a number of Savannah houses in the 1860s and 1870s. In 1870 he remodeled Chatham Academy.

## 117–119 West Perry Street (Figure 26)

These paired frame houses were built for John Morel in 1818 and remodeled in 1869 in the Italianate style with overhanging eaves and brackets. Like a number of corner houses in this area, it appears to be New England in origin, built up with a high stoop, Savannah fashion. Indeed, many New Englanders came to

Savannah as builders and merchants, so that what does not look English or low country about Savannah looks something like New England or Boston.

## 128 West Liberty Street

This late Federal center-hall frame house with its raised stoop and tin-covered hipped roof with close-spaced dormers dates from 1835. Now a bed and breakfast, it is another house that looks like it might belong in New England.

## 116–124 West Liberty Street

This row of masonry three-bay townhouses are good scene setters. They were built for Solomon Cohen in 1873, but they look much more mid-nineteenth century. The flat brick fronts show relatively anonymous faces to the street, hiding possible treasures of moldings, medallions, column screens, and woodwork within.

## PULASKI SQUARE AND PULASKI WARD

Pulaski Square and Pulaski Ward were laid out in 1837. In a retrospective burst of patriotic military zeal, always present in Savannah although benign, the city named the new ward and square Pulaski, after the Polish patriot and hero of the siege of Savannnah.

Benjamin Franklin had met Casimir Pulaski in Paris, where he was in exile, and it was Franklin who called him to the cause of liberty in the New World since the quest for his nation's liberty had failed the young cavalry officer in his native Poland. Sent to Savannah with Continental General Benjamin Lincoln, who had failed in Charleston, Pulaski joined the joint effort of the French and the Continentals to eject the British from Savannah in 1779. The effort failed and Pulaski was mortally wounded on October 9, 1779. Like Sergeant William Jasper, who also died in Savannah after attaining fame in a battle against the British in Charleston, Pulaski had a Savannah ward named after him. Both military heroes were later immortalized in bronze for Savannah squares in yet

**Figure 24**   Aaron Champion house, 230 Barnard Street, Orleans Square 1844, one of Savannah's fore-most Greek revival houses, designed by Charles Cluskey. It is certainly the most monumental with its Tower of the Winds columns extending through both levels from their base on a Palladian-like pier. The high-style house had a third story added in 1895, giving a soupçon of Second Empire style that did not destroy the building proportions. The cast iron fence with its caged cast iron posts is one of the hand-somest in the city. Preservationist Alida Harper Fowlkes left it to the Order of the Cincinnati of the State of Georgia. *Photograph by Goeff DeLorm, courtesy Savannah College of Art and Design.*

**Figure 25** 105–107 West Perry Street. *Photograph by Goeff DeLorm, courtesy Savannah College of Art and Design.*

**Figure 26** Morel houses, 117–119 West Perry Street, 1818. *Photograph by Goeff DeLorm, courtesy Savannah College of Art and Design.*

another burst of characteristic hero worship. Both Pulaski County and the town of Pulaski in Georgia were also named after the colorful cavalry officer.

Pulaski Square and its West Jones Street corridor were the object of the first residential area restoration project for the Historic Savannah Foundation in 1965. It is now hard to imagine the day when rowhouses on West Jones Street, used as tenements or abandoned, could not be sold for $1500. Nor can one imagine that the Savannah gray bricks by the pallet were worth more than a standing structure built of them.

Jones Street, brick paved, tree lined with a wide neutral area between old sidewalks and the street, offers a peaceful, shady stroll through a shaft of 1850s Savannah rows, paired houses, and five-bay center-hall houses, two to four stories in height. Behind brick walls are a number of walled gardens that have been restored or created in the past twenty years. The street as you see it today is largely a creation of the catalytic energy of the Historic Savannah Foundation during the late 1960s and 1970s. During the 1850s, brick rowhouses had been built in such great numbers that they began to symbolize Savannah. By 1950 the same rowhouses symbolized Savannah's downfall. Now, once again, rowhouses like those on Jones Street have been restored to reflect Savannah's fine architecture.

Thirteen acres of compact housing were rehabilitated in a successful effort of volunteerism and community interest whereby $38,000 from the revolving fund produced over $5 million in private restoration activity.

Brick is the medium of Pulaski Square and Greek revival the vocabulary. Remshart Row at **102–112 West Jones Street,** dating from 1854, ranks among the city's finest rows. Paired houses such as **107 West Liberty,** built in the Italianate style, reflect the rental needs of the mercantile city after the mid-nineteenth century. Both detached townhouses and center-hall Greek revival houses reveal Savannah's maturity in economics and good taste from 1840 through the Italianate period, as seen in Pulaski Ward.

**328 Barnard Street** (Figure 27)

This 1915 brick building, the former Jewish Educational Alliance, is a valid part of the street scene. It is one of the more sensitive infills on Savannah's historic lots. The building material, scale, fenestration progression, and size, as well as the portico and cornice, pass the test of aesthetics for Savannah. The corners of the building have an interesting treatment, towerlike, with their fancy brickwork entablature. The building has been preserved as a SCAD dormitory.

**321 Barnard Street** (Figure 28)

This detached frame sidehall townhouse was built in 1845 for merchant Bernard Constantine, who also built the frame townhouse at **218 West Harris Street** in 1839 in this ward, besides the notable paired brick houses in Chatham Ward at **211–215 West Jones Street** (see p. 162) built in 1851.

**Figure 27**   328 Barnard Street, 1930. The former Jewish Educational Alliance, built in 1915, is now a SCAD girls' dormitory. Although this is a replacement twentieth-century building on a trust lot, it preserves the texture, scale, and institutional use traditionally reserved for trust lots. It is one of the more felicitous trust lot infills in the city. *Cordray–Foltz Collection, courtesy Georgia Historical Society.*

**Figure 28** Bernard Constantine house, 321 Barnard Street, 1845. *Photograph by Keith Cardwell, courtesy Savannah College of Art and Design.*

## 331 Barnard Street

Exceptions break the norm, and two of Pulaski Square's trust lots and multiple corner tithing lots have fine frame townhouses such as the Israel Dasher house, dating from 1844. Ths sidehall townhouse has been altered, but it reflects the spirit of its type, with gable ends, double dormers, and a high raised stoop leading to a side entrance beyond which is the requisite stairhall. Even adding a piazza or side veranda to an earlier house is a Savannah tradition.

## 126 West Harris Street

Yet another frame sidehall townhouse with a side veranda is the house Theodosius Bartow built in 1839, with a third story and the veranda added later. The Bartow sons were killed in the Civil War.

## 212–214 West Harris Street (Figure 29)

Handsome paired houses of stuccoed brick were built for Isaac la Roche in 1868. Now the adjacent frame house, said to have been built in 1839 for Bernard Constantine, appears as a frame construction third house trying to match the paired houses. So it goes with flat-faced three-bay sidehall rowhouses: match three porticos and you have uniformity. Here brackets have been spaced between the pierced openings of a one-time entablature.

## 107 West Liberty Street (Figure 31)

In 1870–1871, Charles Groover had this handsome set of paired houses built in brick. Their segmental arched openings and recessed entrances with the handsome pairs of doors are sophisticated touches along with the quoins. Alterations at the first level and adaptation to commercial use at the basement level cannot destroy the houses' contribution to the street scene. After all, the urban street scene, compact and orderly, is Savannah's strong point.

## 201–203 West Charlton Street

Between 1854 and 1856 Celia M. Solomons had this pair of stuccoed brick houses built in the Greek revival style. Flat-fronted, they boast a narrow dentiled cornice beneath a conservative

**Figure 29**  212–214 West Harris Street. *Photograph by Keith Cardwell, courtesy Savannah College of Art and Design.*

**Figure 30**  215 West Charlton Street.
*Photograph by Goeff DeLorm, courtesy Savannah College of Art and Design.*

parapet. Projecting pedimented lintels above recessed entrances are the only decoration besides a touch of ironwork at balconies in front of each pair of first-level windows. Subtle variety within a standard norm is one of the pleasures of the Pulaski Square street scene.

**215 West Charlton Street** (Figure 30)
In 1846, Moses A. Cohen had builder John Studevant erect this fine sidehall detached townhouse in the Greek revival style. Look at the brick chimneys set in the gable end and at the pilastered and pedimented dormers peeking over the parapet. The conservative house intrudes in no way but fits comfortably into the dignified but not pretentious street scene. Not even the stoop infringes on the sidewalk; the house is set back just enough for the portico to touch the property line and a fence to enclose a shallow front space.

**MADISON SQUARE AND JASPER WARD** (Figure 32)

Laid out in 1837 and named after James Madison, Madison Square runs along Bull Street. The ward commemorates Sergeant William Jasper, the patriot of the Continental Army who fell in the siege of Savannah in 1779. Madison Square has two major institutional buildings and St. John's Episcopal Church, which with its center-hall man-

**Figure 31**   107 West Liberty Street. *Photograph by Goeff DeLorm, courtesy Savannah College of Art and Design.*

**Figure 32**   St. John's Episcopal Church on Madison Square, wood engraving from *Ballou's Pictorial Drawing Room Companion* (1857, p. 152). *Courtesy V. & J. Duncan Antique Maps and Prints.*

ST. JOHN'S CHURCH, SAVANNAH, GEORGIA.

sions and Greek revival townhouses makes it one of the richest squares in the city. The Savannah Volunteer Guards at **340–344 Bull Street,** and the Masonic Temple at **341 Bull Street,** both infills of the turn of the century, are as important as some of the original buildings that remain.

### 307–309 Bull Street

This neo-Gothic revival one-story building was built for the Georgia Hussars in 1897. This Spanish–Moorish version of the Gothic style stands out as a fancy or folly in conservative Savannah.

### 326 Bull Street (see pp. 13–16)

This fine two-bay three-story Greek revival townhouse, built for real estate investor Eliza Ann Jewett, has the familiar tripartite windows also found on the Sorrel house across the square. The house is an early example of the Greek revival style, built in 1843. Eliza Ann Jewett built numerous rental properties of fine quality in the area.

The interior has much more architectural embellishment than the exterior would suggest. Corinthian columns act as a divider between the double parlors and screen the stairway from the entrance hall. The windows are wide and have Greek key or trabeated surrounds on the inside.

### 329 Bull Street (Figure 32)

St. John's Episcopal Church was designed by Calvin Otis in 1853 in the neo-Gothic style, which is appropriate to its residential neighbor, the Green–Meldrim house, which is now St. John's rectory. Otis came from Buffalo, New York, not coincidentally, the hometown of architect Calvin Fay. He arrived in 1851 to supervise construction of the church. Church records in 1851 show that he was paid $100 for drawing plans and specifications. His total charge was 2½ percent on $16,000.

### 341 Bull Street (Figure 33)

Hyman W. Witcover designed the Masonic Temple in 1912. Like the

**Figure 33** Masonic Building, 341 Bull Street, 1912. *Cordray–Foltz Collection, courtesy Georgia Historical Society.*

Savannah Volunteer Guards Company building nearby, it has a curving corner and two handsome facades that give the building sophistication and monumentality to match the tripartite facade, with its heavy cornice and handsome engaged columns with pilasters in the midsection. Witcover came to Savannah and started out as a draftsman for A. S. Eichberg in 1891, with offices at 55 Abercorn Street.

### 340–344 Bull Street (see p. 7)

William G. Preston designed the Savannah Volunteer Guards Company building in 1893 in the Richardson Romanesque style, thus related to the old City Hall on Wright Square.

### 14 West Macon Street (Figure 34)

The Green–Meldrim house, built for Englishman Charles Green in 1853 by architect John S. Norris, is Savannah's and perhaps the South's foremost Gothic style house. It is the most expensive nineteenth-century house in Savannah, and the most patently decorative inside, with rococo revival moldings. The exterior features heavy hood molds, "oriel"

**Figure 34** Green–Meldrim house, 14 West Macon Street, 1853. *Photograph by Goeff DeLorm, courtesy Savannah College of Art and Design.*

windows, and a crenelated parapet with fine chimneys above. Notice the clustered iron columns framing the entrance and the tin-covered gallery wrapping around the house.

British owner and cotton merchant Charles Green offered the house to Union General William Tecumseh Sherman when he and his force of 60,000 troops marched into Savannah on their notorious and destructive march to the sea, when much of South Carolina and Georgia was put to the torch in a concerted effort to end what Savannahians and South Carolinians called the War of Northern Aggression. That is when the Civil War lore about Savannah began to reach fever pitch.

After ownership by two distinguished Savannah families, the Greens and Judge Peter Meldrim, the house was acquired by St. John's Episcopal Church.

**2–4 East Jones Street**

The Greek revival corner house dates from 1853 and is probably a John S. Norris design. Alexander A. Smets, the

owner, one of Savannah's earliest and most astute book collectors and intellectuals, was active in the 1830s formation of the Georgia Historical Society. He had come to Savannah from Nantes, France, in 1795, one of a number of refugees from the upheavals during the French Revolution.

**18 East Jones Street**

In 1847, Eliza Ann Jewett had this three-bay townhouse built, one of her numerous buildings on Jones Street. With one dormer at the front elevation, a steep roofline, a stucco facade, and a recessed entrance without sidelights, the house appears Regency in style.

**20–22 East Jones Street**

The estate of Eliza Ann Jewett continued her building traditions with this townhouse for her granddaughter in 1861, just before the Civil War. It continued the Greek revival tradition, with the simple entrance with sidelights and overlight. The two first-story windows are atypical.

**10 West Jones Street**

Architect John S. Norris designed this townhouse, the Noah B. Knapp house, in 1857. Here in the sidehall townhouse he was far more traditional than at the Gothic-style Green–Meldrim house. Notice the full-length windows at the first and second levels, although there is no gallery or balcony to walk out onto. Pedimented hood molds and two pairs of columns at the entrance are the only decoration on the chaste facade.

**5–9 West Charlton Street**

Francis Grimball built the Italianate row in 1879 for Daniel J. Purse, one-time mayor of the city and investor in rental property. He lived in Monterey Ward at **14 East Taylor Street** (see p. 154) about 1870.

**11–17–19 West Charlton Street**

All these houses were built as investments by Daniel Robertson between 1852–1857. The paired brick Greek revival townhouses at **11–17 West Charlton Street** date from 1852–1853 and are typical examples of the period: brick, two stories plus a dormered level over a high brick basement with a gable roof, central chimney, and narrow doors. In 1857 Robertson had **19 West Charlton Street** built. This two-story townhouse over a high basement has the narrow doors and six-over-six windows of an earlier period. It has a plastered facade now, and has lost some exterior details.

### 23–25 West Charlton Street

Paired frame houses built about 1845 were another investment for Daniel Robertson and are fine examples of the rich rowhouse inventory in the ward. These look almost Federal in style.

### 6 West Harris Street (Figure 35)

The Sorrel–Weed house, designed and built by Charles B. Cluskey in 1841 for Francis Sorrel, is the logical descendant in elegance from William Jay's Regency wonders in Savannah. This sophisticated house, although clearly Greek revival,

has a parapet with shallow elliptical arches in the Regency manner. Inside is an exquisite library in the oval form with curving wood doors. The room relates to Thomas Jefferson's work in Charlottesville in the 1820s. Compare this Greek revival house to Jay's earlier Owens–Thomas house museum to see the continuity of form and plan.

### 20–22 West Harris Street

Eliza Ann Jewett had paired brick houses built in 1855 similar in type and style to those of her neighbors. She also had a number of handsome detached townhouses built on West Jones Street in the same ward, such as the one at **16 West Jones Street** in 1857 (windows and doors altered).

### 14–18 West Harris Street

Charles B. Cluskey is said to have designed and built these lovely paired houses, which their father ordered for his daughters Eugenia and Louisa Kerr in 1842–1843. Observe the two-bay design with those tripartite windows so particular to Savannah. Typical of the

**Figure 35**  Sorrel–Weed house, 6 West Harris Street, 1841. *Photograph by Goeff DeLorm, courtesy Savannah College of Art and Design.*

1840s, there are no sidelights or transoms. These are quite early Greek revival townhouse examples.

## LAFAYETTE SQUARE AND LAFAYETTE WARD

Lafayette Square and Lafayette Ward were laid out in 1837 to honor George Washington's French companion in arms, who visited Savannah in 1825. Lafayette, from Auvergne, France, was godfather to a number of Savannah babies, and his name is remembered in many local family names, such as Charles Augustus Lafayette Lamar, Savannah's richest man.

Lafayette Ward is divided by Abercorn Street and has four tithing blocks, among the richest architecturally in the city, although two of the trust lots have been defaced. The first block of East Harris Street, a block on East Charlton Street, and two blocks on East Jones Street are worth special mention. Lafayette Ward has rowhouses, detached townhouses, and five-bay center-hall residences. These exhibit their Greek revival, Italianate, and Second Empire facades.

### 329 Abercorn Street (Figure 36)

This trust lot contains the Andrew Low house, dating from 1849, an early example of architect John S. Norris's work. The house would appear to be Greek revival in style, except for square proportions and the deep overhanging eaves supported by brackets. Otherwise, there is a conservative entrance to a center-hall house, with four rooms besides the hall on each floor. The entrance is flanked by full-length windows having a simple but sophisticated iron balcony at the first level with short windows above.

Andrew Low, one of Savannah's resident British cotton brokers, married Savannahian Sarah Cecil Hunter, whose father was from County Donegal, Ireland, and whose mother was a South Carolinian. They began the house in 1848, but Mrs. Low and their 4-year-old son died before it was finished. Low sent

**Figure 36** Andrew Low house, 329 Abercorn Street, 1849. *Photograph by Goeff DeLorm, courtesy Savannah College of Art and Design.*

his two older daughters to England to his relatives, and five years later married Mary Cowper Stiles, daughter of the U.S. chargé d'affaires in Vienna, Austria. The couple maintained the residence on Lafayette Square, but lived part of the year at family homes in Leamington and Warwickshire and at Liverpool, the major receiving point for Georgia cotton.

The Lows spent several summers in Newport, Rhode Island, in the 1850s, where their son, William Mackay Low, was born. During the Civil War, Andrew Low was imprisoned at Fort Warren in Boston harbor on suspicion of collaboration with the Confederacy.

In 1884, William Mackay Low married Juliette Magill Gordon, who lived nearby at **10 East Oglethorpe Avenue** (then South Broad Street; see pp. 20–22) and whose family was in the cotton factoring business, as were the Lows. Juliette Gordon Low, the founder of the Girl Scouts of the U.S.A., lived in this house and in England, where her husband had various estates and connections (Figure 37). She died of cancer in the Lafayette Square house in 1927.

Juliette Gordon Low's mother was the first president of the National Society of the Colonial Dames of America in the State of Georgia, and the Low house became the state headquarters when the organization acquired it in 1928, just one year after its owner's death. The connection through her mother between Juliette Gordon Low and the Colonial Dames was fortunate for the preservation of one of Savannah's finest houses. Because of the connection, the house was owned by one family from its building to Mrs. Low's death and its acquisition a year later for use as a museum house. The Colonial Dames have interpreted the house in the period of 1849, soon after its construction and when its first mistress, Sarah Low, died there. Period furnishings have been donated and acquired through the Colonial Dames. A visit to the Low house provides an opportunity to see the genre of interiors in a number of Lafayette Square residences.

### 330 Abercorn Street (Figure 38)

The trust lot across Lafayette Square from the Low house contains the Hamilton house, dating from 1873, built for Samuel P. Hamilton after designs by J. D. Hall. In plan the house is standard center-hall on a large scale, with Italianate characteristics. However, paired windows with eyebrow hood molds, a deep mansard roof with crestings of cast iron, above round arched dormers inset into the mansard indicate Second Empire baroque influence. Quoins, multiple balconies, and paired brackets below deep eaves at the lowered arched portico give a patterned surface to the monumental block. Single panes of window glass were possible by the 1870s and are typical of both Second Empire and late Italianate styles.

### 119 East Charlton Street (Figure 39)

The William Battersby house was built in 1852 for Low's partner in the cotton business. Battersby had also married a Savannahian, Sarah Emmelyn Hartridge. The Battersby house is perhaps the only remaining house in Savannah built in the Charleston and West Indies side-piazza type, designed to have the main house entered from the piazza. The outer doors at the street entrance lead onto the piazza, within which the house entrance lies hidden. The plain doors leading from the street to the piazza give no clue to the house type and style within, a monumental center-hall Greek revival house. Two bedrooms at the second level also open onto the piazza. The house retains original fixtures and fittings in the parlors as well as wide trabeated door and window surrounds. The dining room was remodeled in a more ornate style. The house was the residence of Julian Hartridge, Confederate officer and congressman and later U.S. congressman, whose daughter, Mary Adelaide Hartridge, married Edward Moon Green. The Greens' son, Julian Green, a member of the French Academy, lives in Paris. Four generations of Hartridges have lived here over time.

### 201–203 East Charlton Street

John S. Norris is said to have designed this center-hall house in the Italianate style, for John B. Gallie in 1858. One sees its relationship to the Low house in type and style, with its overhanging bracketed eaves and the series of balconies. Major Gallie was killed in action while commanding Fort McAllister on the Ogeechee River during a Union naval attack.

### 207 East Charlton Street (Figure 40)

The estate of William J. McIntosh built this three-bay sidehall townhouse in the Greek revival style in 1856. The simple entrance portico above the steps, filled in with bricks laid in the lattice design, suggests the building date. Georgia prize-winning twentieth-century author Flannery O'Connor's parents lived here, as did the author herself when not in Milledgeville (see p. 45).

**Figure 37** William Mackay Low (1860–1905) on horseback in England, by James Linwood Palmer, 1897. William Low and his wife, Juliette Gordon, lived in Savannah and from 1889 at Wellesbourne House, Warwickshire, where he raised racehorses. Palmer painted Low on one of his favorite mounts, wearing the pink coat and brown cuffed boots of a master of the hunt. *Courtesy National Society of The Colonial Dames of America in the State of Georgia.*

**Figure 38** Turner–Hamilton house, 330 Abercorn Street, 1873. *Photograph by Goeff DeLorm, courtesy Savannah College of Art and Design.*

**Figure 39** Battersby–Hartridge house, 119 East Charlton Street, 1852. *Photograph by Goeff DeLorm, courtesy Savannah College of Art and Design.*

Figure 40  Flannery O'Connor house, 207 East Charlton Street. *Photograph by Goeff DeLorm, courtesy Savannah College of Art and Design.*

Figure 41  211 East Charlton Street. *Photograph by Goeff DeLorm, courtesy Savannah College of Art and Design.*

**211 East Charlton Street** (Figure 41)

This handsome townhouse built for Augustus Barrie in 1853 is, as it appears today, a much more sophisticated design than is common for Greek revival townhouses in Savannah. A pediment with dentils surmounting the facade, an elliptical entrance way with sidelights, pedimented window lintels, and the parapet above the wide portico all bespeak a facade atypical of Savannah. Barrie was a developer in the Victorian district and his name is remembered with one of the wards.

**118–124 East Harris Street**

These fine paired houses built for Joseph Gammon in 1852 in the Greek revival style illustrate the traditional brick flat fronts, here with the pair of projecting entrances on the outside wall of each house.

**204 East Jones Street** (see p. 125)

Built in 1859–1860 for Abraham Minis, this center-hall mansion follows the designs of Stephen Decatur Button (1813–1897). Button was a Philadelphia architect who had come south to design the Alabama State Capitol at Montgomery. The Minis house is another Greek revival center-hall house with Italianate overtones, seen in the wide eaves and balconies and the iron railing running up from a fence at the property line. The stucco that once covered the bricks has been removed.

**112–120 East Jones Street**

This series of rowhouses featuring tripartite windows and stucco fronts was developed by Eliza Ann Jewett in 1852, one more example of her numerous projects in the Greek revival style.

**207 East Liberty Street**

Charles Cluskey designed the Sisters of Mercy Convent in 1845, enlarged in 1869. Its projecting central element recalls John Norris's Greek revival Massie School. Set back on its lot, the complex is enhanced by the handsome cast iron fence.

### Abercorn Street at East Harris Street
(Figure 42)

In 1872–1876, Francis Baldwin designed the Catholic Cathedral, now called St. John the Baptist. Its pair of neo-Gothic revival spires can be seen throughout the city. The church windows were imported from Innsbruck, and the murals were installed by Savannnah artist Charles Murphy. The church was rebuilt in 1898.

## MONTEREY SQUARE AND MONTEREY WARD

The General Pulaski Monument in Monterey Square, designed in 1853–1855 by Robert E. Launitz, is enclosed with an outstanding fence featuring cast iron wreaths. Monterey Square is the last of the squares bisecting Bull Street, just before Forsyth Park, and it is often referred to as the city's most perfect square and ward. Historic buildings fill three of its four trust lots: Temple Mickve Israel, an Italianate man-

**Figure 42** Cathedral of St. John the Baptist; photogravure, about 1899. *Courtesy V. & J. Duncan Antique Maps and Prints.*

sion, and an important set of paired houses in the early Italianate style.

Armstrong College acquired seven properties in this ward, including the Hardee mansion in 1935, after the Armstrong family donated their house at **431–433 Bull Street** for use as a college, using the Armstrong family name. In the 1960s the college bought the trust lot, site of a demolished Presbyterian church next to Temple Mickve Israel, to build a badly proportioned science building. When the college threatened further demolitions, the Historic Savannah Foundation pushed to save the ward and square by acquisition of the seven-building Armstrong College complex. The Lane Foundation supplied property elsewhere for the college, and the historic buildings were sold to individuals for renovation. Now, thirty years later, there is a positive movement afoot to bring a section of Armstrong College back to the historic district, in an appropriate complex on Broughton Street.

East Taylor Street displays a fine group of single-family detached houses and some paired houses. The lane behind Gordon Street in this ward is rich in carriage houses. Most lanes throughout the historic city were faced with nineteenth-century stables, carriage houses, or service buildings, an essential part of the master-house complex. These have not fared well over the years and continue to be demolished.

### 20 East Gordon Street (Figure 43)

Henry G. Harrison designed this building for the Hebrew congregation of Mickve Israel in 1876, and it was modified by J. D. Foley. The architect had come to town to design a church that once stood nearby. The congregation saw an opportunity and had the architect develop a synagogue plan that is more like a church than a synagogue.

The congregation is ancient, begun by settlers arriving on the second ship from London, a group of persecuted Sephardic Jews who had come to

**Figure 43** Temple Mickve Israel. *Courtesy Savannah College of Art and Design.*

London as Marranos from Portugal. With them were a few Ashkenazim German-speaking Jews, including the Sheftalls, Minises, and Cohens. Descendants of these families remain active in the synagogue, which enjoys its reputation as the only such Gothic-style edifice in the country. This is something for the third-oldest Jewish congregation in the United States.

### 423–425 Bull Street (Figure 44)

These elegant paired houses, designed by John S. Norris in 1858 for the Reverend Charles Rogers, a Presbyterian clergyman, recall Grammercy Park in New York. They present an effusive collection of woven wire and cast iron work beside sandstone steps and slate sidewalks. The interiors of the sidehall townhouses reveal large-scale Greek revival detailing.

Paired houses, evident in Savannah as early as the Federal period, appear as one unit on their containing lots and share a common wall. Most often a pair of central

entrances with interior halls and exterior stoops side by side become a design element of the complex. Although they may have different owners, such houses should be treated as a unit by the historic district commission when paint colors, trim, and window mullions and shutter types are considered.

While the interior plans of paired houses match one another, the amount of detail, such as plasterwork, is often different; one of the houses was usually for the owner of the pair and the other a rental unit, sometimes less decorative.

### 429 Bull Street (Figure 45)

The Hugh W. Mercer house, designed in 1860 by John S. Norris and completed after the Civil War in 1871, with further drawings by architects Muller and Bruyn, represents Italianate par excellence in Savannah. The house presents a fine sculptural mass because it is set far back on its containing trust lot behind a cast iron fence. A boxlike structure, the monumental three-bay two-story house gains mass with its large, paired windows crowned with sculptural hood molds of cast iron. Balconies at four win-

**Figure 44** 423–425 Bull Street. *Photograph by Goeff DeLorm, courtesy Savannah College of Art and Design.*

**Figure 45** Mercer house, 429 Bull Street, front and rear elevations. *Photographs by Keith Cardwell, courtesy Savannah College of Art and Design.*

dows and an elegant portico of paired columns make a composition beneath the deep bracketed eaves. The carriage house set behind the handsome rear elevation of the masterhouse completes the trust lot. The rear elevation of the residence is a two-level gallery suppported by huge box columns, unusual in Savannah.

The Mercer house was never occupied by a member of the family because General Mercer went to fight for the Confederacy and sold the unfinished house when he returned. It has most recently been the home of the late Jim Williams, the subject of John Berendt's best-selling nonfiction book, *Midnight in the Garden of Good and Evil* (New York: Random House, 1994).

**2 East Taylor Street** (Figure 46)

This Italianate sidehall townhouse was built in 1880 for Hugh M. Comer, president of the Central of Georgia Railroad. Based on its exterior appearance, with segmental arches and molded lintels, overhanging eaves with paired brackets, and traditional two-story piazza on the east side, the house could have been built in the late 1860s. Inside, however, the house epitomizes the Aesthetic movement, with its elaborate black chimney pieces with mirrored overmantels and fancy coal grates with decorative tile surrounds. The elegant plasterwork on the ceiling, with bosses and opulent molding above a deep set of molded cornices, is indicative of the 1880 date, as are the wide panes in the double-hung full-length windows.

**12–14 East Taylor Street** (Figures 47 and 48)

One side of this pair of townhouses was built for Daniel J. Purse, one-time mayor, the other for Daniel Thomas, in 1869. What you see on the facade and inside today is the 1897 renovation and addition. The surface of the facade has many flourishes in the Second Empire baroque style. The projecting bays were

**Figure 46**   2 East Taylor Street. *Photograph by Clement Speiden.*

**Figure 47**   12 East Taylor Street. *Photograph by Goeff DeLorm, courtesy Savannah College of Art and Design.*

**Figure 48**    12–14 East Taylor Street. The Second Empire baroque manner was an affectation brought to Savannah by Beaux Arts–trained architect Detlef Lienau. *Photograph by Clement Speiden.*

added, extending into the sidewalk area, and the mansard roof was installed.

Architect Detlef Lienau is responsible for bringing the Second Empire baroque fancy to Savannah. This excessive and fluid style applied to Savannah's staid English facades creates an amusing and fanciful street scene.

### 10 West Taylor Street

Built for Edward G. Wilson in 1852 in the Gothic revival style, the sidehall townhouse features Gothic dripstones or hood molds and a multilevel roofline. T. P. Waring owned it about 1904, and after a trip to Holland, where he admired the rounded gables in the Dutch style, he returned to Savannah and had his Gothic revival style house renovated in the Dutch manner at the roofline in time for his wedding. Another remodeling took place in 1916.

### 3 West Gordon Street (Figure 49)

Like its neighbor the Mercer house, the Hardee house, built for Noble A. Hardee beginning in 1860, was not finished until after the Civil War. The massive center-hall house with the handsome high-relief decorative cast iron lintels over lowered-arch windows is one of Savannah's finest versions of the

**Figure 49**    3 West Gordon Street. *Photograph by Keith Cardwell, courtesy Savannah College of Art and Design.*

Italianate craze. The house has an attic story with windows between the paired brackets of the deep eaves and has a fine-looking rear elevation with double galleries.

William J. Hardee was a West Point graduate and author of *Rifle and Light Infantry*, a handbook used by generals on both sides of the Civil War. The Confederate officer was charged with evacuating the city of Savannah before the arrival of Union General Sherman. This member of the family built **212–214 East Gwinnett Street** in 1884 in Stephens Ward, now the Victorian district.

### 7–9 West Gordon Street

The handsome set of paired houses in the late Italianate style built in 1884 for Anson and Lazurus Mohr were designed by Augustus Schwaab, a German-American architect active in Savannah for fifty years until after 1900. Number seven was recently featured in a series of programs on *This Old House*.

### 11 West Gordon Street

This three-bay detached sidehall townhouse with its curving staircase leading to a portico is outflanked by the Hardee and Mercer houses, but is a notable house built during the finest hour of Savannah architecture, for the Reverend Charles B. King in 1858.

### 17–19 West Gordon Street (Figure 50)

This pair of houses was built for John M. Williams in 1879 and 1882. Full arched opening below paired lowered arched windows on the second and third levels make this a sophisticated building. Pilasters and the projecting bays at each end add to the rhythmical composition.

### 1–9 East Gordon Street

Scudders Row, one of the city's outstanding collection of rowhouses, dates from 1852–1853 and was built by and for John and Ephraim Scudder, prominent builders, whose father Amos Scudder had come to the city from New Jersey. Amos Scudder was director of the Savannah and

**Figure 50**   17–19 West Gordon Street. *Photograph by Goeff DeLorm, courtesy Savannah College of Art and Design.*

Ogeechee Canal Company in 1850, and John and Ephraim, with him, were part owners of it.

### 17–19 East Gordon Street (Figure 51)

This high-style Italianate townhouse with piazza and side garden dates from 1881, built for John C. Rowland. Exuberant in its decorative detail, it presents French-style projecting hood molds and a double stringcourse. Fanciful and sophisticated at once, the house shows a lingering affection for the Italianate style along with classical details on sidehall townhouses.

### 450 Bull Street (Figure 52)

The English Consul Edmund Molyneux had this center-hall house built in 1857. When Molyneux returned to England after the Civil War, General Henry Reade Rootes Jackson, Civil War hero and attorney, bought the house, which is now owned and operated as a private dining club, the Oglethorpe Club.

**Figure 51** 17–19 East Gordon Street. *Photograph by Scot Hinson.*

**Figure 52** 450 Bull Street. Built in 1857 for British Consul Edmund Molyneux, one of the most powerful men in the mercantile city, later the home of Henry Rootes Jackson, one of the richest men in Savannah. The house is now the Oglethorpe Club, hosting some 400 of the oldest families and most civic-oriented men and women of Savannah. *Courtesy V. & J. Duncan Antique Maps and Prints.*

Jackson served as minister to Austria-Hungary before the Civil War and minister to Mexico after the war. He was a veteran of the Mexican War and a poet of note.

**443–451 Bull Street** (Figures 53 and 54) Armstrong house was built in 1917 as a private residence for the millionaire and Spanish-American War veteran George Ferguson Armstrong (1869–1924), who had made a fortune in shipping in World War I. In 1935 the Armstrong heirs left the imposing mansion as headquarters for a junior college named Armstrong to be established there by the city of Savannah. Recent celebrity Jim Williams acquired the mansion after the Historic Savannah Foundation mounted a battle

to prevent the college from demolishing the historic buildings they owned in Monterey Ward for a new campus site. After renovating the building, Williams sold it to the law firm of Bouhan, Williams and Levy.

Designed by architect Henrik Wallin, this enameled white brick mansion at the juncture of Monterey Ward and Forsyth Park is the last and most expensive private mansion of first quality to go up in the original historic district of Savannah. The side of the house faces Forsyth Park and the beginnings of the Victorian district. Wallin created a high-style Beaux Arts masterpiece of white brick with limestone trim that fit well into the Savannah vocabulary in plan

**Figure 53** George Ferguson Armstrong mansion, 443–451 Bull Street; photograph signed by the architect, Henrik Wallin, 1920. *Courtesy Walter Charlton Hartridge II, Bouhan, Williams and Levy.*

**Figure 54** Interior of the Armstrong mansion by Henrik Wallin; gouache and watercolor by the architect, 1919. *Courtesy Walter Charlton Hartridge II, Bouhan, Williams and Levy.*

and profile. He brought in Austrian woodcarvers and Italian stonemasons, and craftspeople from across the country were at his disposal. The Armstrong mansion is more Italianate than the Frick mansion in New York City; yet English- and French-inspired decorative details abound in an airy combination. The mansion was featured in *The American Architect*, August 6, 1919. The architect made gouache and watercolor drawings of each room for the Armstrongs, illustrating the crisp paneling and classic European-style detail. Thanks to the vast proportions of the central foyer that focuses on the stairwell, and the large size of the rooms, all having wide and high windows, the house remains open and southern in

feeling rather than pretentious and overdone.

Wallin, a native of Sweden, came to the United States to visit sisters in St. Paul, Minnesota. After association with Henry Bacon in the Astor Hotel design in New York, he came to Savannah to assist with the construction of the Liberty Bank, now demolished. He designed the Bull Street Baptist Church (see p. 196) in the Victorian district and the cigar factory on Abercorn and Bryan streets, now the Christ Church Education building.

### 20 West Gaston Street

The Italianate townhouse with arched openings throughout and an arched motif cornice was designed in 1857 by

John S. Norris for William F. Brantly. The facade seems to have lost hood molds over the arched openings.

### 26 East Gaston Street
One of Savannah's finest revival-style houses was built for Mills B. Lane in 1909 after designs by architects Mowbray and Uffinger.

## TROUP SQUARE AND TROUP WARD
(Figure 55)

Troup Square and Troup Ward were laid out in 1851 and named after the Georgia governor from 1823 to 1827 and later U.S. Senator, George Michael Troup, whose family came from Darien on the Altahama River, another small port town designed by Oglethorpe. Because the Civil War interrupted development of the square along Habersham Street, several of the blocks of rowhouses date from after 1870, and some were built on the trust lots. Only here on these Troup Square trust lots do the rowhouses face one another.

Troup Square is one of the smaller squares in the city and has a Victorian-style armillary sphere as its feature. An armillary is an astronomical model used to display relationships among celestial circles. This charming bronze example is mounted on six bronze turtles in a flight of naturalism in the Victorian period when such devices were all the style, as were sundials. Neighbors call this "dog-bone square" because of the attractive cast iron watering fountain for pets.

### 321 Habersham Street
Moses Eastman, a New Hampshire native and silversmith in Savannah, funded the little Gothic church designed by architect John S. Norris and built by John B. Hogg, dedicated in 1851. The Unitarian congregation originally had a church on Oglethorpe Square opposite the Owens–Thomas House. The Unitarian Association did not survive the Civil War in Savannah, and an African-American congregation of Episcopalians bought the building and named it St. Stephens, hon-

oring the first Episcopalian bishop of Georgia. The church was partially dismanteled and rolled through the streets of Savannah to the present site. Now in a twist of fate the Unitarian church is reclaiming its building.

The Reverend John Pierpont, Jr. was the minister, and his brother James was organist and choir director. James Pierpont composed the Christmas song we know as "Jingle Bells," before the abolitionist beliefs of the congregation caused them to have to close the church. Their nephew, J. Pierpont Morgan, became the great financier.

### 410–424 East Macon Street
The row was built in 1872 for John McDonough and Edward Kennedy after designs of J. J. Dooley. Simple entrances with sidelights and paneled doors make the rowhouses modest versions of the Italianate style. Deep bracketed eaves

**Figure 55**  Troup Square, showing the armillary with houses lining the square. *Photograph by Keith Cardwell, courtesy Savannah College of Art and Design.*

surmount a dentiled cornice. These, with pedimented hood molds, are conservative aspects of the usually elaborate style by the 1870s. The flat-fronted row is built low to the ground without basements and no high stoops, unusual in Savannah, signifying that the sandy streets had been paved when the houses were built. Compare this row to the similarly Italianate row nearby at **405–411 East Charlton Street**.

### 313–315 East Charlton Street
The paired houses were, according to title research, built for Lewis F. Cook in 1852. These sidehall houses hark back to an earlier building style with the tall dormers and steep gable ends. The front-door overhangs and the added cast iron are not in keeping with the original building style.

### 405–411 East Charlton Street
This brick row, known as Cohen Row but built for J. J. Dale in 1882, features raised basements with lowered, segmental arched openings throughout that clearly indicate Italianate style. Note the paired staircases that project onto the sidewalk where the stoop is on city property, a peculiar Savannah custom. J. J. Dale, a lumber dealer, built a number of rental rows in Troup Ward.

### 410–424 East Charlton Street (Figure 56)
One of numerous rows built for John J. McDonough, this row of handsome stucco houses features segmental arches and one and one-half stories of bays as well as curved entrance steps. The Italianate-style row dates from 1882, although it appears to have been built much earlier, since the traditional high stoops are continued and the segmental molded arches are quite sophisticated in treatment.

### 408–410 East Jones Street
These paired stuccoed houses with projecting triple-windowed bays were built for lumberman J. J. Dale with William Noonan as builder. The porticos have paired columns on porticos accessed by

**Figure 56** 410–424 East Charlton Street. Here two fine Italianate rows lie across from one another on Troup Square. *Photograph by Goeff DeLorm, courtesy Savannah College of Art and Design.*

new curvilinear steps. The composition is sophisticated and appropriate to the period, but quite dashing for Savannah's staid streets.

### 420–422 East Jones Street
This pair of brick sidehall townhouses with flat fronts and narrow entrances are set low to the ground. Brick dentils in the Greek revival style below a wide row of bricks acting as parapet are the sole decoration. These date from 1867, built for John Asendorf.

### 346–348 Lincoln Street
Paired, brick, flat-front townhouses built for John Staley in 1852 are almost identical to **420–422 East Jones Street**. Both sets have the simple cornice, two stories, no basement, and single doors without sidelights.

### 322–326 East Harris Street
John McDonough, a heavy investor in

this area, had these paired houses built in 1869. Changes through the years have affected the windows, and the front bays were probably added. However, the bracketed cornice, high stoops, and the six-over-six windows here and there recall the date of the houses. Like many Savannah houses, the basement has become commercial, housing the Troup Square Cafe (see p. 201). The mix keeps the historic district lively, provides convenience for neighorhood residents, and can aid in the upkeep of the residence above through rental income.

## CHATHAM SQUARE AND CHATHAM WARD

Chatham Square and Chatham Ward honor William Pitt, prime minister and Earl of Chatham during the Crown colony period. They were laid out in the 1840s along Barnard Street. The area best reflects the Greek revival period of Savannah's golden age during the 1850s. The ward contains one of the city's best blocks of rowhouses, as well as outstanding paired houses. Here are a few of the many reflections of these predominant Savannah types of brick architecture in the Greek revival style.

**Figure 57** Ironwork at the stoops of Gordon Row. *Photograph by Clement Speiden.*

Jones Street, as always, is architecturally notable, as are two of the trust lots on Chatham Square. Only Whitaker Street, which has suffered along its entire length as an automobile corridor and semicommercial street, is weak. The square is now anchored by Barnard Hall at **212 West Taylor Street** (see p. 164); the Savannah College of Art and Design bought and renovated an abandoned school building in the neo-Egyptian revival style.

### 207–209 West Jones Street

Jesse Mount's paired brick houses date from 1856. The high stoops have a wide arched opening below, and the entrances have delicate columns that articulate the sidelights and overlight.

### 211–215 West Jones Street

Bernard Constantine's paired brick townhouses date from 1851 and exhibit the best of the Greek revival style despite mutilation at one entrance. These paired houses are much like the ones at **113–117 West Jones Street,** also built in 1851, for Louisa Nevitt. Constantine had a frame sidehall townhouse built at **321 Barnard Street** in 1845 (see p. 140).

### 101–129 West Gordon Street (Figure 57)

Chatham Ward has one of the city's most noted rows, Gordon Block, an entire block of fifteen three-story plus raised basement stuccoed and brick rowhouses dating from 1853. Before the establishment of the Historic Savannah Foundation, one could be purchased in the 1950s for $1500. The series of graceful, curved steps with their cast iron railings and newel posts repeating down the block present one of Savannah's many pleasures. The handsome Greek revival entrances have narrow sidelights and overlights above. Sandstone lintels surmount the narrow full-length windows at all levels. These long, narrow casement-style windows give the row an elongated, graceful look.

Savannah's fine decorative cast iron was both made locally and imported. As early as 1818, William Jay was importing cast iron from England. The earliest local cast iron was manufactured at the Hermitage plantation of Henry McAlpin, where architect Jay had advocated that he provide it for Savannah. As early as 1821, McAlpin was advertising in the *Daily Georgian,* "elegant railings, balconies or platforms and likewise for tombs or fences cast from newest patterns." In the 1840s, architect Charles Blaney Cluskey, who lived at the Hermitage, used McAlpin's ironwork on the houses he designed and built. When McAlpin died in 1851, the foundry closed.

The Kehoe Ironworks and Rourke's Foundry made some decorative ironwork locally. David and William Rose of Lancastershire, England, opened a foundry on Indian Street in Savannah, on the west side near the river. An 1854 advertisement recommended their iron for "gates at Laurel Grove, Bonaventure and St. Vincent de Paul [cemeteries]." They moved their foundry to be near the canal between West Broad and Fahn streets. After the Civil War, McDonough and Ballentyne was established.

John B. Wickersham and Janes, Beebee and Company sent down their ironwork from New York for Forsyth Park in the 1850s, and Youle and Sabbaton of New York sold "cast iron doors and frames for stores and dwelling houses, also window frames and shutters, as handsome as wood and secure against fire." These items were used for commercial buildings and along Bay Street and River Street for the ranges and rows of cotton-related buildings.

### 443–455 Barnard Street

The Republican Blues, one of Savannah's volunteer military organizations, still extant, financed this row in their capacity as a building and loan association. The Blues Range, built in 1852, is a row of two-and-one-half-story standard Greek revival sidehall townhouses that have lost their original porticos.

**116–118 West Gaston Street** Chatham Ward must be considered a favored ward with all its free-standing sidehall townhouses dating from the 1850s. John Scudder built this for Gustavus Holcombe. The roof was raised in 1885.

**212 West Taylor Street** (Figure 58)
Anchor to Chatham Square is this school in the Egyptian revival style with an Italian tile roof, built in 1901. Known for many years as the Barnard Street Public School, it closed and lay empty. The Savannah College of Art and Design renovated it for classrooms.

## CALHOUN SQUARE AND CALHOUN WARD

Calhoun Square and Calhoun Ward were laid out in 1851 along Abercorn Street to honor the man considered to be the South's greatest spokesman in the U.S. Senate. John C. Calhoun was from South Carolina, a place that historically Georgians either envy or dislike, or both; thus the honor was enormous.

Gaston and Jones lanes have retained some of their original architectural articulation since some stables, carriage houses, or slave quarters remain. East Taylor and East Gordon streets are magnificent.

Calhoun Square is rich because it was laid out precisely in the decade when architecture in Savannah was at its apex in number of building starts. Paired houses, rowhouses, and detached townhouses in the Greek revival style give the ward its character.

**202 East Taylor Street**
The Reverend William Rogers had this detached townhouse built in 1859. The stucco has been removed and the stoop rebuilt. Ironwork supports are not common in Savannah. The Presbyterian minister was quite a businessman, as he also had the paired houses built after John S. Norris's designs on Monterey Square.

**206–210 East Taylor Street**
The fine pair of townhouses were built by and for builder George H. Ash in 1855. The entrances have been altered

over the years. The Ash family was in building for over thirty years in Savannah. These are not different in plan from the pair at **114–116 West Hull Street** (see p. ii) off Orleans Square, built by John H. Ash, although the latter pair is Federal from 1817, and these are almost Italianate from 1855.

**216–218 East Taylor Street**
Ash also built the more reserved pair of flat-front brick sidehall houses in the Greek revival style. For this venture he was in partnership with Francis Grimball in 1854. They are almost identical to **316–318 East Jones Street** in Troup Ward. Notice that both sets of houses and **206–210 East Taylor Street** have a dentiled cornice of multiple rows.

**426 Abercorn Street**
Ash also built this handsome brick sidehall townhouse, for Easton Yonge in 1855. The detached three-bay townhouse in the Greek revival style looks good with the piazza or side gallery, added in 1909. The house was built at the height of Savannah's prestige as a cotton market for Dr. Yonge, but it is best known as the residence of Juliana and Fred Waring, the author of *Cerveau's Savannah*.

**430–432 Abercorn Street** (Figure 59)
This stuccoed detached sidehall townhouse with its double-level piazza and added bay window makes quite a composition on its trust lot. Benjamin J. Wilson had the simple Greek revival house built in 1868. Portico supports are replacements.

**433 Abercorn Street** (Figure 60)
Wesley Monumental Methodist Church, dating from 1876, was often remodeled after Dixon and Carson, architects, had finished the original design. The chateau-like church with its spires is Gothic revival style, inspired by Queen's Kirk, Amsterdam. The Reverend A. M. Wynn conceived the idea of building the church as a fitting monument to brothers John

**Figure 58** Anchor to Chatham Square is this school in the Egyptian revival style, built in 1901, renovated after it closed and lay empty by the Savannah College of Art and Design. *Courtesy Savannah College of Art and Design.*

**Figure 59**    430–432 Abercorn Street. *Photograph by Goeff DeLorm, courtesy Savannah College of Art and Design.*

**Figure 60**  Wesley Monumental Church, Abercorn and Gordon streets. *Courtesy V.& J. Duncan Antique Maps and Prints.*

(1703–1791) and Charles (1707–1788) Wesley. Charles Wesley wrote the words to about 6000 Christian hymns, including "Hark! The Herald Angels Sing," and John Wesley founded the movement that became the Methodist denomination, first in England, but catalyzed "The Great Awakening" in the United States, particularly the South.

### 201–213 East Gordon Street

Massie School is an important architectural and cultural addition to Calhoun Ward. John S. Norris designed the almost-Regency-looking building in 1856. The segmental openings in the three bays are enframed in a shallow segmental arch outline below a plain pediment. This low-budget project is all the better for the restraint. A good job was done in 1872 and 1886 when the wings were added coherently joining the central facade with the flanking pavilions by small hyphens between.

Peter Massie, its benefactor, was a Scotsman, living in New Jersey before becoming a planter in Glynn County, Georgia. He died in 1841, leaving $5000 for the establishment of a school for the poor in Savannah. By 1856 when the building went up, the fund had grown to $14,008.

### 108–116 East Gaston Street (Figure 61)

Lumberman J. J. Dale and David Wells built these bay-front rowhouses in 1884, using Italianate details. One hint of their late date is the setback to contain relatively low stoops and entrances. The facades of **408–410 East Jones Stree**t (see p. 160) in Troup Ward are similar to these, but the buildings are not set back on the lot. Both sets of rowhouses were built for lumberman J. J. Dale, but with different partners, the same years.

## WHITEFIELD SQUARE AND WESLEY WARD

Whitefield Square and Wesley Ward were laid out in 1851 along Habersham Street to honor Savannah's two most fervent dissenting clergymen, both of whom arrived in Oglethorpe's day. John Wesley, the father of the Methodist church worldwide, got his start in Savannah, first as Oglethorpe's secretary, then as rector of Christ Church. He and his brother Charles were so fervent that

**Figure 61** 108–116 East Gaston Street. *Photograph by Scot Hinson.*

they nearly drove Oglethorpe wild, and they had to be sent back to England despite the fact that Oglethorpe was a friend of their father. George Whitefield was the dissenting clergyman, the kind that found fresh fields of endeavor in the New World, ripe for the evangelical movement. He will forever be remembered because of Bethesda, the orphanage he established in Savannah's earliest years.

He worked hard to commemorate himself and he had the orphans work hard, too. They had to help build the dormitory to house themselves in the 1740s. Whitefield is noted less widely for his stand in favor of slavery. He was among those who defied Oglethorpe and appeared at Georgia House before the Trustees of Georgia to insist that they introduce slavery in Georgia. He knew that men would not get rich in Georgia without slaves. He needed money for the good works he hoped to accomplish. Then, too, natives of the New World and of Africa should be brought together under the aegis of the European Christians, he thought, so they could be saved.

Whitefield Square and Wesley Ward have houses dating from the 1850s, but there is a gap in building during the Civil War. Post–Civil War and late Victorian or Queen Anne frame houses dating from the 1870s and later fill the tithing lots on Taylor and Gordon streets. This return to frame building materials was a presage of the Victorian period that would develop about the turn of the century south of Gaston Street.

Savannah started out as a frame city in 1733, as there were no brick kilns and imported bricks were expensive. Frame construction was logical since the land had to be cleared of its pine and cypress trees to prepare the city lots. Now at Wesley Ward and Whitefield Square, named after two Trustee-period settlers, Savannahians began to build houses of frame construction in great numbers

again. First, the swamps and pine forests southward around Darien were being cleared and lumber was cheap. Second, the industrial revolution had brought saws that made jigsaw work or sawn wood parts for the wood houses. Pattern books were available to the builders, and the projected owner could select from decorative patterns the wood parts he wanted applied to his frame residence. Many houses in Wesley Ward are covered with cypress or pine weatherboard, and have galleries or stoops and entrances made of the wood jigsaw work. These wood houses do not have high stoops because the sandy streets were being covered over with brick or pavement. Galleries crossing the fronts of buildings and returning around the sides brought the inhabitants outside or offered a breeze unavailable with just a stoop or in rowhouses. There are Queen Anne single-family houses. Quadruple rowhouses of frame construction are found built low to the ground. There are series of matching or coordinated single-family frame dwellings built next to one another showing that they were probably rental houses or built for members of a single family.

Wesley Ward is just behind Temple Mickve Israel. Whether that had anything to do with it or not, there were a number of Jewish property owners here having rental rows built after the town got back on its feet following the Civil War.

### 401–405 East Jones Street
There are houses built just as the ward was laid out, like these paired Greek revival houses dating from 1856, with their projecting pedimented cornices over the windodws, almost identical to the houses George Ash built in the adjacent ward. Charles Barnwall and Sabra Ulmer commissioned these.

### 412–414 East Taylor Street
George Ash's work is documented here in Wesley Ward with these paired townhouses built in 1855. They are the same sidehall type of paired houses the family

**Figure 62**  Gazebo in Whitefield Square showing the 1880s frame houses that line the square.
*Photograph by Keith Cardwell, courtesy Savannah College of Art and Design.*

had been building since the Federal style of the early 1800s, but now in the Greek revival style.

### 302 East Gordon Street at Lincoln Street (Figure 63)

Beth Eden Baptist Church was designed by Henry Urban, architect, in 1893 in the neo-Gothic style. Urban was active in Savannah from 1892 to 1905. He had come to Savannah to supervise the rebuilding of the Presbyterian church for architect William G. Preston after the fire of 1899, and he designed the old Desoto Hotel, demolished in 1966 for the Desoto Hilton. He was supervising architect for the east wing of Bethesda Orphanage and the Independent Presbyterian Sunday School, both in 1894. The qualified architect, from Frankfurt, Germany, studied at the Berlin Institute of Art and worked in Berlin and Paris before associating with Preston in Boston, where he found a bride. The little Beth Eden church folds itself onto its containing lot, where a series of deep pediments, crenelated bands, and other Gothic revival motifs add charm to the ward.

### 414–420 East Gordon Street

Wood rowhouses in the carpenter-Italianate style here were built by R. K. Bragdon, builder in 1888 for Abraham Samuels. Porches alternate with projecting triple window bays to create a rhythm emphasized at the roofline, with the wide wood band articulating the bracket course.

### 415–419 East Gordon Street

Wesley Ward even has a storehouse, first built as a house financed by the Workmen and Traders Loan and Building Association in 1886 for Casper Langllia. It was converted to a storehouse in 1895.

### 421 Habersham Street at East Taylor Street

The first church on this trust lot was a frame church built as the First Congregational Church in 1869 during Reconstruction. Missionary students from New England had come to Savannah to the Beach Institute to teach the ex-slaves. In 1895 this small Gothic church was built on the same site for the Congregationalists that came to Savannah. Inexpensive but effective in its simplicity, in the

**Figure 63**   Beth Eden Baptist Church on Habersham and Gordon streets. *Photograph by Keith Cardwell, courtesy Savannah College of Art and Design.*

Congregationalist fashion, the church has a steeply pitched roof covered with tin and a facade that features a large pointed arch stained-glass window beside a bell tower that serves as a church entrance.

### 408 East Gaston Street (Figure 64)

One of the most effective residences on a street filled with eclectic examples of fine single-family homes is this house, built for Laura Jones in 1892. The whimsical Queen Anne house has Gothic window frames and a large turret with portholes and a bracketed cornice beneath a turret roof that looks like a bell, not a bell tower. Paired brackets that look like pediments and wrap around balconies add a whimsical effect to the charming residence.

### 308–310 East Gaston Street

On the same block, Mrs. John Hopkins had these rental apartments built in 1890. The eclectic brick building mixes metaphors, romanesque, and chateau-esque motifs with Dutch-style front gables. This is a double house, with a random floor plan and unmatched projecting elements in the facade. Mrs. Hopkins abandoned the traditional paired houses that were the hallmark of the Greek revival and Italianate buildings in Savannah.

**Figure 64**    408 East Gaston Street. *Photograph by Keith Cardwell, courtesy Savannah College of Art and Design.*

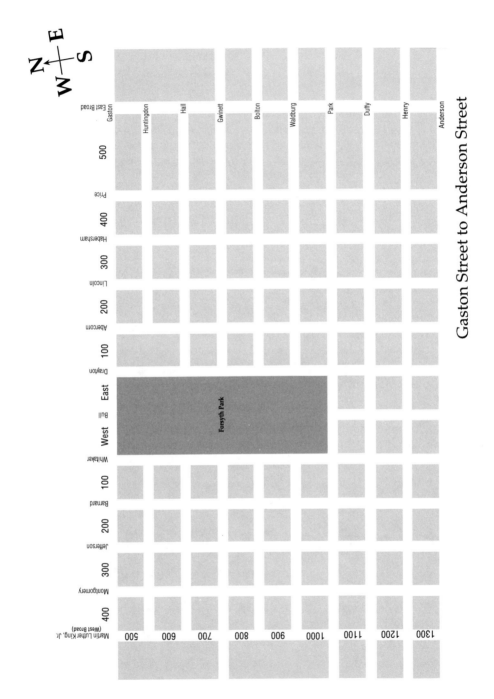

Gaston Street to Anderson Street

# 6

## THE STREETCAR
## SUBURBS

### SOUTH OF GASTON STREET:
### AROUND FORSYTH PARK

Bull Street once terminated at Gaston Street, where Forsyth Park provides a grand finale for the old historic district. William B. Hodgson conceived the idea for the park when he realized that city-owned land was available along with a German landscape designer who had moved to Savannah. The land is part of a series of 4½-acre garden plots, a leasehold that had been assigned to each city tithing lot under Oglethorpe. Wilhelm Christian Bischoff, a Bavarian who had been a landscape gardener for the Nymphenburg Palace gardens near Munich, laid out the park using sophisticated European landscape gardening concepts not yet used in the United States.

Besides the parterre gardens that served as its centerpiece, the park acquired fountains and statues through the decades in the Savannah tradition of outdoor furniture. The cast iron fountain, dating from 1858, is one of Savannah's most popular pieces of street furniture. Janes, Beebe and Company of New York manufactured it along with its twin, located in Cuzco, Peru. Part of the original design was an iron railing, manufactured by John B. Wickersham of New York, to enclose the 10-acre Forsyth Place . This was junked at the end of the century when open spaces became an essential idea in park and lawn design.

Savannahians revere their military heroes, as they concern themselves with military history. Perhaps it's a reverence for lost causes because Savannah was lost twice, to the British, who captured it in 1778 and held it against a siege in 1779, and to Union troops in December 1864. The monument to the

Confederacy, a gift of G.W. J. DeRenne, descendent of military leader Noble Jones from Oglethorpe's day, was designed by British sculptor David Richards in 1874. Robert Reid of Montreal crafted the piece of Canadian sandstone in Canada and brought it to Savannah by ship. Two busts represent General Lafayette McLaws and Brigadier General Francis S. Bartow. Bartow was killed at the first battle of Bull Run, leading the first Savannah company of 106 men in response to Jefferson Davis's call for troops in May 1861. The bronze soldier that terminates the park's southern extension end commemorates Georgians who died in the Spanish-American War.

The park now terminates at Park Avenue and encompasses 26 acres. The southern extension was made possible when the city acquired title from the federal government to the military station or cantonment established there in 1827. This old parade ground of the Savannah Militia was incorporated into the park so that it runs seven blocks deep, from East Gaston Street to East Park Avenue, centered along the Bull Street line, two blocks wide. While the local citizens referred to the park for years as Hodgson's Park, it was officially named in honor of Governor John Forsyth, who had been a U.S. Senator from Georgia and secretary of state (1834–1841) during the Jackson and Van Buren administrations.

The last three wards that terminated at Gaston Street, Wesley, Calhoun, and Chatham wards, had gobbled up the city commons. Forsyth Park obviated the need for the continuation of the traditional wards with public squares, trust lots, and tithing blocks with their lanes. These key elements in Savannah's incremental method of growth were abandoned for typical building squares south of Gaston Street.

The streets bordering Forsyth Park comprise Savannah's Richardson Romanesque and eclectic-style neighborhood of the late nineteenth century (Figures 1 and 2). Clustered along these streets between Gaston, Park, Montgomery, and East Broad streets are the more expensive houses to go up between Gaston Street and Victory Drive.

**Figure 2** Terra-cotta detail in Richardson Romanesque style. *Photograph by Keith Cardwell, courtesy Savannah College of Art and Design.*

**304 East Gaston Street, Wesley Ward**
(Figure 3)
Confederate veteran Captain John David Hopkins had this cross-shaped house, unusual for Savannah, built in 1869. Front bay windows that project below a pair of windows with decorative drip-stones are crowned by a front gable with deep overhanging eaves.

**501 Whitaker Street** (see pp. viii–xi)
The Georgia Historical Society building dates from 1876, designed by Detlef Lienau, whose first clients in Savannah were the Telfair sisters. The building is called W. G. Hodgson Hall, after the scholar who came to Savannah from his diplomatic post in Tunisia as Margaret Telfair's husband. The three-tiered front elevation is conservatively classic in design, suggestive of the architect's Beaux Arts training.

**503 Whitaker Street, Forsyth Ward**
(Figures 4 and 5)
The center-hall mansion, built in 1883 for Guerrard Heywood by Alfred Snedeker, was set back in the new tradition. It is crowned by a Second Empire roof, beneath which double-front galleries curve in outline, unusual in Savannah.

**513 Whitaker Street, Forsyth Ward**
(Figure 6)
Laurence McNeil commissioned G. L. Norman to design this florid neoclassical revival mansion in the then-fashionable yellow brick, with its projecting portico to look like the Roman Temple to the Vestal Virgins. Corinthian columns and a cast iron cresting running above the entablature give the house an elegant profile.

**Figure 3** 304 East Gaston Street. *Photograph by Goeff DeLorm, courtesy Savannah College of Art and Design.*

**Figure 4**   Magnolia Place Inn, 503 Whitaker Street. *Photograph by Clement Speiden.*

**Figure 5**   Magnolia Place Inn, 503 Whitaker Street. This old photograph shows the original paired columns on the front gallery. *Courtesy Magnolia Place Inn.*

**Figure 6**   513 Whitaker Street. *Photograph by Clement Speiden.*

### 803 Whitaker Street, Lloyd Ward

Architect Alfred S. Eichberg designed this spectacular but atypical Queen Anne house for James S. Wood in 1891. Hard brick and terra-cotta above a foundation of rough-faced Georgia marble and the sculptural terra-cotta chimney pots create contrasts of texture.

### 226 East Huntingdon Street, Stephens Ward (Figures 7 and 8)

This Alfred Eichberg design in the Romanesque style was built in 1890 for Irwin S. and George W. Tiedeman. The busy roofline features a hexagonal tower that contrasts with semiround turrets. Chimneys sprout with fancy brickwork and clash with pediments and battlement themes.

### 402–410 East Huntingdon Street, Stephens Ward (Figure 9)

The McMillan brothers built a number of eye-catching and monumental rental rows with decorative facades in the European style around Forsyth Park in the 1880s and 1890s. These include **302–304 East Huntingdon Street.** This one is Ruskinian in style with neo-Gothic motifs on the gallery arches and a multigabled roofline.

### 205–207 East Hall Street, Stephens Ward (Figure 10)

An eclectic combination of motifs, Moorish, classical, and Italianate are combined in this monumental mansion built in 1872 for George W. Saussy and Bridget Clark.

**Figure 7** 226 East Huntingdon Street. *Photograph by Keith Cardwell, courtesy Savannah College of Art and Design.*

**Figure 8** 226 East Huntingdon Street. *Photograph by Keith Cardwell, courtesy Savannah College of Art and Design.*

**Figure 9**   402–410 East Huntingdon Street. *Photograph by Keith Cardwell, courtesy Savannah College of Art and Design.*

**Figure 10**   205–207 East Hall Street. *Photograph by Scot Hinson.*

### 208 East Hall Street, Stephens Ward
(Figure 11)

The long-side elevation of this eclectic-style masonry house is as decorative and handsome as the front elevation. The Italianate motifs seem to have won the battle of styles in the house built for George W. Mills in 1881.

### 213 East Hall Street, Stephens Ward
(Figure 12)

Julius C. Le Hardy wanted a traditional center-hall floor plan in 1884 when he had his Italianate mansion built. A projecting central element behind a front gallery results in a sculptural effect. The whole is framed in quoins and a heavy projecting roofline. The ironwork now supporting the gallery is unusual and outstanding.

### 225 East Hall Street (Figure 13)

George Johnson Baldwin did a lot for Savannah. First he brought architect William G. Preston to Savannah and secured for him the commission for the new city hall. Baldwin, a Savannah boy, had gone to the Massachusetts Institute of Technology after the Civil War, where he met Preston. Second, the enterprising Baldwin was the first president of the Savannah Electric and Power Company. This company owned the first streetcars that launched Savannah's first suburbs.

Preston designed this flamboyant house in the Richardson Romanesque

**Figure 11** 208 East Hall Street. *Photograph by Keith Cardwell, courtesy Savannah College of Art and Design.*

**Figure 12** 213 East Hall Street. *Photograph by Keith Cardwell, courtesy Savannah College of Art and Design.*

**Figure 13**   225 East Hall Street. *Photograph by Keith Cardwell, courtesy Savannah College of Art and Design.*

style in 1887 for Lucy and George Baldwin. It embodies most of the characteristics of the style: smooth, hard imported bricks; a complex footprint and floor plan; a busy roofline; massive round arches; turrets; rondels; rinceaux; and terra-cotta decoration in medieval motifs and waffle patterns. Patterned brickwork combined with terra-cotta create a medley of textures and warm tones.

### 700 Drayton Street (Figure 14)

Architect Alfred S. Eichberg designed this massive hard-brick mansion in the Chateauesque style in 1887. The warm red tones of the hard brick and terra-cotta surfaces and the coned turret, combined with the palm trees of Savannah, cause the mansion to resemble some fanciful medieval castle, true to the romantic movement that came late to Savannah.

### 223 East Gwinnett Street at Lincoln Street, White Ward (Figure 15)

Architect William G. Preston, a native of Boston, designing in Savannah for years, seemed to be nostalgic or southern when in 1891 he designed this raised house for William Hardee, former Confederate general and West Point

**Figure 14** 700 Drayton Street. *Photograph by Keith Cardwell, courtesy Savannah College of Art and Design.*

**Figure 15** 223 East Gwinnett Street. *Photograph by Keith Cardwell, courtesy Savannah College of Art and Design.*

graduate. He combined local and international design features. Double galleries are supported by clustered columns beneath a bracketed cornice, both Italianate customs, combined with the latest innovations in the Queen Anne style, a tall English-style chimney, a turret, and much more.

Queen Anne characteristics as they appeared in frame construction in Savannah included, among exterior features, bay windows, wraparound porches with jigsaw decorations, and decorative cornices created out of components from local millwork pattern books and sash door and blind factories. Gingerbread and brackets abounded until 1900 across front and side porches; rear porches were latticed. Between the brackets and the cornice line, decorative cutout designs were screened to provide ventilation in the attic area. Decorative butt shingles and pressed metal ornamented some Queen Anne houses. Entrances had multipanel doors, often with stained or beveled glass. Multiple small square lights decorated the upper sashes of windows; small round or diamond-shaped upper sashes were also common with a single light below. This house resembles a hip-roof plantation house, with a turret added as an afterthought. The house is far more pretentious than most houses in the vicinity.

Complex multiple forms that juxtapose to create asymmetrical mass characterize these multistoried houses with steep gables, turrets, and massive chimneys below irregular rooflines. A variety of building materials combine in a plethora of surfaces to match an abundance of shapes organized to create a facade.

Interior decoration in the Queen Anne houses focused on the entrance hall. Etched glass and later more expensive leaded glass surrounded doorways, and some doors had panels of etched or leaded glass. Stained glass lit stairwells, some selected from the *Yellow Pine Catalogs*, which offered mail order decorative details, or customers could order them from local lumberyards. Fancy newel posts might have had gas or electric light fixtures as part of the design.

### 305 East Gwinnett Street, White Ward

This sidehall frame single-family house dates from 1888, built for Albert C. Bacon. Two-story bays extend to the roof to meet overhanging bracketed eaves in the Italianate tradition. Many houses almost identical to this one can be found in the Victorian districts, such as that at **123 West Gwinnett Street,** built for George W. Parish in 1887. The other end of the spectrum of the Italianate style is its application to the frame two-bay shotgun at **909 Montgomery Street.**

### 111 West Gwinnett Street, Lloyd Ward

This two-story center-hall house was built for William Estill, Jr. in 1882. The Italianate features are the handsome one-story bays topped with balustrades and the simple brackets below the overhanging eaves. This house is low and boxlike, also an Italianate feature.

### 215 West Gwinnett Street, Lloyd Ward

This 1885 turreted house built for C. H. Dorsett has all the attributes of a good Queen Anne house interpreted in wood. The deep cornice band is its most decorative exterior feature. Inside, the second parlor preserves remnants of brilliantly colored ceiling papers. Both gas and electric connections can be seen in ceiling medallions and walls. Illumination by gas continued from 1884 until about 1912. Some parlor fixtures that were manufactured for only about twelve years combine gas and electric fittings. The electricity was at first untrustworthy, or thought to be so, and the usual gas fittings were used as backup on the same chandeliers. Jacob Kraft's 1913 house at **301–305 West Duffy Street,** Gue Ward, electrified at the outset, retains many original fixtures.

# MORE STREETCAR SUBURBS
## TO ANDERSON STREET

Beyond Forsyth Place at Gwinnett Street, the original 1851 section of Forsyth Park, the real working-class streetcar suburb began. Acres of houses of frame construction remain today to reveal the variety and ingenuity used in the design and decoration of inexpensive turn-of-the-century housing. Bolton, Waldburg, and Park streets came first, then the area from Duffy Street to Anderson Street was developed, now called the Victorian district, but houses of the same style continued south from Anderson Street to Victory Drive, now officially the south Victorian district. 33rd through 36th streets between Abercorn and Barnard streets illustrate the Savannah late Victorian look, where the picturesque quality of wood late Victorian architecture blends with Savannah's particular environmental essence. 36th Street retains its brick paving, and live oaks hung with moss arch over the street to create the effect of an enclosed passageway. Thomas Square, bound by Duffy Street and East Broad Street, presents an effort to continue the traditional squares of old Savannah. Dixon Park was created by city purchase of land in 1906. The nearby railroad cuts a diagonal swathe through the south Victorian district, adding a touch of industrialization to the Victorian districts. St. Paul's Academy for Boys in the square bound by Jefferson, Montgomery, and 38th and 39th streets illustrates the neighborhood custom whereby large institutional buildings of brick or stone anchor the surrounding neighborhood. St. Paul's was once part of the Greek Orthodox complex, and the church, along with an adjacent city park, enhances the area's potential.

In 1867 the city passed an ordinance authorizing horse-drawn carriage railways. The electric streetcar line introduced by George J. Baldwin was hailed as a great improvement in 1888, and Baldwin is responsible for the large patterned brick complex on Gwinnett Street extended to the east. He probably arranged the commission for architect William G. Preston to build the monumentally massed buildings where the streetcars were stored and where the repair yards and electric works were located, and later the waterworks (Figure 16).

Between 1888 and 1920, a vast streetcar suburb of frame houses developed from Gwinnett Street south to Victory Drive, bound by the traditional West and East Broad streets. The streetcar suburb of Savannah was not plotted by the city until 1884, long after Bull Street's extension had become the paved high ground access to southern and eastern Chatham County. As early as 1920, however, streetcar lines like the one on Whitaker Street were being removed, since the automobile had become the dominant mode of transportation.

As early as 1873, city regulations had allowed interior water closets to replace privies. The Mutual Gas and Light Company began to lay gas mains in

**Figure 16**   Gwinnett Street extended. City water works, previously streetcar storage and electric works, designed perhaps by William G. Preston for electric streetcar developer George J. Baldwin. *Photograph by Keith Cardwell, courtesy Savannah College of Art and Design.*

the Victorian districts in January 1884. Two electricity supply companies came to Savannah in 1882. The absence of fire zoning made simple its establishment as a huge district of frame construction. The suburb's development also paralleled the clear-cutting of the pine forests and swamplands along the Altahama and Ogeechee rivers, a time when lumber cost next to nothing.

The Victorian district was the first urban sector to benefit from the Oglethorpe-assigned 45-acre farm or tillage acreage assigned to each tithing lot dweller inside the city. The farm lots extended from present-day Gwinnett Street southward 3 miles, to the east nearly to the Wilmington River, and to the west 4 miles. The development of farm lots was begun in 1843 by James Frew, a dealer in lumber and building supplies, and Amos Webb. Their development efforts failed because of the inaccessibility of the area. Much of the Victorian district was the Drouillard plantation, subdivided in 1847 by the Drouillard grandchildren. The master house remains at **2422 Abercorn Street.**

By the 1880s, though, development went apace. Mutual loan associations and railroad companies with housing needs for their workers helped develop the Victorian districts. The German-American Loan and Building Company aided German and German-Russian immigrants. The Home Building Company, a local agency for cheap loans for frame houses costing $5000 and under, used plans in *Shoppell's Modern Houses*, a Philadelphia publication that provided house plans. *The Savannah Morning News* of 1885 indicated that with 10 percent down, a $2000 house was available. The association built, then financed, the building, with the buyer being given ten years to pay for the house. The minimum sum was $22.50 a month for the 120 months. At the end of that time the owner had paid $2700, exclusive of the first deposit of $200. The purchaser paid only $900 more during the ten years than he would have paid in rent under the then-current terms and conditions.

Acres of these inexpensive frame houses, single, paired, or in rows, dotted the newly laid-out blocks. Besides the 20-foot house setback, the city demanded a 7-foot tree area between the sidewalk and street so that brick streets would quickly become tree-lined in the tropical climate of Savannah. Fences instead of stoops, and frame construction instead of brick, set the visual image of the Victorian district. The central focus for each enclave of residences was a brick institutional building. Public or parochial schools, hospitals, or churches, together with the yards around them, anchored each neighborhood, replacing the concept of squares as anchors for the surrounding buildings.

The Georgia Infirmary, said to be the oldest asylum-hospital in the United States established solely for African-Americans, moved into its Greek revival institution in 1837. Mary Telfair's will established the Telfair Hospital, designed in 1886 by Fay and Eichberg at **17 East Park Avenue.**

At **14 West Anderson Street** at the corner of Bull Street, the Lawton Memorial was built as a civic auditorium, now St. Paul's Greek Orthodox church (Figure 17). The Benedictine order started projects in Savannah in 1874 when they built a school on Habersham Street between 31st and 32nd streets. The Little Sisters of the Poor came to Savannah in 1890 and established the buildings at 37th and Lincoln streets in 1894. With its beautiful chapel, the complex is slated for renovation as a home for the elderly after an avoidable fire nearly ruined it.

**Figure 17** St. Paul's Greek Orthodox Church, 14 West Anderson Street, formerly Lawton Memorial Auditorium; photogravure from Charles Edgeworth Jones, *Art Work of Savannah and Augusta* (Chicago: Gravure Illustration Company, 1902). *Courtesy V. & J. Duncan Antique Maps and Prints.*

A Carnegie library designed by J. De Bruyn Kops that provided one of these anchors was built in the Prairie style in 1914. It emphased the horizontal and was a style popular in the midwest and brought here by magazines. The Savannah Public Library, begun in 1903, moved into a new library in the 2000 block of Bull Street, designed by H. W. Witcover, architect of City Hall, in 1915 and provides a focus for the vicinity, along with the adjacent open square.

Plans and elevations for inexpensive homes afforded by railroad workers and City Hall clerical workers could be ordered from advertisements in the newspapers. John Henry Newson, an architect in Cleveland, Ohio, offered "Homes of Character" in 1913.

*Shoppell's Modern Houses*, published in Philadelphia, gives Savannahian J. J. Waring as a reference. The house at **203 East Gwinnett Street** is design number 521 in *Shoppell's Modern Houses*. Most of these offerings were Queen Anne style with an open interior plan. The Co-operative Plan Association from New York also provided plans.

*W. H. Hughes and Sons Catalog*, the *Yellow Pine Catalogs*, and in 1906 the first *Sweet's Catalog*. provided details for the Victorian district. In 1884, Andrew Hanley's store on Whitaker Street provided an array of doors, sashes, blinds, moldings, stair rails, balusters, newel posts, oils, varnishes, and plain and decorative wallpaper. After 1896, tiles often came from the Beaver Falls Art Tile Company of Beaver Falls, Pennsylvania, but some were from Zanesville, Ohio, where the popular arts and crafts pottery was made.

By the time a 182-acre-area working-class streetcar suburb was fully built up, between Gwinnett and Anderson and from East Broad to West Broad streets, it had close to 1000 buildings of historic value that reflect the life of a southern port city from the 1880s through World War I.

The houses are frame vernacular interpretations of the high styles of the period, built mostly without architects. Builders sometimes followed the catalog plans exactly; however, Savannah builders often lifted a few ideas or used the jigsaw-patterned wood they could order but continued to follow traditional Savannah house types or floor plans.

Paired houses, a Savannah trademark, remained popular, but now with a return to wood construction. They harken back in appearance to the Federal paired houses of the early nineteenth century. Those in the Victorian district have applied wood decoration made possible by the steam power of the industrial revolution. The familiar six-bay two-story facade was garnished with the varied decorative styles made popular by late-nineteenth-century pattern books. The same facade was used repeatedly in various wards. For example, paired turrets above two-story bayed rooms flanking recessed central entrances appear with minimum variations at **405–407 East Gaston Street, 608–610 Habersham Street,** and **301–303 Henry Street** (see p. 189).

The sidehall plan for single-family dwellings remained the preferred house type, built of wood. The same sidehall plan used in the old historic district rowhouses is repeated in frame rows throughout the Victorian districts. Citizens continued to prefer these traditional conservative floor plans despite the books with a rich variety of floor plans and the new complex house footprints with rooms around a large entrance "parlor," complete with mantelpiece. It is surprising to find that about 700 of the Victorian districts' frame houses are single-family dwellings.

Simple frame center-hall cottages continued to be popular. The most modest houses in the districts were doubles, one or two stories, having two bays for each unit, two-room houses without halls. Storehouses are the rule for corner lots. The buildings changed in appearance stylistically through applied ornament, usually sawn work, bay windows, and turrets.

The Waring family's development of much of the northeastern side of the Victorian district in Lee and Waring wards illustrates how the vast sea of frame houses came to fill block after block, then acre after acre of former farm lots. James J. Waring (1829–1888), a Harvard-educated physician, liberal in thought by family tradition, advanced in his thinking because of education and travel, is responsible for draining the swamps surrounding what is now the Victorian district, to eliminate the mosquito breeding sources. He advocated indoor plumbing and the eradication of the outdoor privy, a source for mosquito breeding and bacteria collection.

As early as 1865, Dr. Waring had several cottages built in Portland, Maine, and shipped to Savannah. He called them "Democratic houses" and had them put up near the Savannah, Albany and Gulf Railroad for workers' houses. In 1866 he bought a tract bounded on the south by Anderson Street and on the north by Fairlawn, the remnant of an old plantation site, for $10,000. He stipulated in the lot deeds of conveyance that owners must set the front line of their buildings back 25 feet from the street. This was the first time that setbacks became a consideration in Savannah's urban planning.

Seeing that the advent of the horse-drawn trolley system would make logical the extension of the city, Waring wanted to develop his former farm lot in 1871. He traded rights-of-way with the city by opening streets in exchange for public drainage construction, an essential request since drainage was critical to the area. Water mains were installed in 1871.

Other major developers of the Victorian district include Charles Seiler, born in Ronneburg, Altenburg, Germany, in 1839. Arriving in Savannah just before the Civil War, he opened a butcher shop in the city market on Ellis Square. In addition to a saloon, which he bought in 1879 for $5500, records show that the successful immigrant owned farm lots, bogs, and woodlands.

Louis A. Fallgant, a native Savannahian active in civic affairs and a prominent physician and alderman, constructed a number of small workers' cottages in the south Victorian district. Other developers are remembered by the wards that bear their names.

### 918 Abercorn Street at Waldburg Street, White Ward

This Queen Anne house featuring flamboyant porches and an oversized corner tower was built in 1896 as rental property for George A. Mercer, lawyer and president of the Board of Education. Harvey Granger, who lived in the house in 1898, developed Chatham Crescent in 1910, one of Savannah's first "automobile suburbs," in which he included a public park system. The house became head-quarters for Savannah Landmarks Re-habilitation Project, Inc., which has initiated rehabilitation of several hun-dred houses in the area.

### 217–225 East Bolton Street, White Ward

Rowhouses continued to be built, but they are of wood construction in the Victorian districts, like these examples in the Italianate style built in 1896 for Margaret Flaherty.

### 313 East Bolton Street Between Lincoln Street and Habersham Street

This clapboard one-story house was built in 1885 for and by John Joseph McMahon, contractor and native of County Clare, Ireland. It was a center-hall cottage, measuring 32 feet by 52 feet 6 inches, a facade decorated with jigsaw work. When he died in 1935, McMahon was the oldest living member of the Irish Jasper Greens, a military company in Savannah.

### 114–118 West Bolton Street, Lloyd Ward

This elegant Second Empire house was built in 1871 for Isabella Van Horn and Eliza Roberts. Typical of the style, the doorway is set back from the main facade. Deep cornices with wood brack-ets support the eaves below the mansard roof. Classical ornament is seen in pan-eled corner boards.

### 213 West Bolton Street Between Barnard Street and Jefferson Street, Lloyd Ward (Figure 18)

One of the oldest houses in the Victorian districts, the L-shaped cottage is the only example left of its kind, built in 1868 for William B. Sturtevant, commission mer-chant. The floor plan and the wood verge board recall Andrew Jackson Downing's country house plans adver-tised by his book in many editions from 1849. Ironwork craftsman Ivan Bailey renovated this house at one time.

### 10 West Duffy Street, Gallie Ward
(Figure 19)

Built in 1877 for Charles A. Drayton, this small center-hall cottage illustrates con-servative vernacular Italianate elements like the brackets beneath overhanging eaves and the spindle course between columns on the front porch.

### 14 and 16 West Duffy Street, Gallie Ward (Figures 20 and 21)

The Home Building Company financed the construction of these two almost

Figure 18  213 West Bolton Street.
*Photograph by Keith Cardwell, courtesy Savannah College of Art and Design.*

**Figure 19** 10 West Duffy Street. *Photograph by Keith Cardwell, courtesy Savannah College of Art and Design.*

**Figure 20** 14 and 16 West Duffy Street. *Photograph by Goeff DeLorm, courtesy Savannah College of Art and Design.*

**Figure 21** 14 West Duffy Street, detail.
*Photograph by Geoff DeLorm, courtesy Savannah College of Art and Design.*

identical frame Queen Anne houses in 1890 and 1891. Projecting elements, bays, a variety of galleries having decorative bands between columns, and wide decorative cornice bands combine to create a symphony in wood.

Such houses were as fanciful and fulsome inside as they were on the facade. Picture moldings were standard late Victorian installations, gilded in the more expensive houses. Borders, friezes, and dados as well as ceiling papers were popular in the 1880s and 1890s. At the turn of the century, white-on-white ceiling papers with an overall floral design came into vogue. Overall floral patterns in wallpapers as well as geometric patterns in vivid colors were popular. Decorative fireplace tiles became standard in both inexpensive and more costly houses.

The Queen Anne style, popular in the Victorian district between 1885 and 1905, originated in England in the 1860s, based on rural medieval traditions. The Philadelphia Centennial Exposition of 1876 popularized the style in the United States.

**107–109 West Duffy Street, Gallie Ward** (Figure 22)
The Burrel L. Boulineau house, built in 1867, illustrates how various decorative motifs can be combined successfully to create a fanciful design that is yet formalized. Greek revival entrance, Gothic front bay, Italianate cornice, and stick-style front pediments are used discriminately. Burrel L. Boulineau, master of machinery of the Central of Georgia Railroad, borrowed $3000 from the Workingman's Mutual Loan Association to build the house in 1867 and paid it back at the rate of $30 a month. It is the eastern half of a two-story paired house. The clapboard sidehall house measures 23 feet 3 inches by 63 feet 3 inches.

**Figure 22** 107–109 West Duffy Street.
*Photograph by Geoff DeLorm, courtesy Savannah College of Art and Design.*

### 201–209 East Duffy Street, White Ward

Two units of three-story wooden row-houses were built in 1886 for DeWitt C. Bacon, lumber dealer. The plan is side-hall, two rooms deep, in two stories plus a full brick basement. They are characterized by three-story bay windows, a molded cornice with wood dentils, and wide, bracketed eaves, and a standing-seam hip roof. The entrances are protected with a projecting overhang that becomes part of the rhythmical progression of forms. The original front steps are wood on brick piers, trimmed with turned balusters and square newels.

### 210–212 East Duffy, White Ward

These frame paired houses date from 1891, built for Maria W. Sexton and Robert Beytagh. The rectangular frame building with small dentils at the cornice does not look much different from the Federal type except for the jigsaw work on the front gallery at the first level and the two-over-two windows.

### 517–519 East Duffy Street

Clues to this simple colonial revival building lie in the triple windows, columns on pedestals, and uneven fenestration. Vernacular examples of the colonial revival are simple, boxlike structures with one or more "colonial" details. Palladian windows and multilite upper sashes with single-lite lower sash are typical.

### 220–228 East Henry Street, White Ward (Figure 23)

Three identical Second Empire frame sidehall houses date from 1881, built for John O. Smith. The multiplication of a dramatic house style adds to the effect. One-level front bay windows, recessed entrances, and the ever-present mansard roof pierced with dormers characterizes the style.

The Second Empire style, popular in the Victorian district between 1870 and 1890, was brought to America from

**Figure 23**  220–228 East Henry Street. This one of three Second Empire style houses in a row were built for John O. Smith in 1881.
*Photograph by Keith Cardwell, courtesy Savannah College of Art and Design.*

France, where it flourished during the reign of Napoleon III. The few examples in Savannah appear Italianate in style, with a mansard roof added, providing a full story at the attic level via a double-pitched roof with a steep lower slope. Profiles may be straight, concave, or convex, and the roof is pierced with a variety of dormer widows. Slate shingles multicolored and arranged in patterns cover the roofs.

### 301–303 East Henry Street, White Ward

Henry Seeman had these paired houses built in 1890. Queen Anne in style, the buildings have pedimented and porched central elements, flanked with curving turrets in a Moorish motif roof. There are other examples of the same facade in the area.

### 521 East Henry Street

A two-story house has battered porch piers, wood shingles, and exposed structural members that suggest the bungalow style. The deep eaves are Italianate, but the double and triple windows that have numerous lites in lozenge form above single panes are City Beautiful or Colonial revival style.

### 525 East Henry Street

Percy Sugden was the architect in 1915, and William Ayres the builder, for this house that features neoclassical revival details. Neoclassical revival, a term that loosely covers Georgian revival, Edwardian, and the many gable-roofed vernacular buildings with classical columns and details, flourished in the Victorian district between 1900 and 1929.

### 115 East Park Avenue, Cuthbert Ward

This small, two-story, tin-roofed, gabled-end house with brick chimneys at each end dates from 1870 and was built for Ann Hopkins. It illustrates the frame vernacular Greek revival center-hall house.

The Greek revival style, so popular in the older section of the city during Savannah's richest years before the Civil War, provided the precedent for the early houses of the new working-class suburb, vernacular interpretations in wood construction, continuing in popularity into the twentieth century.

### 119 West Park Avenue, Gallie Ward

This brick center-hall Greek revival raised villa is unusual in Savannah and perhaps is the only example of its type in the city. Although it looks much earlier, it was built between 1865 and 1870.

### 118 East Waldburg Street, Cuthbert Ward (Figure 24)

This Italianate sidehall townhouse dates from 1886, built for Catherine Ward. The Italianate style, influenced by the rural architecture of northern Italy, was introduced in the United States in the 1830s but did not abound in Savannah until the late 1850s. Then it took hold and became a standard vernacular style in frame construction.

### 414–416 East Waldburg Street Between Habersham Street and Price Street

These masonry rowhouses with marble trim date from 1900. Use of tile and the curvilinear outline of the gable over the bay window recalls the Spanish revival style.

**Figure 24**   118 East Waldburg Street. *Photograph by Keith Cardwell, courtesy Savannah College of Art and Design.*

**209 West Waldburg Street, Lloyd Ward**

A flat facade is embellished with front porches extending across the entire front elevation in this house built for Clement Saussy in 1872.

## SOUTH VICTORIAN DISTRICT

Frame Victorian housing continues in the south Victorian district to Victory Drive. The entire area, much in need of rehabilitation, recalls uptown New Orleans, also a sea of frame late Victorian and Edwardian eclectic housing. The New Orleans neighborhood has fared better than its Savannah counterpart and is presently better preserved.

The New Orleans frame uptown district does not have the inventory of rowhouses and townhouses evident throughout the Savannah Victorian district. However, New Orleans double shotguns are a one-story equivalent of the Savannah paired houses. Comparison of the two, similar neighborhoods in terms of architectural inventory and dates of development,

would be advisable to thrust the Savannah area into a rehabilitation mode.

**1921 Bull Street** (Figure 25)

Grocer Cord Asendorf had this late Victorian confection built in 1889. The builder of the two-story frame house with its wraparound gallery made felicitous use of the spindles and sawn work available at local lumberyards. These galleries show how individual taste, imagination, and carpentry skills could vary the look and quality of assembled industrially manufactured woodwork.

**222 East 32nd Street at Lincoln Street** (Figure 26)

Juxtaposed masses, including a two-level piazza, projecting bay windows on two levels with a one-story entrance projecting further toward the sidewalk characterize this frame late-nineteenth-century house. The extensive use of latticework catches the eye when passing this corner house set back on its lot on the piazza side.

**Figure 25**  1921 Bull Street. *Photograph by Keith Cardwell, courtesy Savannah College of Art and Design.*

**122 East 36th Street at Abercorn Street** (Figure 27)

Colonial revival dressed in shingles is somewhat unusual. It works well with the pretentious broken pediments on the three dormers and the triple first-level windows. Above a traditional portico and entrance with sidelights and overlights is a triple bay window set behind a balustrade. The facade, with its woodwork lifted from classical styles, resembles a piece of eighteenth-century American furniture more than an early twentieth-century house.

**East 39th Street at Drayton Street** (Figure 28)

A double gallery wrapping the two-story house on two elevations creates an eye-catching composition combining a handsome deep Italianate bracketed cornice with spindle work galore. Bands of spindles connect columns; spindles are combined to create a balustrade pattern.

Figure 26    222 East 32nd Street at Lincoln Street. *Photograph by Keith Cardwell, courtesy Savannah College of Art and Design.*

Figure 27   122 East 36th Street at Abercorn Street. *Photograph by Keith Cardwell, courtesy Savannah College of Art and Design.*

**Figure 28** 100 East 39th Street at Drayton Street. *Photograph by Keith Cardwell, courtesy Savannah College of Art and Design.*

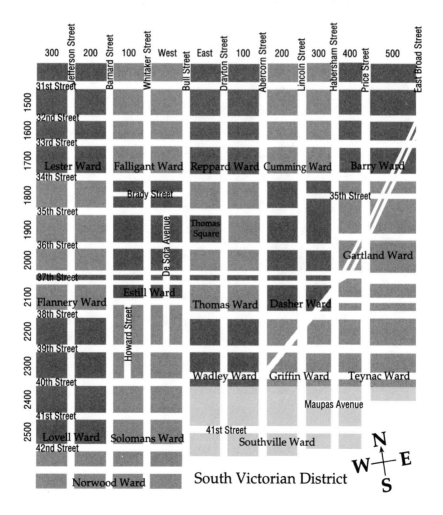

South Victorian District

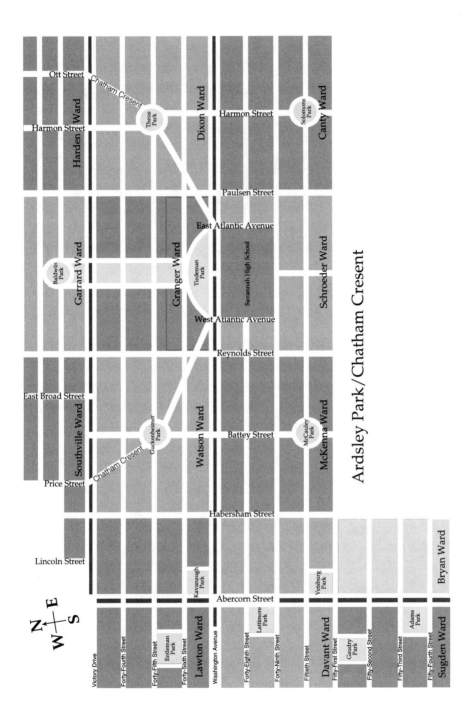

Ardsley Park/Chatham Cresent

# 7

## AUTOMOBILE SUBURBS TO THE ATLANTIC OCEAN

### VICTORY DRIVE, ARDSLEY PARK, AND CHATHAM CRESCENT

Ardsley Park and Chatham Crescent, the first automobile suburbs of Savannah, were thoughtfully designed under the influence of the Beaux Arts and City Beautiful movements, thanks to the interest of Henry Hays Lattimore, the developer. Victory Drive, designed to be the grand street of the new subdivision, became Route 80 leading to Tybee beach. Lots were sold to be filled with upscale, architect-designed brick houses set deep into wide, fence-less lawns running the gamut of revival and eclectic styles. Abercorn Street was conceived as the north–south centerpiece, with open public squares staggered on each side at alternating streets between 46th and 50th streets. These squares, named Kavanagh, Vetsburg, Lattimore, and Adams, serve as entrances to the private side streets, so that houses do not face Abercorn Street.

You may experience Ardsley Park at its best along 45th to 59th streets off Victory Drive and Abercorn Street. There is, at Barnard and 53rd streets, an old-time square that bisects Barnard Street much in the fashion of the squares in the old historic district. The double-drive, tree-lined Washington Avenue (which would have been 47th Street), starts at Bull Street and extends to Waters Avenue, where it becomes a single street. Greek revival-style houses set back in their large lots along Washington Avenue were built in the 1920s. The junction of Abercorn Street and Washington Avenue has about five quadrants, with fine revival-style houses built after 1911. Look for Spanish castles, Greek-provenance mansions, Italian villas, and even Louisiana plantation houses among the selection of residences dating from between 1910 and World War II between Victory Drive, Bull Street, Waters Avenue, and 54th Street. Include Baldwin Park, a part of Chatham Crescent north of Victory Drive.

Savannah's architects active in the Ardsley Park–Chatham Crescent district after the turn of the nineteenth century indicate that Savannah was a port city. Olaf Otto, who immigrated to the United States from Norway, designed about two dozen houses in the Ardsley Park–Chatham Crescent area. Percy Sugden of Halifax, England, arrived in Savannah by 1888 from Liverpool, where he apprenticed as an architect. Gottfried L. Morman specialized in schools in the 1890s. Henrik Wallin from Sweden, who studied architecture in France and Italy, assisted Henry Bacon with the Astor Hotel in New York and came to Savannah to assist Hyman Witcover in construction of the Germania Bank. He stayed to become the first president of the South Georgia Chapter of the American Institute of Architects. He designed Hull Memorial Presbyterian Church at **122 East 36th Street** and the Oliver Apartments. Hyman Witcover, first president of the Savannah Society of Architects, designed the main branch of the Savannah Public Library on Bull Street in the south Victorian district. His legacy remains a number of public buildings in Savannah built near the turn of the twentieth century. He designed the buildings at **22 East 34th** and **111 East 36th** streets.

Beyond Ardsley Park, Chatham County exhibits its history along roads that offer glimpses of the salt marshes that surround Savannah and the winding rivers, creeks, and streams that provided transportation, livelihood, and protection.

Chatham County was named for William Pitt, the Earl of Chatham and friend of America, in 1777 when the county system replaced the parish system. The county is bordered on the north by the Savannah River and by the Ogeechee River on the south. Oglethorpe-period garden and farm lots related by name and plan to the original wards of the town have been absorbed into the city limits. Beyond these were agricultural villages and private estates such as Wormsloe and Beaulieu. Plantations covered islands such as Wilmington, Ossabaw, and Wassaw in the eastern part of the county. After emancipation, former slaves established communities, generally near the water, such as Coffee Bluff, Nicholsonboro, Pin Point, Sandfly, and Grimball Point.

Skidaway Road accesses the southeastern section of the county, the Isle of Hope, a National Register historic district, and nineteenth-century river resorts "on the salts," as these salt marsh–view communities were called.

Bonaventure Cemetery lies along the Wilmington River. The cemetery and its land provide glimpses into the heart of Savannah's history. The land was settled by English Colonel John Mulryne about 1760 during the Crown colony years. He named the place Bonaventure, and his brick plantation house was built in time to host the 1761 marriage celebration of his daughter Mary to Josiah Tattnall of Charleston. This brought the Tattnalls to Savannah, but the Revolutionary War brought them a divided family. John Tattnall and his father Josiah sided with the Tories and had to depart to England. Their property was confiscated by the patriots. Josiah Tattnall, Jr. returned to Georgia when he was 18 to fight under Revolutionary General Nathanael Greene, thereby recovering his grandparents' estate, Bonaventure. His decision to support the patriots was fortuitous for Georgia because this English-reared son of Savannah became a member of the U.S. Congress and governor of Georgia when he was in his thirties. He died in 1804 at 38 and is buried with his wife at Bonaventure. His orphaned son Josiah Tattnall III was raised in England by his grandfather. He too returned to America to join the Navy. He fought in the War of 1812 against England, and served as commodore for the Confederate States of America. Once Tattnall breached America's neutrality by aiding the British fleet fighting in Chinese waters. His remark when reprimanded, "Blood is thicker than water," brought international attention to the incident. It also summed up the dilemma of many Savannahians during the years of the American Revolution.

Bonaventure passed out of the Mulryne–Tattnall ownership in 1850, when Captain Peter Wilberger, owner of the Pulaski House, bought the place to use as a cemetery. In 1907 the city bought it, placing the waterfront under the Park and Tree Commission. This appropriate move reflects the positive attitude in Savannah relative to cemeteries. Cemeteries have always been promenades and places for strolls and visits in the Victorian tradition. John Muir, the Scottish naturalist, reached Savannah in 1867 and spent five days camping at Bonaventure. He recorded that he discovered there "one of the most impressive assemblages of animal and plant creatures I have ever met," along with a similarly impressive "company of...tillandsia-draped oaks of Bonaventure."

Because of a cemetery scene in John Berendt's *Midnight in the Garden of Good and Evil*, (New York: Random House, 1994), visits and picnics at Bonaventure have again become *de rigeur*. It is, in fact, a return to an age-old custom. Notice that the tombs are often situated with a parlorlike or yardlike setting in front of them, with cast iron furniture suitable for visits to the environment of the deceased.

The road to the largest bridge over the Wilmington River takes you to Thunderbolt, now a fishing village in transition running alongside the river. Thunderbolt was established by Oglethorpe as part of his agrarian–military outpost scheme to protect the settlement of Savannah from the Spanish. Laid out on the site of an abandoned Indian settlement, his fortified farming village was almost deserted by 1740. Roger Lacy managed to get a 500-acre grant of the area from King George II during the Crown colony years. French troops encamped there during the 1779 siege of Savannah in an abortive effort by French and patriot troops to eject the British from Savannah. Among the French troops from St. Domingue was 12-year-old Henri Christophe, an African, born a slave in Grenada, who later emerged as hero of the Haitians in their fight for independence from the French in colonial St. Domingue. Most of Savannah's Italians clustered in Thunderbolt in the late nineteenth century. The Blessing of the Fleet is an annual celebration held in late May or June.

Judge Peter W. Meldrim, president of the American Bar Association in 1912–1913, helped bring the Georgia Industrial College, founded in 1890 for African Americans, to Savannah and served on its first board of commissioners. Now Savannah State College, its first president was Richard R. Wright, whose son became the first graduate of the college to receive a Ph.D. degree, which he earned at the University of Pennsylvania. Hill Hall is a National Register building.

The Isle of Hope retains its picturesque aspect along the banks of the Skidaway River. Piers reaching out into the water and fishing craft can be seen from the old-fashioned screen-porched frame cottages raised on brick piers. Such summer retreats or fishermen's cottages date from the 1840s to World War I. They exhibit little change in plan or decoration, a wide center hall with equal-sized rooms ranged along each side. A wide gallery usually surrounded such a house on four sides.

Among National Register properties in the county that should be seen is the Bethesda Home for Boys. The Reverend George Whitefield, a dissenting minister, worked with James Habersham, Savannah's leading merchant, to establish the orphans' home. Its first orphans were installed in 1740, during Oglethorpe's time.

On Wilmington Island, the former General Oglethorpe Hotel, a 1920s Florida-style establishment with cottages and the Florida look, recalling Henry Flagler's hotels, served as a point of embarkation for the Olympic sailing venue in 1996.

The little fishing village at Wilmington Island had shanty Irish fishermen clustered at one end of the island, and Porpoise Point had some old cottages. To get to Pin Point, Georgia, a village filled with Chinquapin trees, shrimp boats, and screened-porch frame cottages, you had to pass through Sandfly. The shrimp boats went out at 3:30 or 4:00 in the morning, and the sounds of their departure barely disturbed the little town. The boats chugged back about noon. The Pin point shrimpers were both black and white. Supreme Court Justice Clarence Thomas lived at one end of Pin point, where his grandmother took in laundry.

Vernonburg was laid out in 1742 upon the petition of German indentured servants who had completed their five-year service. They had come with Oglethorpe, having been recruited from the Palatine along the Rhine River. The river beside Vernonburg had already been named the Vernon, honoring Georgia Trustee James Vernon or his brother, Edward, an admiral of the Royal Navy. The town was incorporated in 1865 and was a summer resort until after World War II. The earliest surviving houses date from the 1840s. Typical nineteenth-century riverside houses are elevated with porches to catch the breezes. More modest one-story bungalows front a creek and date from the early twentieth century.

As early as 1851, steamers were taking visitors to Fort Pulaski and Tybee for outings to enjoy the salt breezes. The only permanent residents were the lighthouse keeper and his family. Serious development began in 1873 when John Tebeau developed a plan to subdivide the island for the Tybee Improvement Company. The Ocean House went up in 1876 on the southern end. A horse railroad ran through groves of oak, pine, and palmetto to transport passengers for a swim in the inlet or to dance to the Guards Brass Band. In 1886 the Tybee Railroad Company began the rail connection with Savannah, and for forty years Tybee was the only Georgia coastal barrier island with public access by land transportation.

Tomochichi and Toonahowi; photo-lithograph by Julius Bien of the original mezzotint from *The History of Georgia*, Vol. I, by Charles C. Jones, Jr. (Boston: Houghton Mifflin). Toonahowi, adopted son of Yamassee (Creek) Chief Tomochichi, visited England with Oglethorpe. The lands that would have been part of his Creek heritage were taken up by the English settlers and Toonahowi disappeared into the mists of history. *Courtesy V. & J. Duncan Antique Maps and Prints.*

E. Shaver Booksellers 326 Bull Street, Madison square. *Esther Shaver's bookstore has been a gathering place for decades. This drawing by Louise Y. Streed.*

# "RECEIPTS," GOOD EATS, LODGING, ANTIQUES, AND BOOKS

## "RECEIPTS"

James Edward Oglethorpe, Savannah's founder, established the Strangers' House and the communal oven on trust lots near Ellis Square, now the city market area, on the northwestern side of historic Savannah. The inhabitants brought their bread to be baked and their meat to be cooked to the communal

Troup Square Cafe, 322–326 East Harris in the basement of an 1869 paired house. *Photograph by Clement Speiden.*

ovens there. This saved firewood and kept the small houses cool in the devastatingly hot and humid coastal climate. How long the communal oven was used in Savannah is not recorded, but the custom of communal ovens owned by the city continued on Greek islands into the 1950s.

Recipes, called "receipts" in Savannah, are papers you receive from friends explaining how they cook food. A handwritten set of receipts bound in brown faux-marble paper and hand-stitched was collected by Georgia Lamar Malone, daughter of Charles Augustus Lafayette Lamar. Many of these were given to her by a "Mrs. Habersham." The receipts have been handed down to Cornelia McIntire Hartridge from her grandmother. The book of receipts indicates that families were extended and visited each other often. Large numbers were expected to dine from any recipe.

"Georgia Lamar Malone's Receipts," Harriet Ross Colquitt's *Savannah Cook Book*, (Charleston, S.C.: Walker, Evans and Cogswell Company, 1933), and the cookbook by Savannah historian and journalist Margaret Way DeBolt, *Savannah Sampler Cookbook*, (Whitford Press: 1978) reveal Savannah's traditional way of cooking as well as a lot about the city's lifestyle. A reprint of Colquitt's cookbook is available from Mrs. Raskin at the Book Lady, and the *Savannah Sampler Cookbook* is available at the Ballastone Inn store. Damon Lee Fowler is an author and southern cooking specialist. His new book, *Classical Southern Cooking* (New York: Crown Publishers, 1995), reveals new research and lots of little-understood aspects of southern cooking.

Savannahians, they say, are like the Japanese because they eat rice and worship their ancestors. Certainly, rice is first and foremost in their minds. Besides making Savannah wealthy in the eighteenth and nineteenth centuries, rice became a key part of every meal, from breakfast fritters to curry and dessert. Even today, it's served at least once a day.

Ground artichokes (Jerusalem artichokes), a root vegetable, not the California-grown stalk common in the grocery stores today, were found in the woods and grown in gardens from the earliest days. Jerusalem artichokes are best just scrubbed, leaving on much of the skin. Throw them into cold water to keep them from turning dark. Better yet, have your salted water boiling in a saucepan and pitch them in to cook until tender. Test with the tines of your fork. Drain and add butter and a bit of chopped parsley for taste and looks. It's a delicate and subtle dish.

Fresh shad and shad roe are on the menus at home and in Savannah restaurants. Grits usually accompany these fish, but occasionally, shad roe appears with rice. Never serve shad itself with rice. Rice with fish is unheard of except in an old tale that all the families tell. A guest in a Savannah home asked for rice with his fish. "Sir," replied the butler, embarrassed for the poor guest's gaffe, "in this house we don't eat rice with our fish."

In Savannah nearly everything, including rice cakes and sweet potatoes, is fried at one time or another. Leftover pone and grits are fried. Hoecakes, originally a dough of cornmeal and water, were fried on the iron hoe over a fire scratched together in the rice and cotton fields by slaves or in the field by soldiers. Even desserts are fried (fritters).

Miss Mary Telfair's notebooks describe some yummy desserts, among them snow balls, fried. Here it is: 1 pint of milk, 1 pound of flour, ¼ pound of butter, 10 eggs, 6 ounces of sugar. Boil the milk, stir in the flour and butter, and when cool, add eggs and stir in sugar. Fry in spoonfuls.

In Savannah there is always something sweet on the side of your dish of meat and rice. A little curry is added to raisins, or stewed tomatoes with sugar, or lemon or orange marmalade, sometimes made from fruit in the garden. Ginger is very important, too. The sweet side dish custom is said to have arrived with the English from the Caribbean islands. While rice was grown locally, its serving as a curry dish was brought by the British from their Asian colonies.

The sweet tooth may have started during the eighteenth century when the coastal plantations tried to grow sugarcane. They could not compete with the Caribbean or Louisiana in growing sugar, but Savannah beat out New Orleans in the refining business. The Savannah Sugar Refinery was once the only refinery between Philadelphia and New Orleans. New Orleans' Sprague and Oxnard families built a new refinery on the Savannah River, and they brought almost 400 families, employees for the refinery, to Savannah from New Orleans soon after World War I. Their fame lies in "Dixie Crystals."

African food found its way to Savannah kitchens, becoming essential to each meal. Although owning slaves was illegal in the colony between 1733 and 1750, slaves were rented from Beaufort, Port Royal, and Charleston. Others were brought in from the English West Indies. After 1750, slave ships from Africa brought black-eyed peas, okra, and probably African sweet potatoes—what we also call yams, their African name.

The large yellow yam is the one of African origin, they say, and certainly the name is forever attributed to Africans. One line of thinking is that *yam* is a contraction of the Gullah word *nyam*, which means to eat and which also may be the origin of *yum yum*. Samuel Stoney in *Black Genesis* (New York: The Macmillan Company, 1930) traces the word yam to the African word *unyamo*. As for the plain old white potato, the coastal Negroes called them "buckra yams," *buckra* being the Gullah word for white man.

Whether it came to Savannah via African slave ships or was slipped over by Spaniards at St. Augustine, who knew of it from South American Indians, the yam was once essential to the Savannah diet. Once, when breakfast was a meal to be reckoned with, fried sweet potatoes provided a side dish. Peel and slice the raw sweet potato, sprinkle with salt, and fry in hot fat. Better yet, cut up yesterday's cold boiled sweet potatoes or candied yams and fry them up the same way.

As for okra, you've got to love it if you live in Savannah. And like everything else in Savannah, you can fritter okra. Boil 1 quart of okra. Since you're going to mash it, the length of time doesn't matter much. Drain the water and mash. Season with salt and pepper and beat in two eggs, 2 teaspoons of baking powder, and enough flour to make a stiff batter. Drop a tablespoonful at a time in deep fat and fry.

Corn was a staple in the earliest days of the colony. It was fed to servants, slaves, livestock, and in the houses of the gentry. Indeed, during the attack on British Savannah by the French and the American patriots, the French commandant, le Comte d'Estaing, was appalled at the food served to him by the Americans. The American chefs had no flour and when the count dined with the "insurgents," he was served what he referred to as "a massive cake of rice and corn cooked under the ashes of the fire on an iron platter."

Hoe cakes—pancakes made of cornmeal and water, cooked over the fire after being spread on iron hoes in the absence of skillets—never tempted the Frenchman. "I absolutely forbade my two brother commanders [Noailles and Dillon] to put themselves for more than a year on [American] General Lincoln's diet," quipped le Comte.

Hoecakes went out of style when money came back to Savannah. But now hoecakes are making a comeback with those interested in historical cuisine. Mix 1 pint of cornmeal with cold water and 1 teaspoon of salt into a stiff dough. Dust the grid iron with meal and lay on in thin cakes. No butter, please.

Just as recipes are called "receipts" in Savannah, grits were called "grist," carried to the grist mill and ground coarsely. Or grist may be ground from corn that has been first processed as hominy through the use of lye, then dried and ground as hominy grits. Either way, it's corn ground and boiled with water and served with salt, pepper, and butter as accompaniment to shad or fried fish, beneath stews, shrimp, seafood, or meat, or beside eggs for breakfast.

Next-day grist would be cut up cold into blocks and fried as fritters or stirred with milk and eggs, poured on a griddle, and served as pancakes with butter and sorghum or cane syrup.

Here are some of Mrs. Habersham's "receipts" from Cornelia McIntire Hartridge's nineteenth-century handwritten cookbook. Try them when you have lots of people coming. They are generous.

### *Sweetbreads served with mushrooms for 16 persons*

1 dozen sweetbreads

1 quart cream, or 1 pint cream and 1 pint milk

some of the liquor in which the sweetbreads were cooked

½ pound best butter

a little grated nutmeg

pepper and salt to taste

a large glass of wine (chablis)

1 cup (cups were cans to Mrs. Habersham) mushrooms

4 tablespoons sifted flour

"Throw sweetbreads in boiling salt water and cook for 25 minutes. Take them out and, when cold enough to handle, peel and cut off gristle or dark parts, and cut up into size of dice.

"Melt the butter and add flour, some of the cream gradually, a pinch of the nutmeg, salt, pepper and then mushroom liquor. Mix the prepared sweetbreads with all the above ingredients.

"Add wine, then the mushrooms and rest of the cream, and sweetbread liquor as needed." Mrs. Habersham.

Terrapin meat was in the repertoire of most housewives. Terrapin, Savannahians are quick to point out, are not sea turtles but small tender turtles. Mrs. Habersham told Mrs. McIntire how to fix them.

## Terrapin

"To Prepare Terrapin, cut off their heads; dip each one into boiling water a very short time and peel off the outer skin. Peel them open with a hatchet and sharp knife and take out the eggs and put them in cold water. Take out entrails, gall bags and throw away. The bag is attached to the liver, but the liver must be put with the meat.

"The shell must be put into a large soup pot with salt and the onion. Cover it up tight and boil until perfectly tender. Take the meat out and strain it. Throw the shells and bones away and the long dark string down the back. Cut the meat and the fiber very fine. To prevent it from being stringy, put the meat in one bowl and the water in another bowl where it will jelly.

### Three terrapin boiled and cut up

yolk of six hard-boiled eggs

½ pound best butter

3 tablespoons sifted flour

juice of one lemon

half a grated nutmeg

1 pint fresh cream

a thimbleful of sherry

some of the jelly in which the terrapin were cooked

red pepper

1 tablespoon Worcestershire sauce

terrapin eggs

salt

"Put yolks of eggs, butter, flour, together in a bowl, put over the terrapin jelly to cook in a pot. As it boils, add the terrapin eggs mixture in the bowl, Worcestershire sauce, nutmeg, and let boil. Then throw in the terrapin meat and boil for five minutes; then add cream, wine and lemon, stirring all the time to prevent bruising. Serve with onion." Mrs. Habersham.

As politician Mark Hanna put it: "I care not who makes our Presidents as long as I can eat in Savannah."

### Green corn pudding

Corn pudding is big in Savannah. Here's the green corn pudding receipt from the Gordon family: Grate 1 dozen ears of young corn to make 3 cups. Mix with 1 pint of milk, two eggs, 1 spoonful of butter, and black pepper and salt to taste. Bake about 45 minutes in a 350°F oven.

### Red rice

Savannah's red rice receipt came from the Bethesda Home for Boys, where they've been eating rice since the 1740s. Stir rice with a fork (not a spoon) and don't let any water or steam condense on it. Rice grains must be separate and apart.

¾ cup diced onion

½ cup chopped green pepper

1½ pounds cooked ham, chopped

2 8-ounce cans tomato sauce

2 8-ounce cans water

½ teaspoon salt

2 tablespoons sugar

2 cups rice

Sauté onion and pepper in oil. Add ham, cook a bit more, then add tomato sauce, water, salt, and sugar, and mix. Add raw rice. Bring to a full boil, then cover and let simmer over low heat about 15 minutes. Stir with a fork. If water and liquid are not absorbed, continue to cook without the top until the moisture is absorbed.

### Chatham artillery punch

I don't think Comte d'Estaing, French commandant at the siege of Savannah, had any, but Chatham artillery punch is a Savannah festival tradition. Never made in small batches, strong men mixed it for big events, and still do. Here is the smallest recipe I could find, for just 10 gallons:

1 pound green tea

2 gallons cold water

juice of 3 dozen oranges

juice of 3 dozen lemons

5 pounds brown sugar

1 quart maraschino cherries

3 gallons Catawba or Rhine wine

1 gallon rum (I like dark)

1 gallon brandy

1 gallon rye whiskey

1 gallon gin

1 pint Benedictine liqueur

champagne

Let the green tea stand in cold water overnight. Add fruit juice and strain. Add sugar, cherries, and liquor, cover, and allow to ferment for two to six weeks in a large stone crock. Strain off the cherries and put the liquid in bottles. Store in the refrigerator. Mix 1 gallon of chilled stock with 1 quart of chilled champagne or chilled charged water at serving time. Pour over ice in a punch bowl and serve.

## Good Eats

Where do you go to get the old Savannah food? The Oglethorpe Club is private, so you'll have to find turtle soup elsewhere. With Savannah restaurants, don't expect the works; you might get good food and bad service, or good food and service without atmosphere, as at Williams Seafood on the road to Tybee.

You don't go to Savannah for nouvelle cuisine. You go for traditional Savannah cooking and seafood. Savannah seafood, fresh and eaten on the water, soul food at Nita's, or some Savannah-style cooking at Elizabeth's on 37th will do just fine. Don't forget, for iced tea this is sweet tea territory; just say yes and ask for lots of lemon on the side.

**SAVANNAH'S CANDY KITCHEN, 225 East River Street, 233-8411.**
This shop on the Savannah River has the best pralines I've eaten out of a private kitchen. The folks there will give you a sample.

**EXPRESS CAFE, 39 Bernard Street at the City Market, 233-4683.**
This is my favorite stopping-off place for breakfast or lunch or reading the paper with coffee. Stop there after an early morning walk to the Savannah River or a stroll around the squares off Barnard Street. Hours are 7 a.m.to 4 p.m. Wednesdays through Fridays and from 8 a.m. to 4 p.m. Saturdays and Sundays.

**RAY'S FAMOUS CAFE, 146 Montgomery Street, 232-4155.**
Scattered all over the wall are illustrations by Streeter of Savannah of famous Georgians. It's a good hangout for breakfast and lunch across from the courthouse.

**JOHN AND LINDA'S, 313 West St. Julian Street, 233-2626.**
Eat in the patio and have a good time in the city market area.

**606 EAST CAFE, 319 West Congress Street, 233-2887.**

This restaurant has surprisingly good food considering the kooky atmosphere in the city market area, and features off-the-wall decoration, including laundry on the line mixed with psycodelia. It is loud and fun with good waitresses and lots of young people. Moderately priced.

**DEBIE'S, 10 West State Street off Wright Square, 236-3516.**

Near the post office is where you'll find lots of local professionals downing inexpensive generous sandwiches or traditional hot lunches, all served by attentive, if busy waitresses, who bring sweet tea in huge glasses with lots of fresh lemon. Skip dessert. It's old time, small town.

**WALL'S BAR B QUE, 515 East York Lane, 232-9754.**

The Walls dispense divine crabcakes and barbecue out of their little cottage. It's take out, and you owe it to yourself to see the old lane here.

**45 SOUTH, 20 East Broad Street, 233-1881.**

Coat, tie, reservations, and lots of money are needed. This is a quiet restaurant with attentive service. The chef is serious, if flawed, about his presentation: no mint sauce served with the lamb.

**THE OLDE PINK HOUSE, 23 Abercorn Street, 232-4286.**

Alida Harper saved this early building built by merchant James Habersham in the eighteenth century by opening a tearoom here when she was a young woman in the 1930s. Half a century later it remains one of the city's traditional dress-up dinner restaurants. You have to go to see the old building, one of the city's finest and oldest. The bar downstairs is particularly appealing.

**CHUTZPAH AND PANACHE, 251 Bull Street at Liberty Street, 234-5007.**

Where else can you sit at tables with Provençal cloths and order a lamb sandwich with ratatouille? It is also a wearable art dress shop, which hardly prevents men from coming.

**JUICY LUCY'S UPTOWN CAFE, 241 Abercorn Street, 231-1707.**

What a surprising name for a restaurant where you are likely to be served by Savannah's Junior League members. The chef is a lovely young woman who speaks Spanish.

**CLARY'S, 404 Abercorn Street, 233-0402.**

Fried eggs, grits, and biscuits for breakfast used to be it for Clary's. Now there's much more. Good old-time milkshakes or a Caesar salad with grilled chicken will hold you until dinner.

**MRS. WILKES BOARDING HOUSE, 107 West Jones Street, 232-5997.**

This is the home of Savannah's home-cooked food, a long-time favorite where you sit at communal tables in the basement of a historic townhouse. Note the hours: breakfast 8–9 A.M.; lunch 11:30–3 P.M. Monday–Friday.

**CRYSTAL BEER PARLOR, 301 West Jones Street, 232-1153.**

Traipse over at noon or nighttime for crab soup or oyster stew, good burgers, and beer. Locals go there when there's no time to cook.

**NITA'S PLACE, 140 Abercorn Street, 238-8233.**

Nita and her help are handsome and full of personality and good humor. She's had her portrait painted to look like Aunt Jemimah on the window, and the place is full of photographs of her with famous people who've found her little hole in the wall. Where else can you get rutabagas cooked well and hoecakes served with good fried chicken and a squash casserole? You pick it out and Nita and company bring it to you. Everyone's carrying on one big conversation even though you have your own table.

**TROUP SQUARE CAFE, 321 Habersham Street, 231-8037.**

This is a hangout for breakfast in the southern part of town in a residential neighborhood not far from the Victorian district. Lunch is quiet, but you can still order breakfast after 3 in the afternoon, including any number of crepe combinations. Lots of the locals and SCAD art students in strange garb eat there, adding to the local atmosphere.

**JEAN LOUISE, 321 Jefferson Street, 234-2311.**

This restaurant is behind Pulaski Square near Orleans Square on the west side. The chef used to work for Donald Trump. Now he's providing fine dinners and working on his big Queen Anne house near Kroger's.

For ethnic eating in old Savannah, don't miss:

**PEPE'S, 325 East Bay Street, 236-0530.**

Mexican food and beer are served in a casual ambiance near the river.

**TAJ, 110 West Congress Street, 231-9815.**

This is in the Market Square district, has good food and good service, and is quiet.

**IL PISTACCIO, 2 East Broughton Street, 231-8888.**

This lunch, dinner, and deli market is an effort at high-style dining with a lively atmosphere and art gallery upstairs. It has done a lot for Broughton Street, too.

If the bar scene is you, here's what's fun.

**PINKIE MASTERS LOUNGE, 318 Drayton Street, 238-0447.**

With its jukebox, Pinkie's is always popular. It looks the same as it did the day Jimmy Carter passed by with local Democrats before he was governor of Georgia.

**BAR BAR, 312 West St. Julian Street, 231-1910.**

This is a popular hangout of some locals in the Market Square area.

**HANNAH'S, 20 East Broad Street, 233-2225.**

A feature of Hannah's is live jazz; in the Trustees Garden area above the Pirates House.

**SIX PENCE PUB, 245 Bull Street at Liberty Street, 233-3151.**

Near the Desoto Hotel, this bar and restaurant is a convenient stop for soup and sandwiches, day or night.

Heading south to the Victorian district, on to Ardsley Park, and east toward Tybee, you'll find lots of seafood and everything from elegance at Elizabeth's on 37th to sawdust and newspapers with a hole in your table for the shrimp and crab shells at Teeples.

### ELIZABETH'S ON 37TH, 105 East 37th Street, 236-5547.

The Terrys have opened a world-class restaurant in an imposing mansion in the Victorian district. It's an occasion to go there. You'll be around a chef and proprietors who are interested in Savannah's future and work hard to help it. You may want the cookbook they've compiled.

### JOHNNY HARRIS RESTAURANT, 1651 East Victory Drive, 354-7810.

Open between 11:30 A.M. and 10:30 P.M. This restaurant is a must if you're in the Ardsley Park area or on the way to Wormsloe or Bonaventure Cemetery. Savannah's oldest restaurant, it is a vintage automobile suburb and speakeasy combined, with huge walled-off booths and fake stars on the ceiling, good seafood and desserts too.

### TUBBY'S TANK HOUSE, 2909 River Drive, Thunderbolt, 354-9040.

Tubby's features good fresh fish and atmosphere.

### TEEPLES RESTAURANT, 2917 River Drive, Thunderbolt, 354-1157.

Teeples is the place for fresh steamed seafood in a shack.

### LOVE'S, Highway 17 South, the old Ogeechee River Road, 925-3616.

(Officially at 6817 Basin Road on the old way to St. Simons Island.) Love's is located on the water. The seafood, such as the fried flounder, and the service are good. It's old-time and comfortable. Love's is a good stop on your return from outings to Ebenezer, with its 1767 Jerusalem Lutheran Church, built on the site of the 1741 church, and the Salzburger Museum and Cemetery, commemorating the Salzburger contribution under the Reverend John Martin Bolzius to Oglethorpe's settlement. Love's is a good dinner stop after a trip to Guyton, a little sand ridge village where many Savannahians have summered since the nineteenth century.

### GOODFRIEND'S GALLEY, BULL RIVER MARINA, U.S. Highway 80 east of town, 897-0990.

This restaurant is out on a pier en route to Fort Pulaski and Tybee. Open for lunch and dinner, it's a new project of Linda of John and Linda's Restaurant at the city market. Try their grilled seafood and look at the water and Savannah grass.

### WILLIAMS SEAFOOD, U.S. Highway 80 east of town, 8010 Tybee Road, 897-2219.

This is the place to go if you want good fried seafood from a family that's been serving it since the 1930s. It's across the highway on the left from Goodfriend's Galley, going toward Tybee, just before the Bull River bridge.

### THE CRAB SHACK AT CHIMNEY CREEK, 40 Estill Hammock Road, Tybee, 786-9857.

Eat steamed seafood outside under oak trees and moss, with a view of the water. Insects are part of the scene. Bring repellent or borrow it from other guests.

**HUNTER HOUSE,** 1701 Butler Avenue, Tybee, 786-7515.

The energetic owners of Hunter House have tried to bring something of turn-of-the-century Tybee back with a good restaurant in a renovated historic building on Tybee. They also offer a few bed-and-breakfast rooms.

**NORTHBEACH GRILL,** Van Horne Drive, Tybee, 786-5984.

Eat in the tiny screened porch area or outside at this laid-back place next to the Tybee Museum. Its specialty is Jamaican food. Visit the old-time Tybee Museum and walk along old Fort Screven's ruins.

**THE BREAKFAST CLUB,** 1500 Butler Avenue, Tybee, 786-5984.

Everybody is there for breakfast, tourists and locals alike, so it has to be fun. It's been there as long as anyone remembers.

## LODGING

Savannah has a long history of both gracious and notorious lodging. Oglethorpe used Trustees' money to build a "Strangers' House" in one of his first four wards. He himself relied on his old tent that had seen him through the German campaigns. He even brought his yellow damask curtains to decorate his tent, thrown up not far from the river. On his third voyage he rented rooms along Broughton Street, a situation not too different from our bed and breakfasts of today.

The City Hotel, of William Jay's time when he made Savannah into a Regency city after 1816, may one day be restored even though it has been sitting roof-

Gaston Gallery bed and breakfast, 211 East Gaston Street. *Photograph by Goeff DeLorm, courtesy Savannah College of Art and Design.*

less on Bay Street for decades. Pulaski House on Johnson Square was the most popular place to stay in the 1840s. It has been replaced on Johnson Square by Morrison's Cafeteria (that southern chain, established at Mobile, is worth a visit).

Mary Marshall's Marshall Hotel was all the rage in the 1850s and housed Union soldiers during the Civil War. It, too, could possibly be restored if the mutilating fake front were removed. Savannahians had a fancy dress ball to mourn the demolition of the Richardson Romanesque pile of the Desoto Hotel in the 1960s. Only the name and the location is preserved at the Desoto Hilton at Liberty and Bull Streets. The craze for inns and bed and breakfast lodging has swept Savannah along with the rest of the country. But Savannah knows how to entertain. You'll enjoy any of the historic lodgings, and remember that where you stay is part of the grand ritual that is Savannah.

**RIVER STREET INN, 115 East River Street, 234-6400/800-253-4229.**

Facing both Bay Street and the Savannah River, this inn has a romantic location with potential for walking out the door to riverfront activities: a boat ride to Calibogue or Daufauskie islands, a tour of the riverfront by boat, shopping and eating along the waterfront, and eating delicious pralines at the candy factory.

**OLDE HARBOR INN, 508 East Factors Walk, 234-4100/800-553-6533.**

This inn faces both the river and Emmett Park, a new landscape where cotton bales and barrels of naval stores were once stored. This inn provides a romantic setting in a lovely brick building.

**EAST BAY INN, 225 East Bay Street, 238-1225/800-500-1225.**

Facing Bay Street just off Reynolds Square between Abercorn and Lincoln streets on the east side of town, this hotel offers a quiet walk through Warren, Washington, Columbia, and Greene squares to Trustees Garden. Or walk across the street to the commercial River Street attractions. Like a small hotel, the inn has a restaurant and provides the anonymity attractive to travelers who do not wish to interface with inn owners and other guests. Good hotel bathrooms are a feature, along with ice machines in the hall. The inn combines hotel and bed and breakfast services effectively.

**PRESIDENT'S QUARTERS, 225 East President Street on Oglethorpe Square, 233-1600/800-233-1776.**

A hot tub and patio are set between a parking lot and the historic house, which dates from 1853. It is located near the Richardson–Owens–Thomas and Davenport House Museums, the Olde Pink House restaurant, and the central business district.

**THE KEHOE HOUSE, 123 Habersham Street on Columbia Square, 232-1020/800-820-1020.**

The Consul Courts' luxury European-style inn is housed in a lavish 1892 mansion belonging to the Kehoe iron foundry family. Joe Namath, the football legend, owned the building prior to renovation.

**1790 HOUSE, 307 East President Street, 236-7122/800-487-1790.**

This hotel and fine restaurant, on the east side of the historic district, near the Richardson–Owens–Thomas house and museum, offers the Savannah look in decoration, with attention to textiles and some authentic antiques housed in a Federal-style paired house that faces Lincoln Street. The restaurant and tavern have atmosphere and fine crabcakes and key lime pie.

### BALLASTONE INN AND TOWNHOUSE, 14 East Oglethorpe Avenue, 236-1484/800-822-4553.

In 1873, Captain Henry Blun had architect William G. Preston enlarge George Anderson's 1838 house, and now, after recent extensive restoration, you can enjoy it. The inn is centrally located on what used to be the southern border of the original town plan. A good gift shop and a fine bar add interest to the inn. The present owners, interested in historic preservation, are civic minded. Some of your room rental may go to the S.P.C.A.

### FOLEY HOUSE INN, 14 West Hull Street, Chippewa Square, 232-6622/ 800-647-3708.

This inn, based in a handsome 1896 residence designed by Henry Urban for Honora Foley, offers 19 rooms, some of them in a vine-covered four-story service wing of brick is visible from the Independent Presbyterian Church. Such service wings are rare in Savannah. Walk to Telfair Square with its Telfair Museum and enjoy live theater on Chippewa Square, where William Jay built Savannah's first theater about 1818.

### BED AND BREAKFAST INN, 117 West Gordon Street, 238-0518.

All the locals recommend this 14-room 1853 inn in Chatham Ward, as does the Telfair Museum staff. It's friendly, inexpensive, and deep in a residential area.

### MAGNOLIA HOUSE INN, 503 Whitaker Street near Gaston Street, 236-7674/ 800-238-7674.

Next to the Georgia Historical Society, this 1878–1883 center-hall mansion was built for Guerrard Heywood by Alfred Snedeker. The innkeepers can discuss deconstructivism and other scholarly subjects with you. The man who had the house built died soon afterward and his widow used it as a boardinghouse. Once again it offers thirteen guest rooms. Conrad Aiken's parents were boarding there when he was born; they soon moved to their house at Marshall Row on Oglethorpe Avenue.

### LIONS HEAD INN, 120 East Gaston Street, 232-4580/800-355-lion.

This spacious galleried late Italianate style mansion dates from 1883, when William H. Wade had John R. Hamlet build it. Today, it houses one of the most extensive argon lamp collections in America. The owners brought the lamps with them from Chicago along with a massive collection of monumental antiques. Large rooms and a Victorian atmosphere with lavish period antiques characterize the inn. You will feel like wearing an antique white nightgown with a nightcap to get the full effect of the six guest rooms.

### GASTON GALLERY, 211 East Gaston Street, 238-3294.

This late Italianate paired house was built in 1876 for Samuel B. Palmer and Henry A. Dresser. You will be at home in its expansive kitchen and garden visiting with the owners, who collect and sell antiques and write books.

### THE GASTONIAN, 220 East Gaston Street at Lincoln Street, 232-2869/800-322-6603.

This inn, in a house that wealthy grocer Aaron Champion had built in 1868 on the southeastern side of town, and another dating from 1869 built for Robert H.

Footman, is within walking distance of the residential Chatham, Monterey, and Whitefield Squares. The Gastonian, offering sixteen rooms, is the inn of choice for honeymooners.

## ANTIQUES AND COLLECTIBLES

Take a stroll along Bay Street for great antique shops with interesting proprietors. The cast iron, granite, stone, and Savannah gray brick fronts of the shops back up to the Savannah River. Among those shops clustered there are Melonie's, Once Possessed, Southern Lady, and more.

### CHRISTOPHER'S ANTIQUES, 126 East Bay Street, 912-232-0277.

Christopher retired from the Long Island Railroad to come to a real railroad town, Savannah. His shop specializes in the antique white clothing and linens his wife finds. The collection of Pinchbeck jewelry is worth the trip.

### JERE'S ANTIQUES, 9 North Jefferson Street, 912-236-2815.

For years Jere's has filled a big riverfront warehouse with everything known to man: imports, American, everything, on floor after floor.

### YOUMAN'S FURNITURE WAREHOUSE, 314 Williamson Street, 232-7161.

It's a must—best junk place in town—has everything.

### ALEXANDRA'S ANTIQUE GALLERY, 320 West Broughton Street, 912-233-3999.

Jane Kimball, a Savannah native, returned to her hometown, bought two 1891 commercial buildings on Broughton Street, and renovated them for an antique mall that

Eliza Thompson house, 7–9 West Jones Street. *Photograph by Keith Cardwell, courtesy Savannah College of Art and Design.*

makes an effective statement. She has dealers from Maine to Jacksonville and antiques from Tiffany sterling and eighteenth-century American silver to outsized period posters and moderne vintage clothing and costume jewelry. Four floors of booths should not be missed, nor the buildings, originally the Chatham Brickworks and Mercantile and the Savannah Buggy Company. Jane's mother was the renown antique dealer Audrey Norris. Jane has been shopkeeping since she was 13. She knows her stuff.

**PINCH OF THE PAST**, 109 West Broughton Street, 912-232-5563.

Noreen Parker has architectural accessories and old hardware, refinished and ready to use. They polish brass there, too. Talk to her about preservation.

**NO BULL ANTIQUES**, 110 Bull Street, 236-2625.

A hole in the wall between Broughton Street and West State Street, it's the king of junk shops, where you'll find some little something special. Besides the inventory, you'll get a kick out of the proprietor, who can repair anything.

**ARTS AND CRAFTS EMPORIUM**, 234 Bull Street, 912-238-0003.

Check out the handmade items that are brought in by the artists.

**S. HINSON**, 116 West Hull Street, 912-232-5644.

Scot specializes in moderne and the kind of funky and sophisticated things for house and garden you see in *World of Interiors* magazine.

**MICHAEL V. DECOOK ANTIQUES**, 20 West Hull Street on Chippewa Square, 912-232-7149.

Go in to see the antiques and take a look at the simple but nice Greek revival house with builder John Scudder's trademarks.

**BOB CHRISTIAN DECORATIVE ARTS**, 12 West Harris Street, 912-234-6866.

Bob has done faux finishes for museums and private homes in Savannah. He knows his historical details.

A little cluster of shops beginning at Madison Square includes:

**THE JAPONICA SHOP**, 13 West Charlton Street, 912-236-1613.

**JOHN TUCKER FINE ARTS**, 5 West Charlton Street, 912-231-8161.

**THE MULBERRY TREE**, 17 West Charlton Street, 912-236-4656.

On to Jones Street and then south:

**ARTHUR SMITH ANTIQUES**, 1 West Jones Street, 912-236-9701.

This is where locals have been buying the Savannah look for years.

**DELOACH ANTIQUES**, 12 West Jones Street, 912-238-1387.

This shop illustrates another Savannah look, which has to do with color, a casual mix of styles of antiques, an eclectic collection of silver, English china and accent pieces, lots of silk, and avoidance of the kinds of chintz that spell country house and Virginia estate. Savannah leans to Chinese export rather than Old Paris or

Staffordshire. Sheraton is to Savannah what high country is to Virginia. Walnut is out. Curly and tiger maple and exotic woods and burls are in. Inlay on a Baltimore piece added a soupçon of sophistication in the nineteenth century.

**TAYLOR HOUSE ANTIQUES, 10 West Taylor Street, 912-234-5520.**

Five rooms in the basement of an old Waring family house on Monterey Square comprise this shop. You get a glimpse of old-house garden and interior facets from the estate pieces she has collected. It is one of those shops that successfully mixes old and new.

**FREIDMAN'S ART STORE, 116 Whitaker Street, 912-234-1322.**

Freidman's has been there as long as I can remember, and it's always a good browse. You might just find a print you can't do without. After all, Catesby and John James Audubon passed through Savannah, as did William Bartram.

**CLAIRE WEST FINE LINENS, 411–413 Whitaker Street, 912-236-8163.**

Claire has done a fine job of combining two buildings and renovating them to enhance Whitaker Street. She has also successfullly combined chic antiques with high-end linens and decorative accessories to achieve an exciting look. Her shop is a definite event, as is Claire, whom you must engage while in the shop.

**CHECKERED MOON, corner of Whitaker Street and Taylor Street, 912-233-5132.**

This shop features Betsy Crawford and her painted furniture. She also represents local artists who trained with her.

**COBBS GALLERIES, 417 Whitaker Street, 912-234-1582.**

Albert L. Cobb says he offers the largest selection of art pottery in the South. Rows of Roseville, Van Briggle and other pottery line his shelves. Go upstairs for his $5 cookbooks. I found a good one ten minutes after he brought it in.

**RENAISSANCE GALLERY, 345 Abercorn Street and 405 Whitaker Street, 912-236-3542.**

If you like sophisticated stuff such as swags, tapestries, paste jewelry, and continental antiques, run into the shop next to Claire West and visit with Donna.

**BLATNER'S ANTIQUES, 347 Abercorn Street, 912-234-1210.**

The owner works hard seeking unusual local lore and objects, and it shows. You can make a real find among the litter and glitter at Blatner's. If you're lucky, you'll find the owner's father shopkeeping. He's full of lore about the marshes and rivers around Savannah. He knows where to fish among the offshore islands, too.

**FRANCIS MCNAIRY ANTIQUES, 411 Abercorn Street, 912-232-6411.**

Skeeter has the more traditional Savannah look with English and American antiques and a few show pieces from the continent. Fine antiques and art from William IV to American Hepplewhite appeal to him.

**THE LITTLE HOUSE, 107 East Gordon Street, 912-232-1551.**

This shop is owned by Laura Reid and run by her mother, Lanette H. Reid, a Savannah native. Laura is the fifth owner after the Little House's establishment by ladies of the Barrow family. Located near the Wesley Monumental Methodist Church, the Little House, set back in a garden, was once the Sprague carriage house.

The Sprague house is gone; a parking lot is on the site and the carriage house is fronted by an addition.

**ALEX RASKIN ANTIQUES, 441 Bull Street, 912-232-8205.**

In addition to the eclectic collection that Alex, with his fine eye, has put together, don't miss this Italianate mansion with its plethora of cast iron, fencing, balconies, and monumental cast iron lintels above the openings. The house is among the city's most sophisticated. It is associated with a number of notable owners, most recently the Ashcraft family, connected with Coca-Cola.

**COTTAGE SHOP, 2422 Abercorn Street, 912-233-3820.**

Although it's not exactly antiques, fine gifts and linens are displayed in an 1848 cottage built by John Maupas on his mother's share of the old Drouillard plantation.

Don't forget the museum shops and sales desks at the various museums and parks. The Savannah School of Art and Design offers Exhibit A Gallery at **342 Bull Street,** where they sell photographs, paintings, weaving, and fine prints executed by students.

## BOOKS

For 25 years the Beehive Press has helped to preserve the culture and architecture of Georgia and the deep south by publishing special editions about the south. All are now listed in *Books in Print.* Founder Mills B. Lane's *Savannah Revisited*, in its fourth edition (Savannah: Beehive Press, 1994), is their most widely sold book, the revised second edition of a pictorial history that was first published by the University of Georgia Press, Athens, in 1969.

Henry James said it takes a lot of history to create even a little literature. Beehive knew they were delivering both history and literature when they republished the memoirs of the Butler women, who lived at Pierce Butler's plantations at St. Simons, Little St. Simons, and Butler's islands in the nineteenth century.

*Journal of a Residence on a Georgian Plantation in 1838–1839* (Savannah: Beehive Press, 1992), by Frances Anne Kemble, the English Shakespearian actress who married the rich Philadelphian Pierce Butler II, recalls the 1838–1839 growing seasons at the hereditary Butler rice and cotton plantations. Fanny had a rude awakening at her husband's Georgia coast plantations, where she learned that absentee ownership of slave-holding property was among the worst of fates for slaves. She found that the heat, humidity, and mosquitoes of a coastal Georgia plantation can and did kill. She suffered from knowledge that her wealth and that of her children were gained from the abhorrent system referred to locally as the "peculiar institution." An abolitionist, she published her journals two decades later, from England, during the Civil War.

Her daughter, Frances Butler Leigh, the fourth generation to own the land, lived on the same plantation after the Civil War and wrote about it in *Ten Years on a Georgia Plantation* (Savannah: Beehive Press, 1992). Absentee owners for the most part, she and her father could not find an adequate overseer after the Civil War and moved to Georgia's sea islands to take over the plantations. The story of adaptating the slavery task system to a share crop system written by a well-educated woman raised in the north and in England makes for poignant reading.

Van Jones Martin is a photographer and publisher whose work has contributed to preserving Savannah's history and culture, thus the city itself. His projects include: *Classic Savannah, History, Homes and Gardens* (New Orleans–Savannah: Martin–St. Martin Publishing Company, 1991), text by William Robert Mitchell, Jr., photographs by Van Jones Martin; *Coastal Georgia*, (Savannah: Golden Coast Publishing Company, 1985), text by Beth Lattimore Reiter, photographs by Van Jones Martin (Beth is one of Savannah's most knowledgeable and productive architectural historians and active citizens); *The Architecture of Georgia*, (Savannah: Beehive Press, 1976), text by Frederick D. Nichols, photographs by Van Jones Martin.

Van Jones Martin is also related to the Joneses of Liberty County, who were the subject and authors of the letters in *The Children of Pride, A True Story of Georgia and The Civil War*, edited by Robert Manson Myers (New Haven, Conn.: Yale University Press, 1972; or in three volumes from Popular Library, New York). The Charles Colcock Jones family produced generations of ministers, scholars, and Georgia leaders. C. C. Jones, Jr., whose wife and one daughter died of scarlet fever during the Civil War, wrote one of the first definitive histories of Georgia.

Ashantilly Press of Darien, Georgia, has published special editions by local scholars, including *Anchored Yesterdays*, by Elfrida DeRenne Barrow and Laura Palmer Bell, (Ashantilly Press for the Little House of Savannah, copyright 1923, 1966).

Mac Bell and his wife, Muriel, have contributed to the preservation of Savannah architecture and history through their publications and photographs. Among them are: *Shadows: Survival Studies Among the Georgia Coastal Negroes* (Athens, Ga.: University of Georgia Press, 1940), Savannah Unit, Georgia Writers' Project, Works Projects Administration, foreword by Guy B. Johnson, photographs by Muriel and Malcolm Bell, Jr.; *Major Butler's Legacy, Five Generations of a Slaveholding Family* (Athens, Ga.: University of Georgia Press, 1987), Malcolm Bell, Jr. After his retirement from banking in Savannah, Mr. Bell produced this informative biography of coastal island rice and cotton plantations owned by the Butler family. Also, *Savannah* (Savannah: Historic Savannah Foundation, 1977), text by Malcolm Bell, Jr., photographs by N. Jane Iseley; *Savannah* (Savannah: Chamber of Commerce, 1937), compiled and written by Savannah Unit, Federal Writers' Project in Georgia, Works Progress Administration.

When I asked Bill Abbot, a friend and professor at the University of Virginia, to tell me about Georgia's role among the thirteen colonies, I didn't even know he was from Louisville, Georgia, upcountry near Augusta, where the Telfairs of Savannah had lots of land. His book, *The Royal Governors of Georgia, 1754–1775* (Chapel Hill: University of North Carolina Press, 1957), published for the Institute of Early American History and Culture at Williamsburg, is a thoughtful illumination of Georgia's three royal governors. It reveals the Crown's contribution to what Savannah is today.

Bill presented me with a copy of *Georgia Plan: 1732–1752* (Berkeley, Calif: Institute of Business and Economic Research, University of California, 1972), by Paul S. Taylor. The late Mr. Taylor spent his career advising emerging nations as to the manner in which they might set up their governments. During his studies, he came upon Oglethorpe's trustee colony. He felt that the Trustees' purposeful and brave plan for Georgia, a state without slavery with small landholdings and religious farming families surrounded by undisturbed Indians to trade among, might have succeeded given time and the absence of Eli Whitney's cotton gin. Indeed, is that not what happened after Reconstruction ended in 1876? Tenant farmers lived and worked on small plots divided off from vast plantations formed during the Crown colony days.

Macon Toledano, my son, wrote his thesis in 1989 at the Harvard Graduate School of Design on contemporary intervention in the original plan of Savannah. He envisioned residential infill in the mutilated sections of Crawford Square. He felt that Oglethorpe's plan was urban and suburban at once and might be unitized and multiplied as needed should it be applied to a new city. He illustrated that citizens in 1733, 1833, and 2033 may need similar amenities. This paper, "Transforming the Historical Context: A Proposal for Contemporary Intervention in the Original Plan of Savannah, Georgia," is available at the Georgia Historical Society and at Harvard.

Novels about Savannah help to elucidate the attitudes of Savannahians. Julian Hartridge Green, Académie Française diarist and novelist, was born of Savannah parents in Paris, where his father represented cotton interests after the Civil War. Over 90 years old, Green has recently begun to write about the city his parents described while he was growing up. He knew his grandfather's home, the Gothic revival Charles Green House on Madison Square. Green's novels are being translated from the French now, including *The Distant Lands* (Paris: Seuil, 1991), translated by Marion Boyars.

Another Savannahian, J. Frederick Waring, was not only editor of an edition of *Uncle Remus* (New York: Appleton, Century, 1935) by Savannah newspaperman Joel Chandler Harris, published while Waring was a student at Cambridge, but the English professor wrote *Cerveau's Savannah* (Atlanta, Ga.: Georgia Historical Society, 1973).

Eugenia Price captures the feeling of coastal Georgia with her historical novels, including a series set in and around Savannah. Her use of research in the Henry James manner, setting the stage, results in creative literature. Another historical novelist, Conrad Aiken's daughter, Jane Aiken Hodge, wrote *Savannah*

*Purchase* (New York: Fawcett Crest, 1971), a rewarding read about the city. Harry Hervey wrote *The Damned Don't Cry* (Garden City, N.Y.: Sun Dial Press, 1942), set in Savannah in the 1930s. Out of print, it evokes the city at that time.

Other books helpful to me were *Savannah; A Historical Portrait* (Virginia Beach: The Donning Company, 1976), by Margaret Wayt DeBolt; *Eden On The Marsh: An Illustrated History of Savannah* (Northridge, Calif.: Windsor Publications, 1985), by Edward Chan Sieg, produced in cooperation with the Coastal Heritage Society; *Georgia Historical Markers: The Complete Texts of 1752 Markers* (Valdosta, Ga.: Bay Tree Grove, 1973) (much careful research presented succinctly); and *Savannah* (Columbia, S.C.: Bostick and Thornley, 1947), by Walter Charlton Hartridge, etchings and drawings by Christopher Murphy, Jr. Murphy may be the best native artist Savannah has produced. His drawings and etchings of Savannah capture scenes unavailable to the camera. Walter C. Hartridge devoted his life to Savannah scholarship. The book *Historic Savannah* (Savannah: Historic Savannah Foundation, 1968), is an essential tool for studying Savannah; both the 1968 and 1979 editions need indexes. Let us hope the upcoming third edition abandons the survey format and analyzes titles, thereby presenting social and cultural history as well as associative information. The addresses of the buildings inventoried and the collection of information should be presented adjacent to the photograph, deleting code numbers.

Emmaline and Polly Cooper's new *Guide to Savannah* (Charleston, S.C.: Wyrick & Company, 1995) is personal, carefully researched, and very convenient. Pick one up at any of the stores around town and follow the Coopers' directions.

Nancy Rhyne's *Touring the Coastal Georgia Backroads* (Winston-Salem, N.C.: John F. Blair, 1994), is a good treatment of the complex Gold Coast area with its eighteenth- and nineteenth-century plantations and towns, such as Darien, Ebenezer, Sunbury, and Midway, which you should visit. Rhyne handles the intricate history of the sea islands informatively and with verve. Take her tours.

Beth Lattimore Reiter's *Savannah Victorian District Building Survey and Evaluation* (Savannah: 1980) provided the base of information for the Victorian districts' inventory.

Finally, preservationist and antiquarian Jim Williams's misfortunes and tortured demise have brought great fortune to historic Savannah. Ironically, John Berendt's book *Midnight in the Garden of Good and Evil* (New York; Random House, 1994) featuring Jim has made more money than Jim did on antiques and historic houses. I hope John invests some of it in historic Savannah.

Go to some of Savannah's historic district bookstores to get your books. Since you'll have a list, you may strike up a conversation with the book dealers and learn much more about Savannah.

**E. SHAVER BOOKSELLERS,** 326 Bull Street on Madison Square, 912-234-7257.

Esther Shaver was going strong thirty years ago when I first came to Savannah. A visit is a Savannah ritual for meeting locals and uncovering the local literary and preservation lore. Chairs are set about and you don't feel embarrassed looking through the books at your leisure. A full selection of new books and a full-service store would make the Shavers competitive anywhere.

**V. & J. DUNCAN ANTIQUE MAPS AND PRINTS,** 12 East Taylor Street on Monterey Square, 912-232-0338.

This shop offers much more than antique maps, prints, photographs and books. John Duncan has long been active in the preservation of historic Savannah.

**THE BOOK LADY,** 17 West York Street, 912-233-3628.

Anita Raskin is intimate with Savannah and its literary and social history. Like her son at Raskin Antiques, she and her shop are a resource for the Savannah experience. Stop by the new adjacent coffeehouse to read what you've bought.

**JACQUELINE LEVINE BOOKS,** 107 East Oglethorpe Avenue, 912-233-8519.

By appointment.

**THE PRINTED PAGE,** 211 West Jones Street, 912-234-5612.

Call ahead.

**BOOKS ON BAY,** 11 West Bay Street, 912-231-8485.

This new store near the City Hotel (which is slowly being restored), features used books and a coffee bar.

Savannah River

N
W — E
S

Factor's Walk

River

Bay  Tybee Beach ➡

Martin Luther King, Jr. (West Broad)

Indian

400  Montgomery  300  Jefferson  200  Barnard  100  Whitaker  West  Bell  East  Drayton  100  Abercorn  200  Lincoln  300  Habersham  400  Price  500  Houston  600  East Broad

Bryan

Franklin Square  Ellis Square  Johnson Square  Reynolds Square  Warren Square  Washington Square  St. Julian  Trustees Garden

Congress

Franklin Ward  Decker Ward  Derby Ward  Reynolds Ward  Warren Ward  Washington Ward

Broughton

State

Liberty Square  Telfair Square  Wright Square  Oglethorpe Square  Columbia Square  Greene Square  President

York

Liberty Ward  Heathcote Ward  Percival Ward  Anson Ward  Columbia Ward  Greene Ward

◄ U.S. 17A & I-95

Oglethorpe

Hull

Elbert Square  Orleans Square  Chippewa Square  Colonial Park Cemetery  Crawford Square  McDonough

Perry

Visitor's Center

Jackson Ward  Brown Ward  Crawford Ward

Round House

Liberty

Harris

Pulaski Square  Madison Square  Lafayette Square  Troup Square  Macon

Charlton

Pulaski Ward  Jasper Ward  Lafayette Ward  Troup Ward

Jones

◄ I-16 & I-95

Taylor

Chatham Square  Monterey Square  Calhoun Square  Whitefield Square  Wayne

Gordon

Chatham Ward  Monterey Ward  Calhoun Ward  Wesley Ward

Gaston

## Downtown Savannah

# Index

Note: An index is made to help the reader and the reseacher and, in this case, the curious. This index focuses on architects, builders, artists and first-time owners of buildings. Large buildings are indexed, and city planning from an historical perspective prompted entries. Lists of contemporary names are omitted as are the preface, acknowledgements, foreword and Chapter 8, dealing with lists of books, lodgings and restaurants. Names that appear in full in the text are shortened to first-name initials in the index to provide more space for entries.